SPICE

SPICE

Flavors of the Eastern Mediterranean

ANA SORTUN WITH NICOLE CHAISON

PHOTOGRAPHY BY SUSIE CUSHNER

ReganBooks
An Imprint of HarperCollinsPublishers

ReganBooks
An Imprint of HarperCollins Publishers

SPİCE

For information, address HarperCollins Publishers Inc.,
10 East 53rd Street, New York, NY 10022.

HarperCollins books may be purchased for educational,
business, or sales promotional use.
For information please write: Special Markets Department, HarperCollins Publishers Inc.,
10 East 53rd Street, New York, NY 10022.

FIRST EDITION

Designed by Erica Heitman-Ford for Mucca Design

Printed on acid-free paper

Library of Congress Cataloging-in-Publication Data
Sortun, Ana, 1967–
Spice : flavors of the eastern Mediterranean / Ana Sortun with Nicole Chaison.– 1st ed.
p. cm.
Includes index.
ISBN 10: 0-06-079228-0 (alk. paper)
ISBN 13: 978-0-06-079228-2

1. Cookery (Spices) 2. Cookery (Herbs) 3. Cookery, Arab. I. Chaison, Nicole. II. Title.
TX819.A1S6534 2006
641.6'383–dc22   2005055186

06 07 08 09 10 QW 10 9 8 7 6 5 4 3 2 1

In memory of my brave and loving father, Gary Sortun,
who gave me creativity.

Contents

Introduction

What makes each country's food taste unique? What gives it life? In the Arabic foods around the Mediterranean and Middle East, the answer is spice.

In cooking school in Paris, I was taught that the way to add flavor to a dish was with fat. The rule still lingers that where there is fat there is flavor, and so French-influenced chefs regularly use extra butter or heavy cream to add richness to a dish. I have nothing against the use of fat, but my experience has taught me that it is not the only way to achieve flavor.

All chefs think about how dishes taste and appear, but few consider how the food makes people feel after they've eaten. In my travels to the eastern Mediterranean region, I learned that the cuisines feel rich and are full of flavor because of the artful use of spices and herbs, flowers, nuts, and cheese. I've brought these lessons home to Oleana, my restaurant in Cambridge, Massachusetts, where we make dishes absolutely alive with flavors that leave guests ready for a night of dancing–not weighed down and ready for bed.

My journey as a chef started with my grandmother Betty Johansen, who was an excellent home cook and who instilled in me the love of eating good food. My grandmother was a simple cook, but she made everything from scratch, using the freshest seasonal ingredients, straight from the family farm in Kent, Washington. She made her own bread, butter, ice cream, salad dressings, pickles, and canned fruits. The memory of her homemade rolls–fresh and warm out of the oven, slathered with homemade butter–still makes my mouth water.

At age fourteen, I started washing dishes in a small neighborhood restaurant called the Santa Fe Café in Seattle. That led to other kitchen work, and I soon began assisting at a local cooking school

in order to learn more basic skills. Meanwhile, I studied French privately and intensely for over two years, until I passed a fluency requirement exam, and when I turned nineteen, I left for Paris. It was there that I trained in classic, regional French cooking and wine at La Varenne, while working at the school to pay for my education. The best lesson I learned in France is the importance of fresh, high-quality ingredients. I learned to shop at farmers' markets, where I began to recognize the difference between truly fresh vegetables and those that had been shipped.

Back in the United States, I worked for Moncef Meddeb–a Tunisian-born chef famous for bringing upscale, cutting-edge Mediterranean and French food to a Boston dining scene steeped in traditional New England fare–as the chef at Aigo Bistro, in Concord, Massachusetts. Under his tutelage, I came to understand how the Arabic world has influenced French cuisine.

Moncef pushed me toward a deeper understanding of food and flavors. I was twenty-four at the time, working out my own style and identity in the kitchen. One night after work, he called, and I told him I was starving. He told me that I should keep fruit around for late night snacks, but all I really wanted was bacon and eggs. At this point, Moncef launched into a 20-minute discussion about oranges. He described in depth the fragrant spray of oils releasing as the skin of the orange is broken and the juices running down one's hand as the fruit is peeled. After listening to him, my hunger for that orange was nearly unbearable. What happened to me that night as a chef was a milestone: I understood food more intimately. I was able to taste food when I thought about food.

As the chef at Casablanca restaurant in Harvard Square, where I worked for five years, specializing in the cuisines of the Mediterranean rim, I began to come into my own. It was on my trip to Turkey in 1997 that I had a revelation, and my journey in spice began.

That year, the owner of Casablanca, Sari Abul-Jubein, sent me to Gaziantep in southeastern Turkey, the country's gastronomic capital. The very thought of Turkey was foreign to me—I envisioned flying carpets and covered women hidden deep in the veils of purdah. I flew through Istanbul and went straight to Gaziantep, where I stayed with Ayfer Unsal, a friend of Sari's and a journalist and author of Turkish cookbooks.

Ayfer welcomed me with a lunch staged by some of the townswomen. Each of them had brought her family's specialties in my honor: everyone had a different version of the bulgur-based *köfte* or *kibbeh*, some with lamb, others with potato and pumpkin; salads dressed with sweet-tart pomegranate molasses; fresh and intriguing vegetables spiked with the spice and herb combinations which are now staples in my kitchen. It was a feast, the likes of which I had never before experienced. I stayed with Ayfer for just over a week, studying her as she cooked, going with her to the market—where ordinarily women do not go—as well as baklava shops, pita bakeries, pistachio growers, and artisans' shops.

I left Gaziantep for Istanbul where Ferda Erdinc, a friend of Ayfer's, took me on yet another intense food adventure. Ferda is active in the food world, both as a writer and restaurant owner. Through these two women, my misconceptions about Turkey were replaced with a deep respect for the country's culture and cuisine. Istanbul itself was a revelation. More westernized than Gaziantep, the city offered food and dining experiences that were more sophisticated than what I'd found in the south. I continued to dine, sometimes eating elaborate, multicourse meals. Inevitably, these occasions would end in dancing, and I got hooked on the culture as well as the cuisine. It was during this trip that I began to home in on the Arabic use of innovative herb and spice blends to extract maximum flavor in cooking. I had found spice.

Later, back in Boston, I began processing what these two women had shown me and gradually incorporated what I had learned. Other than the sophisticated fusion of Western technique with the exotic spice blends of the Middle and Near East, what impressed me most about my experiences with Turkish cuisine were those delicious multicourse meals after which everyone left feeling energized. So I decided to open Oleana, a restaurant that introduced people to the exciting foods of the Arabic Mediterranean, where customers would leave their tables ready for a night of dancing.

So many Mediterranean restaurants focus on the cuisines of Spain, the south of France, and Italy, where large meals usually put me in bed, feeling heavy and tired. I want people to experience the Arabic flavors of North Africa, the eastern Mediterranean region, and the Ottoman empire, as these cuisines have contributed hugely to world gastronomy but haven't been explored much in the United States.

At Oleana, we make healthful, seductive, and exotic food approachable to a wide variety of customers. Arabic foods intrigue me so much that I can't sit still when I eat at a great Turkish restaurant. I get so excited about the flavors and curious about their kitchens that I practically jump out of my chair. I'd like to share that enthusiasm with you—my readers, friends, and customers—and welcome you in finding spice.

How This Book Is Organized

People ask me so many questions about spices and herbs—their usage alone and in combination. What can I do with coriander? What spices go well with lamb? What can I do with all the mint in my garden?

Unlike other cookbooks, which are most often organized by meal order (salads, appetizers, main courses, etc.) or ingredients (chicken, vegetables, etc.), this book is organized by spice and herb groupings or families. In chapter 1, for example, I've grouped cumin, coriander, and cardamom together because they complement one another and can be used in similar applications. This way, you can become familiar with the wonderful individual qualities of each spice as well as the ways you can combine them to enrich your dishes. And you'll learn which spices go well with different foods.

By organizing the book this way, I'm hoping to provide you with a map that you can use as you embark on your own spice journey.

Enjoy!

PART I
Spices

1
THE THREE Cs
Cumin, Coriander, and Cardamom

Cumin, coriander, and cardamom are wonderfully fragrant and warm spices that complement one another: cumin is earthy, coriander is citrusy, and cardamom is sweet. They cannot be used interchangeably, but they balance one another when blended to add depth to a dish.

These spices work well with rich proteins like beef, braised pork, lamb, or salmon. They also bring fragrance to simple legumes like chickpeas or lentils, and they brighten up sweet carrots, silky avocados, or dishes with dried fruits. Sweet cardamom is particularly good when added to the chocolatey, bitter flavor of coffee.

CUMIN

The pungent aroma of cumin lingers and is warm and slightly sweet. Combined with chickpeas and tahini, cumin is the spice that makes hummus taste like hummus. Cumin is wonderful on lamb and beef; with chickpeas, lentils, cabbage, savory apple preparations, eggplant, and cooked tomato; or combined with spices like dried mint, paprika, coriander, and saffron. It's also perfect with garlic or fennel.

It's best to buy cumin whole and grind it fresh every time you use it. I like to grind my own spices and use a coffee grinder or an Arabic coffee hand grinder designated for just one spice that I use often, like cumin. Arabic coffee grinders grind spices very finely, even more finely than a pepper mill. You can purchase them at www.arabiannights.ca.

CORIANDER

Dried coriander seed is bright and citrusy and has a slight sage or herbaceous note. It's acidic and perfumey. Combined with oranges, orange zest, rosé wine, sugar, and eau de vie, coriander makes a delicious aperitif. Coriander grew in the Hanging Gardens of Babylon, and Charlemagne ordered it to be grown on the imperial farms in central Europe. In the Middle Ages, love potions were crafted from the seeds.

On one of my trips to Turkey, I returned with a box full of candied, coated coriander seeds. Turks use them at the end of meals to clean the breath like Indians use fennel seeds. I made my staff crazy at a special dinner at the James Beard House in New York City when I asked them to stuff the little candied seeds into raspberries to accompany a rich chocolate tart.

Coriander is the seed of the cilantro plant. When cilantro bolts at the end of its growing season, the plant produces little green berries which are wonderful to eat fresh. One little seed cleans your breath in a second. I also sprinkle fresh, green coriander seeds on fish and in fish broths.

Dried, ground coriander seed is good over grilled mushrooms, in chicken stews, and with apples in either sweet or savory preparations, and it's even better combined with nuts and cumin, as in the Egyptian spice mix called *dukkah* (page 6). It is also delicious mixed with fennel seed or saffron or cinnamon.

CARDAMOM

Cardamom has a refreshing eucalyptus scent as well as an herbaceous tea quality. Buy the dried cardamom whole, in the green pod, and open the pod and remove the black seeds as necessary. The pod will keep them fresh. The pod is fibrous, so don't grind the whole cardamom–just the black seeds. Like cloves, this is a spice that should be used with a careful hand: too much can overperfume a dish. A little goes a long way.

Cardamom is delicious with coffee, and in fact, it is the spice that gives Arabic coffee its unique flavor. The little black cardamom seeds are oily, like freshly roasted coffee beans. Try crushing some green pods by smashing them with the back of a knife or crushing them with a rolling pin and adding them to your French-pressed coffee.

Enjoy cardamom in cakes, mulled wine, gingerbread, dates, squash, and on grapefruit with sugar for breakfast.

TRICK FOR REVIVING SPICES

If you come across a jar of cumin, coriander, or fennel seeds in your cupboard and you aren't sure how long it's been kicking around, here's a good trick to revive your spice. Put the seeds in a small skillet. Swirl the skillet around and around over a low flame for 3 to 4 minutes until you see a little steam come off the spices and the seed oil starts to release. At this point, you should begin to smell the spice. It's not necessary to toast the spice or change its color, because doing so could alter its flavor completely. Cool the seeds and grind them, and you should have a more lively tasting spice on your hands.

Oleana 3C Ale

As we started building Oleana, I decided that we should offer our own style of beer—one that would pair well with our food and get us involved in the beer-making process. I called many local brewers and found Randy Hudson, who owns Cisco Brewers on Nantucket. Randy was willing to work with us on a signature beer, for sale only through the restaurant. I took a ferry over to Nantucket to learn how Randy makes beer and to discuss some recipe possibilities. I learned a great deal from Randy and his team and was very impressed with the quality of Cisco Brewers' product. I had originally envisioned *flowering* the beer—that is, adding an infusion of fresh roses into the beer while it was fermenting. We tried to do it, but the flowers ruined the fermentation. I was discouraged but still determined to create a beer that matched Oleana's cuisine.

We began to brainstorm, and decided to try adding spices to the beer. I was nervous that the additions would make our brew taste overly spiced, like bad Christmas beer, but I had complete confidence in Randy's skill.

Oleana was still under construction, and I was overwhelmed with pre-opening details, so I asked my sous-chef Nookie to take a trip out to Nantucket and pick up with Randy where I left off. He learned a lot about beer making, made some friends, and developed a delicious signature beer for our restaurant. Nookie and the Cisco team used cumin, coriander, and cardamom to add a subtle fragrance to the Belgian-style brew. We named it "Oleana 3C Ale," and we sell loads of it at the restaurant. We've even paired the beer with some desserts. Our customers frequently comment on the refreshing and delicate spice tones.

Nookie is very proud of his beer and all that he learned from Randy on Nantucket. His story is on the label.

RECIPES WITH CUMIN, CORIANDER, AND CARDAMOM

Carrot Purée and Egyptian Spice Mix with Nuts and Olive Oil

I discovered this Egyptian spice mix called *dukkah* when I had the pleasure of working with Claudia Roden during a lecture she delivered on Middle Eastern food at Boston University in November 2000. Together, we gave culinary students and friends of the university a sense of the flavors and history of Arabic cooking. With the addition of coconut to the spice and nut mixture, we offered a twist on the more traditional dukkah.

Dukkah is incredibly versatile. I've seen versions that include nigella seeds and dried mint. It can be eaten as a simple bread condiment along with olive oil, but it's also delicious on seared sea scallops and duck, or in a salad of raw fennel and orange. Dukkah is also fantastic in the summertime sprinkled on sliced tomatoes.

At Oleana, our menu begins with the *prêt-à-manger*, which are bread condiments. This recipe is for two of the most popular ones.

— SERVES 8 —

For the Carrot Purée

2 pounds carrots, peeled and cut into 2-inch lengths

6 tablespoons extra-virgin olive oil, plus more for dipping

2 tablespoons white wine vinegar

4 teaspoons harissa (page 152)

1 teaspoon ground cumin

½ teaspoon ground ginger

Torn pieces of French baguette

Salt and pepper to taste

For the Dukkah

½ cup blanched almonds

3 tablespoons coriander seeds

2 tablespoons cumin seeds

2 tablespoons sesame seeds

¼ cup unsweetened dried shredded coconut

½ teaspoon salt

½ teaspoon freshly ground black pepper

To Make the Carrot Purée

1. In a large saucepan over high heat, cover the carrots with water and bring to a boil. Reduce the heat to medium and simmer until tender, about 20 minutes. Drain the carrots and return them to the saucepan. Cook for 30 seconds over medium heat to thoroughly dry them. Remove the carrots from the heat and coarsely mash them with a fork or whisk. You should have a coarsely ground carrot purée that sticks together but still has rough pieces throughout.

2. Stir in the olive oil, vinegar, harissa, cumin, and ginger. Season the mixture with salt and pepper.

To Make the Dukkah

1. In a medium skillet over medium heat, toast the almonds until golden, about 4 minutes. Transfer the almonds to a work surface to cool, and then finely chop them.

2. Put the coriander and cumin seeds in the same skillet and toast, stirring, until fragrant, about 2 minutes. Transfer the seeds to a spice grinder and allow them to cool completely before coarsely grinding.

3. In a medium bowl, combine the almonds with the ground spices.

4. Put the sesame seeds in the skillet and toast them over medium heat, stirring until golden, about 2 minutes. Transfer to the spice grinder.

5. Toast the coconut in the skillet over medium heat, stirring constantly until golden, about 2 minutes. Add the toasted coconut to the grinder and let it cool completely.

6. Grind the sesame seeds and coconut to a coarse powder. Combine with the almond and spice mixture and season with salt and pepper.

7. Serve the dukkah and carrot purée in separate bowls with torn chunks of crispy baguette and olive oil. Dunk the bread in the oil, dredge it in the dukkah, and spread on the carrots.

Chickpea Crepes

In Nice, they call these crepes *socca*. In the north of Italy, they call them *farinata*. The crepes are made from chickpea flour, which can be found at Indian markets or online at www.kalustyans.com. Chickpea crepes are served hot and with plenty of freshly ground pepper and sometimes lots of grated Parmesan cheese. I like to use cumin in them because it pairs so beautifully with chickpeas.

These crepes aren't thin like French crepes, but they are thinner than pancakes–about ⅛ inch thick. Crispy on the outside and soft on the inside, they're delicious served instead of bread with Carrot Purée and Egyptian Spice Mix (page 6). You can make the crepes ahead of time and warm them in the oven with the cheese and oil, just before serving. Cut them into wedges and pass them around for a great snack or hors d'oeuvre.

MAKES SIX 8-INCH CREPES THAT SERVE 6 TO 12

1½ cups chickpea flour	1½ cups water
1 teaspoon salt	¼ cup extra-virgin olive oil plus about 3 tablespoons for cooking and drizzling
½ teaspoon freshly ground black pepper	
1½ teaspoons ground cumin	4 tablespoons grated Parmigiano Reggiano cheese

---

1. Preheat the oven to 350° F.

2. In a small mixing bowl, combine the chickpea flour, salt, pepper, and cumin. Whisk to combine. Slowly whisk in the water and continue whisking until it forms a batter. You may see some small lumps that will dissolve while the crepes are cooking, but whisk the mixture until it's as smooth as possible.

3. Whisk in the ¼ cup olive oil and 2 tablespoons of the cheese and let the mixture sit at room temperature for at least 15 minutes.

4. Using an 8-inch nonstick skillet over medium-high heat, heat 1 teaspoon of oil and add a little less than ½ cup of the batter to the pan, swirling the pan so the batter evenly coats the bottom of the pan to the edges. Reduce the heat to medium

and cook for 5 to 6 minutes, until the batter crisps around the edges and the crepe flips easily without breaking. It needs to cook a bit longer than most other pancakes or crepes because the chickpea flour is dense. Make sure the first side is a little brown, and then flip and cook the other side for 2 to 3 minutes.

5. Place the crepes in a single layer on a heavy baking sheet, the smoother side facing up.

6. Repeat the crepe-making process until the batter is gone (if you use a smaller skillet, it may make more pancakes).

7. Sprinkle each crepe with a little of the remaining 2 tablespoons of Parmesan and drizzle less than a teaspoon of olive oil over each. Bake for about 4 minutes until the edges crisp up and the cheese melts. Cut each crepe into 4 to 6 wedges and serve immediately with more freshly ground pepper.

Fried Haloumi Cheese with Pear and Spiced Dates

Haloumi is a sheep's milk cheese from Cyprus. It's brined like feta but it has a firm texture that is perfect for frying. There is no need to bread or flour the cheese before frying; you don't even need to use oil in the pan. The cheese browns naturally from the sugar in the brine and keeps its shape. Haloumi is often flavored with dried mint, which goes perfectly with pears and dates. It's also beautiful paired with grilled peaches and red peppers during the summer months. To add drama, sugar, and a slight anise flavor, carefully flambé the dish with ouzo at the table.

You can make the dates ahead of time and brown the pear in a separate pan, at the same time you're browning the haloumi, to speed up the process a bit.

—⌁ SERVES 4 ⌁—

Zest and juice of 1 lemon

1 tablespoon brown sugar

½ teaspoon ground cumin

½ teaspoon ground coriander

¼ teaspoon ground cardamom (just the oily black seeds from within the green pod)

¼ teaspoon black pepper

8 dates, cut in half and pits removed

2 tablespoons olive oil

¾ pound haloumi cheese, cut into 8 slices

1 pear, quartered, seeded, and sliced into 8 pieces

3 tablespoons ouzo

---

1. Preheat the oven to 350° F.

2. In a small sauté pan, big enough to hold the dates, mix the lemon juice, lemon zest, and brown sugar and cook over medium heat, stirring, until the brown sugar melts. Add the spices and dates and cook until the dates soften a little, about 5 minutes. Stir in 1 tablespoon of the olive oil and set the mixture aside.

3. Heat a large nonstick pan over medium-high heat. Arrange the cheese slices in the skillet,

being careful not to overlap or crowd them. Brown the cheese, about 2 minutes on each side, or until golden brown on each side. Transfer to a heavy gratin or baking dish, placing the haloumi slices side by side.

4. Using the same sauté pan, heat the remaining 1 tablespoon olive oil on medium-high heat and then add the pears. Brown the pears for 4 to 5 minutes on one side. Remove the pears from the pan and add them to the baking pan with the haloumi. Spoon a date onto each piece of haloumi and place the pan in the oven until it gets hot and the cheese gets a little softer, 6 to 8 minutes.

5. Remove the pan from the oven, place it on the table, and without waiting, add the ouzo to the pan and carefully ignite it. Stand back when you light the dish, as the flames can reach 5 inches. The fire will burn off the alcohol, and after about a minute, it will leave the sweet flavor of the ouzo.

Red Lentil Köfte with Tomato, Cucumber, and Pomegranate

Köfte is bulgur-based pâté or dough. It's also known as *kibbeh* in Arabic. It is combined with lentils, meat, squash, potato, and so on and can be baked, fried, or eaten raw. You must use finely ground bulgur to make köfte; coarse bulgur will not bind. The bulgur as well as the Aleppo chilies and pomegranate molasses in this recipe can be found online at www.kalustyans.com. Pomegranate molasses can also be found at most Middle Eastern markets or online at www.zingermans.com.

My friend Ferda Erdinc, who owns Zencefil restaurant in Istanbul, inspired this recipe. Zencefil (see page 15), which means "ginger," is a vegetarian restaurant in the Taxim neighborhood. The flavors in her menu are so rich, I never even missed the meat during a meal there.

Ferda makes a tangy salsa with finely chopped cucumber, pomegranate, and tomato to accompany her köfte. This dish is great as a salad course or accompanied by grilled fish.

MAKES 8 MEDIUM KÖFTE TO SERVE 4 TO 8

For the Köfte

2 tablespoons butter

1 medium white onion, minced

1 carrot, peeled and finely chopped

1 tablespoon tomato paste

1 teaspoon ground cumin

2 teaspoons Aleppo chilies
  or medium-hot paprika

1 cup red lentils

4 cups water

1 cup finely ground bulgur

¼ cup extra-virgin olive oil

Salt and freshly ground pepper
  to taste

For the Salsa

1 small red onion, finely chopped

1 medium European cucumber, peeled, halved, seeded, and finely diced

1 small green bell pepper, finely diced

1 pound tomatoes, seeded, finely diced, and drained of most of their water in a sieve for about 10 minutes

6 tablespoons extra-virgin olive oil

1½ tablespoons fresh lemon juice

1 tablespoon pomegranate molasses

¼ cup pomegranate seeds (about ½ pomegranate)

Salt and pepper to taste

¼ cup minced fresh flat-leaf parsley or mint

8 romaine lettuce leaves, torn into large pieces

To Make the Köfte

1. Melt the butter in a medium saucepan over moderate heat. Add the white onion and carrot and cook, stirring occasionally, until softened, about 5 minutes.

2. Stir in the tomato paste, cumin, and Aleppo chilies, and then add the lentils and water and bring to a boil over high heat. Reduce the heat to medium-low and simmer until the lentils are tender and have absorbed about ¾ of the liquid, about 8 minutes.

3. Stir in the bulgur and olive oil and remove from the heat. Let this stand until the liquid is absorbed and the bulgur is softened, about 20 minutes.

4. Season the mixture with salt and pepper, transfer it to a rimmed baking sheet, and spread in an even layer to cool.

To Make the Salsa

1. Toss the red onion with the cucumber, bell pepper, and tomatoes.

2. In a small bowl, make the dressing by whisking the olive oil with the lemon juice and pomegranate molasses and seeds.

3. Pour all but 2 tablespoons of the dressing over the salsa, season with salt and pepper, and toss. Stir in the parsley.

continued

To Assemble the Köfte

1. When the lentil mixture is cool enough to handle, form it into patties by scooping up about 2 tablespoons at a time and rolling the patties between your palms to make a round ball, and then flatten them slightly. For a fancier presentation, you can also form them into quenelle shapes by using two spoons as a mold to press them into the shape of small footballs. Make a thumbprint in the center of each patty to catch the juice from the cucumber salsa.

2. In a large bowl, toss the romaine with the remaining 2 tablespoons of dressing and arrange on a large platter. Set the köfte on the lettuce.

3. Spoon the salsa on top, nestling most in the thumbprint, and serve.

ZENCEFIL

I met Ferda Erdinc in 1996 on my first visit to Turkey. She owns Zencefil, a small vegetarian restaurant in a very hip neighborhood called Taxim in Istanbul. Ferda was a teacher to me and became a dear friend. She took me to restaurants and into friends' kitchens on my mission to study Turkish food. This first trip to Turkey changed my life. I initially knew nothing about the culture or cuisine, but came back wanting to know more. And I started to change the way I cooked and ate. Ferda introduced me to flavors I had never tasted before. I began to understand that food can be made rich and satisfying by carefully blending spices and ingredients and without using too many fats.

When I arrived at Zencefil, I walked into Ferda's kitchen. The cooks were cleaning mallow, a wild weed that can be stewed and has a texture like okra. For dinner, we ate a composed salad of black-eyed peas, pickled beets, lettuce, and tomato, followed by some stewed mallow with garlic and olive oil that tasted to me like a cross between broccoli and artichokes. We also ate Ferda's red lentil köfte and had sweet-sour soup with chickpeas, barley, and pomegranate molasses. We ate special greens from the Black Sea that were sautéed and sprinkled with a cheese that Ferda called "dried feta." I do not think I've ever eaten such an exciting meal as that one at Zencefil. And it was so healthful. I would give up meat if only Ferda's restaurant were around the corner.

Moroccan Ras el Hannout

I think the best way to describe this spice mixture is Moroccan curry. *Ras el hannout* means "head of the shop," and there are as many variations on this blend of spices as there are shop owners in Morocco, some using more than the seven spices we use at Oleana. Ras el hannout has many uses, and it works well as a condiment for cooked chickpeas, fried squid, fish, and vegetables. However, I think it really shines with chicken, which takes on the reddish hue of the paprika and the slight sweetness of the ginger, saffron, and cinnamon.

⌁ MAKES ABOUT 1 CUP ⌁

¼ cup cumin seeds

¾ teaspoon saffron

1½ teaspoons ground cinnamon

1 tablespoon turmeric

1 teaspoon ground ginger

1 tablespoon freshly ground black pepper

½ cup paprika

1. In a small skillet over medium-low heat, toast the cumin seeds for 2 minutes, until fragrant. Place the seeds in a spice grinder and cool completely. Add the saffron to the spice grinder and grind with the cumin seeds.

2. Remove the saffron and cumin mixture to a small mixing bowl and combine with the remaining spices.

Fried Squid with Avocado Hummus

Hummus means chickpeas, but I make it from a variety of ingredients such as squash and parsnips (see page 188). But nothing is as creamy and unctuous as the avocado. Avocado hummus can be eaten on its own with bread or with raw vegetables for dipping.

It's important to use a good brand of tahini when making hummus. Tohum brand is a dark-roasted organic tahini from Turkey (you can find it at www.tohum.com). Tohum also carries organic heirloom chickpeas and wonderful sun-dried red pepper paste. I love Tohum tahini because it's not chalky, and it's rich and oily instead of bitter and dry.

With this dish, you might enjoy a medium-bodied white wine with silky qualities, like an Australian Semillon.

— SERVES 4 —

2 ripe avocados, split, seeded, and scooped	¾ cup milk
¼ cup tahini	½ cup all-purpose flour
1 tablespoon chopped garlic (about 3 cloves)	¼ cup fine cornmeal
3 teaspoons ground cumin	2 teaspoons salt
4 tablespoons freshly squeezed lemon juice (about 1 lemon)	Fresh black pepper to taste
¼ cup extra-virgin olive oil	1 teaspoon Aleppo chilies or medium-hot paprika
Salt to taste	4 to 6 cups vegetable oil for frying
1 pound small squid bodies, cartilage removed and washed in cold water	1 tablespoon chopped fresh parsley
	4 lemon wedges

1. Blend the avocados, tahini, garlic, 2 teaspoons of the cumin, the lemon juice, olive oil, and salt to taste in a food processor, fitted with the metal blade. Blend until the mixture is smooth and creamy, like sour cream. Cover tightly with plastic wrap, placing the wrap directly on top of the avocado so that no air gets into it to turn it brown. Set it aside.

continued

CUMIN, CORIANDER, AND CARDAMOM

2. Slice across the squid bodies to make ½-inch rings and place them in a small mixing bowl. Cover the squid rings with the milk.

3. In another small mixing bowl, combine the flour, cornmeal, 2 teaspoons salt, the pepper, Aleppo chilies, and the remaining 1 teaspoon cumin.

4. Heat the vegetable oil to 350°F in a medium-large, deep saucepan over medium heat or follow the instructions of a small countertop deep-fryer.

5. Drain the milk from the squid and toss them evenly in the flour mixture.

6. Carefully drop the squid rings, one by one, into the hot oil, being careful not to crowd the pan, and fry them until golden brown, about 3 minutes. Depending on the size of your pan, you may need to fry the squid in two batches.

7. Remove the squid with a slotted spoon and drain them on paper towels. Sprinkle with salt to taste.

8. Spoon the avocado mixture onto 4 plates and top with the squid and parsley. Serve with lemon wedges.

SALMON

Ninety percent of the salmon caught in the United States comes from Alaska, where the fish is still abundant because fisheries are well managed and the spawning rivers and streams have been well preserved. King salmon is usually available year-round, but much depends upon the weather: when the seas are too rough and the air too cold for fishermen to do their job, the supply drops and prices increase. Salmon fishing regulations are strict, and fishing is also frequently shut off so that the salmon population won't be depleted.

Wild salmon taste better than farm-raised salmon because of their diet. Wild salmon eat naturally from what is in the wild–lots of shrimp, for example, which lends color to the salmon's meat–while farmed salmon are fed fish food made from soy, and sometimes dyes and preservatives, not food found in its natural environment.

Salmon labeled *day boat* will be exceptionally fresh, because the fishing boat will have gone out and come back in the same day. Some fish are kept on ice for days when boats go out for long periods in deep water. *Line caught* means that the fishermen haven't dropped nets and dragged for a huge catch. There is less impact on the marine environment when fish are line caught. Line fishing is more selective, causes less damage to the seabed and fish stock, and provides more jobs, as it is a more labor-intensive method of fishing. Choose only line-caught fish, even though it is usually more expensive.

The best way to get good fish is to get to know your fishmonger and ask where and how the fish were caught.

There are five varieties of wild Pacific salmon:

· **sockeye or red**
available mid-May through September

· **coho or silver**
available July through mid-September

· **chum**
available June through September

· **pink**
available in July and August

· **king or chinook**
available year-round

Seared Salmon with Egyptian Garlic and Coriander Sauce

I'm from the Pacific Northwest, and grew up eating salmon. This makes me biased: I prefer the deeper flavor and richer texture of wild Pacific salmon over the farm-raised variety widely available on the East Coast. My favorites are sockeye and king salmon, because they have the wonderfully marbled, high-fat content, producing a deliciously creamy fish. For people living on the East Coast, the taste of farm-raised salmon is probably more familiar, and it's also easier to find than wild salmon. Either one is fine for this recipe, but if you have never had wild Pacific salmon, it's worth seeking out.

I like to sear salmon on one side until it's crispy, cooking it from the bottom up. Salmon's high oil content (the good kind of oil: omega-3 fatty acid) will render as it cooks to form a crisp bottom, leaving the top side creamy and soft.

The tomato sauce in this recipe, which is just acidic enough to cut through the fish's richness, is brightened and emboldened with the sweet coriander and toasted garlic. And as a finishing touch, I sprinkle peanuts on the salmon, adding a nutty layer of flavor and texture. I like to use peanuts, too, in honor of my friend Mona Mourad, who managed Oleana for two years and whose family hails from Alexandria, Egypt. There, the peanut crop is abundant, and Egyptians eat a lot of them: as snacks, sprinkled over pilafs, and in dukkah, a spice mix with nuts and seeds. This recipe is dedicated to Mona and her young twins, Nur and Ali.

Serve the salmon with some seared Swiss chard (page 53) or green beans and Rice Cakes (page 65).

A white Chateau Neuf du Pape that is aromatic with citrus, sage, and mineral notes will pair well with the density of the salmon.

⟶ SERVES 4 ⟵

1 tablespoon butter	Salt and pepper to taste
2 tablespoons olive oil	Four 7-ounce salmon fillets, boned and skinned
1 tablespoon finely chopped garlic (about 3 large cloves)	2 tablespoons lightly toasted, roughly chopped peanuts (see page 91)
2 cups peeled and seeded tomatoes (see page 104), roughly chopped	2 tablespoons chopped fresh parsley or cilantro for garnish
2 teaspoons lightly toasted, ground coriander	

1. In a small saucepan over medium heat, melt the butter with 1 tablespoon of the olive oil until the butter starts to brown. Stir in the garlic and cook, stirring constantly until the garlic toasts and turns golden brown, 4 to 5 minutes. The garlic will start to release its sugar and stick to your spoon just before it browns.

2. Immediately stir in the tomatoes and coriander. Reduce the heat to low and simmer the tomatoes for about 20 minutes, until they are soft and make a sauce. The consistency of the sauce may vary, depending on how juicy the tomatoes are. If it seems too dry, add a teaspoon or more of olive oil and a teaspoon of water.

3. Season the sauce with salt and pepper and set aside.

4. Season the salmon fillets with salt and pepper on both sides.

5. In a large sauté pan over medium-high heat, heat the remaining 1 tablespoon olive oil. When the pan is hot, place each salmon fillet on its skinned side (the oily side, which browns the best) in the pan and cook for 6 to 7 minutes until a nice golden-brown crust begins to form. Lower the heat to low and cover the pan with a lid or heavy foil. Continue cooking the salmon on this side for another 6 minutes, until it's almost completely cooked except for a little rare spot in the thickest middle part of the fillet. Turn off the heat and flip each fillet over to cook the rare spot, letting the fillets sit for about 3 minutes.

6. Remove the fillets and place each on a dinner plate, crispy side up.

7. Top each fillet with ¼ cup of the tomato sauce and sprinkle them with the peanuts and parsley. Serve immediately.

Spoon Lamb

I also call this dish "lamb sauce" because the lamb becomes so tender that you can serve it with a spoon. The use of pomegranate molasses is tricky because it can often be too tart. Always be sure to balance it with lemon juice. Somehow the acidity of the lemon softens the degree of the pomegranate's tartness. Spoon lamb is great served over a rice or grain pilaf with fresh peas and fresh mint.

Drink a grenache from Gigondas in the Rhone Valley with this dish. Other Rhone blends work well, too, as they're robust wines that stand up to the intense flavor of the pomegranate molasses.

⌐ᴎ SERVES 4 ᴎ⌐

---

2 tablespoons canola oil

Four 10- to 14-ounce lamb shoulder chops, 1½ to 2 inches thick

2 cups dry red wine

1 cup water

1 tablespoon ground cumin

4 teaspoons garlic, peeled, split, and mashed (about 4 cloves)

1 large carrot, peeled and sliced into ¾-inch rings on the bias

1 large white onion, peeled and quartered

2 tablespoons pomegranate molasses (see Resources, page 358)

4 tablespoons butter, cut into 4 equal pieces (optional)

Salt and freshly ground pepper to taste

Juice of ½ lemon

---

1. Preheat the oven to 350°F.

2. Heat a medium-large skillet over medium-high heat. Add 1 tablespoon of the oil and 2 of the lamb chops. Cook them for about 4 minutes on each side or until they are golden brown. Remove the chops and set them aside in a roasting pan big enough to hold all 4 chops. Remove the

skillet from the heat and carefully pour off any fat that has rendered and add ¼ cup of the wine to the browning pan. Scrape up the sugars stuck to the bottom of the pan and strain the liquid through a strainer over the meat. Wipe the pan clean and repeat the browning process with the remaining 2 chops and 1 tablespoon oil and another ¼ cup wine.

3. Sprinkle the cumin over the lamb chops. Add the garlic, carrot, the remaining 1½ cups wine, and the onion to the pan and top it off with enough water so that the liquid reaches halfway up the chops. Cover twice with baking foil and seal tightly, or cover with a lid that fits tightly. Braise in the oven for 2 to 2½ hours, until the meat begins to fall apart with the poke of a fork.

4. Remove the lamb chops from the pan and strain the braising juices into a bowl. Reserve the carrots for garnish.

5. Refrigerate the braising liquid until the fat rises to the surface and can be easily skimmed off and discarded (at least 1 hour). Skim and pour the juices in a saucepan. Boil the liquid over medium-high heat for about 20 minutes or until reduced by half.

6. Stir in the pomegranate molasses and butter, if using. Season with salt and pepper and add the lemon juice.

7. Look at the lamb closely and remove any little chunks of excess fat from around the edges of the chops with your fingers.

8. Reheat the lamb and carrots in the sauce by simmering them over low heat for about 10 minutes. Turn the lamb to coat it nicely with the sauce after 5 minutes and serve.

Galette of Tender Pork with Cumin and Cider

Arabic cooking doesn't include pork because of Muslim dietary restrictions, so this is a dish with a little Spanish inspiration. The Moors in Spain cook with pork using Arabic flavors. The savory cumin, combined with cinnamon and sweet cider, gives this dish its sweet/sour signature and great autumn flavors. The pork is cooked in cider and spices until it pulls apart easily with a fork. It makes a great filling for Spanish-style empanadas (using puff pastry) or stuffed into an apple or pumpkin and baked again.

A German rosé (see page 357) made from *spatburgender* grapes (the German name for pinot noir) pairs very well with this dish.

⟶ Makes 8 galettes to serve 4 to 8 ⟵

---

4 pounds pork butt (boneless shoulder meat), cut into 4 equal pieces

¼ cup salt

3 tablespoons ground cumin

4 tablespoons chopped garlic (about 12 cloves or 1 head)

4 cups apple cider (if you can't find cider, use apple juice and add 3 or 4 sliced apples to the braising liquid)

2 cups white wine

1 cinnamon stick

3 eggs

1 cup dry bread crumbs

Salt and pepper to taste

2 tablespoons butter

2 tablespoons canola oil

USING SALT

Salt is one of the most important ingredients to understand because its use is crucial in drawing out flavor. Salt must be used with balance. It is important to season with salt throughout the cooking process, adding it little by little. If you season a dish with salt only after it has finished cooking, the ingredients will not have had enough time to absorb the salt, and you will taste it on the outside of the food. Generally, slow-cooked dishes like Galette of Tender Pork with Cumin and Cider require a heavy hand with salt, as do potatoes and green beans. Whenever possible, use sea salt or kosher salt. Sea salt is pure salt that all other commercially produced cooking salts try to mimic. Kosher salt is salt with added minerals. Avoid iodized salt. It is highly processed with chemicals and leaves a harsh flavor on food.

1. Preheat the oven to 350°F.

2. Season the pork butt generously with the ¼ cup salt. Rub it with cumin and garlic, and place the meat in a heavy braising pan. Add the cider, white wine, and cinnamon stick to the pork, then cover the pan with three layers of baking foil, or use a lid that fits tightly.

3. Braise for 2½ to 3 hours or until the meat is tender and can be pulled apart with a fork.

4. Drain and reserve the braising liquid and let the meat and liquid cool for at least 1 hour (as long as overnight). Skim the fat off the braising liquid and reserve 1 cup. Keep the rest of the liquid for other uses, like soup. It freezes well.

5. When the meat is cool enough to handle, begin roughly shredding it with a fork or by hand, discarding any fat or tissue.

6. Combine the pork with the eggs, bread crumbs, and 1 cup braising liquid and season with salt and pepper. Form the meat into 8 patties.

7. In a medium or 10-inch sauté pan over medium-low heat, combine 1 tablespoon of the butter and 1 tablespoon of the oil. Brown the patties 4 at a time and cook until they are golden brown and crispy outside and hot in the middle, about 5 minutes on each side. Brown the remaining 4 patties with the remaining 1 tablespoon butter and 1 tablespoon oil.

8. Serve the pork patties with Chickpea Crepes (page 8).

Grilled Skirt Steak with Tomato, Caramelized Butter, and Cumin

This is a twist on a classic Turkish kebob called *Iskander*, which is typically served as chunks of grilled meat on a small pita, topped with tomato, brown butter, yogurt, and hot peppers. I like to use skirt steak because it's full of flavor and the price is right. Quality (organic or natural) beef in prime cuts is expensive. You can substitute sirloin for this recipe if your butcher can't provide skirt steak and your budget allows it.

This recipe will work best if you use Greek yogurt, which is thicker and creamier than other yogurts and has a consistency like sour cream. You may find it in some markets, such as Trader Joe's, and in most Arabic, Greek, or Armenian shops. Old Chatham Sheepherding Company makes good tangy yogurt you can use as a substitution (on the Web at www.blacksheepcheese.com or at whole foods markets). For this recipe, the yogurt doesn't necessarily have to be thick, but it does need to be tangy and made with rich, whole milk.

Pair this dish with a Chianti Classico or other Sangiovese-based wine.

⌒ SERVES 4 ⌒

---

4 cups canned diced tomatoes, drained (28 ounces)

2 tablespoons olive oil

2 teaspoons chopped garlic (about 2 cloves)

Salt and freshly ground pepper to taste

1 stick plus 1 tablespoon butter

4 long, thin, green sweet or hot peppers or 2 green bell peppers

4 teaspoons ground cumin

2 teaspoons dried oregano

1 teaspoon ground Aleppo chilies or medium-hot paprika

3 pounds skirt steak, trimmed of fat and any silver skin, and cut into 6- to 8-inch-long pieces

1 tablespoon canola oil for searing

2 large pita breads, cut in half

1 cup plain yogurt, preferably Greek

---

1. Preheat the oven to 375°F.

2. In a medium saucepan over medium heat, simmer the tomato chunks with 1 tablespoon of the olive oil, the garlic, salt, and pepper for about 20 minutes, until the tomatoes break down and become soft and saucy.

3. Meanwhile, in a small skillet, melt one stick of butter on low heat and simmer for about 12 minutes until the butter turns nut brown and smells like hazelnuts. The solids will begin to separate and then fall to the bottom. Butter turns from brown to black very quickly, so watch closely. Immediately remove the butter from the heat and strain through a fine sieve into a dry container. Set aside to cool. The butter is very hot, so be careful not to spill any water in it as it cools; otherwise, the butter will spit and bubble, the way hot oil does.

4. Stir half of the caramelized butter into the tomato sauce and purée it in a blender until smooth. Reseason it with salt and pepper and set it aside.

5. In a medium mixing bowl, put the peppers in the remaining 1 tablespoon of olive oil and season them with salt and pepper. Place the peppers on a baking sheet and roast them in the oven until they are soft and collapsed, 8 to 10 minutes. Set them aside but keep them warm.

6. In a small mixing bowl, combine the cumin with the oregano and Aleppo chilies and sprinkle the skirt steaks evenly on both sides with the spice mixture.

7. Grill the steaks over charcoal (see Grilling Tips, page 100), or sear them as follows. In a large, heavy skillet or cast-iron pan over medium-high heat, mix ½ tablespoon of the canola oil and ½ tablespoon of the remaining butter. When the butter turns brown, add the steaks and sear them on the first side, allowing them to brown for about 5 minutes. Lower the heat if the pan becomes too smoky or if the spices begin to burn. Turn the steaks over and brown the other side. Cook for another 5 minutes if you want them more well done. Put them on a platter to rest and wipe the pan out. Brown the remaining steaks with the remaining ½ tablespoon of butter and oil.

8. Arrange the pita halves on 4 plates. Remove the steaks from the pan and rest them on the pita. As the meat rests, the juices will soak into the bread. Top with tomato sauce, yogurt, and the peppers and serve with the extra caramelized butter to drizzle over all.

COFFEE

Arabic coffee is ground as fine as powdered sugar and flavored with cardamom. It's brewed slowly and carefully on a stovetop in a small, long-handled copper or stainless steel urn. The cardamom is either ground and brewed with the coffee, or the cardamom pod is smashed and you will find it floating in the coffee, where you sip around it.

Turkish coffee is ground ultrafine like Arabic coffee and prepared on the stovetop, but the Turks do not use cardamom to flavor their brew. I have seen many different preparations of Turkish coffee. Some people add lots of sugar. Some add very little sugar. Some let the coffee rise only once while swirling the pot from time to time. When I saw the coffee boiled on hot sand at Kokkari, a Greek restaurant in San Francisco, it turned out thick as custard sauce. The ultimate goal, however, is to achieve the *crema* (foam).

The Turkish coffee recipe included in this book (page 32) was taught to me by Mark Mooridian of MEM Tea, who is Armenian and sells beautiful wild herbal teas from his home country. Mark blends our Turkish coffee and grinds it fresh every week. One commercially available blend I recommend is called Kurukahveci Mehmet Effendi, and you can find it at www.tulumba.com.

You drink Arabic or Turkish coffee until you reach the silt at the bottom of the cup, and then you turn the cup over onto its saucer and leave it to rest for a minute. The silt forms patterns that predict your future. The ritual is to sit around and tell stories, predicting the future by reading the patterns of the grounds.

I once spent almost 2 weeks with a woman named Ayfer Unsal who lives in Gaziantep in southeast Turkey. Ayfer is a journalist and food writer who now lives in Istanbul and is one of the most charismatic people I have ever met. She had organized a gastronomic tour for me that kept me busy every minute from 7 a.m. to 10 p.m. Gaziantep, or Antep, is 1 hour from the Syrian border and is famous for its kebobs and pistachios, and considered to be the gastronomic capital of Turkey.

When I first arrived, Ayfer had organized a potluck luncheon in a park, and twenty of her female friends were there to greet me. They all brought a family dish to demonstrate that the best food in Gaziantep is cooked by women at home. We feasted on salads of purslane with tangy pomegranate molasses; seven different kinds of *köfte*; lamb, beef, and nutty pilafs. At the end of this unforgettable lunch, we drank Turkish coffee. Ayfer told me that when I finished my coffee, I should turn the cup upside down and let it rest on its saucer for about five minutes. We spent the rest of the afternoon watching Ayfer make her way around to tell each lady a story about her future.

Ever since my special lunch with Ayfer, I've enjoyed the ritual of drinking Turkish coffee. The reading of the patterns of the grounds inside the cup can last as long as the meal and is a time for bonding, playfulness, hopefulness, and serious life conversations.

Ayfer Unsal's Guide to
Reading Fortunes in Your Coffee Grounds

Rectangle: You will receive some goods.

Triangle: You will receive either a present or money.

Circle: You will have good fortune. You could get married or receive a job promotion.

Cube: You will have a happy family.

Bow: Some happy event is very near.

Star: You will take a short trip or you will make a good investment.

Rising sun: Your dreams will come true.

American football: You must sacrifice to win somebody's heart.

Woman's purse: You will receive money in the near future. Be frugal.

Palm tree: You will have a fantastic holiday and meet new people.

Key: You will move into a new home. You will win somebody's heart.

Leaf: You will hear from an old friend or make a new one.

Eye: Somebody is jealous of you.

Butterfly: Be careful of a new friend.

Ear: Don't believe everybody. Be careful!

A bunch of little dots: You are spending too much money. Please be careful.

Arabic Coffee Pot de Crème

Pot de crème is French for pudding. At Oleana, we leave some coffee grounds in this creamy custard to strengthen the coffee flavor. The grounds are so fine they don't ruin the smooth texture. They settle to the bottom of each crème to form a thin layer of grounds as they bake, so you can read a fortune in your pudding, too!

You can infuse the cream with the crushed espresso and cardamom a day ahead of time, storing it in a tightly sealed container.

This dessert is delicious served with Turkish Coffee (page 32).

⌁ SERVES 8 ⌁

1 cup espresso beans	¾ cup sugar
2 tablespoons whole green cardamom	2 tablespoons brewed espresso, cooled
2 cups heavy cream	1½ tablespoons very finely ground espresso
1½ cups whole milk	1 cup heavy cream (whipping cream)
6 egg yolks	

1. Crush the espresso beans and cardamom by placing them together in a thick plastic bag and lightly pounding them or crushing them with something heavy (a rolling pin or wooden mallet works well). The espresso beans should have the texture of coarsely chopped nuts and the cardamom pods should split open.

2. In a medium saucepan, bring the cream, milk, and crushed espresso and cardamom to a boil. Remove the saucepan from the heat. Cover the mixture and let the coffee and cardamom steep in the cream for about 1 hour.

3. Preheat the oven to 300°F.

4. In a small bowl, whisk the egg yolks and the sugar together until thoroughly combined. Strain the cream (which is now infused with cardamom and coffee) through a fine sieve into the yolks, while whisking.

5. When combined, strain again through the fine sieve to remove any pieces of cooked or lumpy yolk. Stir in the brewed espresso and espresso grounds.

6. Fill eight 4-ounce espresso cups or ramekins with the mixture, pouring almost to the top, and place the cups in a large ovenproof baking dish. Pour some lukewarm water into the baking dish until it reaches halfway up the sides of the cups or ramekins. Using a small spoon, skim any fine bubbles that form on the top of each custard. This will ensure a smooth and creamy top.

7. Cover the pan tightly with foil and bake for 45 to 50 minutes. Carefully remove the foil, because escaping steam can burn fingers. Test for doneness by shaking the pan gently; the crèmes should be set around the edges and not quite firm in the center. Remove the crèmes immediately from the pan and set them onto a baking sheet or tray, allowing them to cool for 5 to 10 minutes.

8. Refrigerate the crèmes for several hours to chill and set. Top with whipped cream beaten to soft peaks and serve.

Turkish Coffee

For this classic drink, you will need a medium-size Turkish coffee pot (available at www.kalustyans.com) and 4 demitasse cups.

4 tablespoons finely ground espresso, as fine as powdered sugar

4 teaspoons sugar

4 demitasse cups full of cold water (about ⅓ cup)

1. Place coffee, sugar, and water in the coffee pot, and do not stir. Cook over high heat until the sugar starts to melt and the coffee looks shiny, about 3 minutes. The coffee will get hot and the mixture will start to collapse. At this point, remove from the burner and stir the coffee with a spoon. Place the mixture back on the heat. Holding the pot, watch and wait until the coffee is not quite ready to boil, but begins to rise to the top of the pot.

2. Remove from the heat and let it sit for 1 minute, then turn the heat on high and wait for the coffee to rise to the top of the pot again. This should take only 10 to 15 seconds, so make sure to watch the pot carefully. Repeat the process once more, for a third rising.

3. After the third rising, carefully skim a little bit of the foam—or *crema*—from the top and divide it equally into 4 demitasse cups.

3.

4.

4. Slowly pour the coffee into each cup, equally
dividing the coffee. There should be a little *crema*
on the top of each coffee.

5. Sip the coffee to the grounds, turn the cup over
onto the saucer, and let the grounds settle. Refer
to Ayfer Unsal's Guide to Reading Fortunes in
Your Coffee Grounds (page 29) for interpretation.

Künefe with Champagne-Cardamom Syrup

Künefe is an eastern Mediterranean dessert that is made with shredded phyllo dough (called *kadafi*) and filled with a sweet cheese. It's baked until golden and crispy and soaked in a sweet syrup.

I had tasted several different künefes in the United States, but I finally understood what is so special about this dessert when I ordered one at a kebob restaurant called Hamdi, in Istanbul, next to the Egyptian Baazar. Hamdi's künefe was the best, sweet, caramely, hot, crunchy, toasted cheesecake I had ever tasted. Hamdi used just the right amount of syrup, and the künefe was thin, crisp, and golden brown, with a sweet cheese center. In Turkey, they serve künefe with *kaymak*–a cream so thick that you can practically cut it–made from buffalo milk.

Maura Kilpatrick, who has been Oleana's pastry chef from the day we opened (and whose skills leave me speechless), makes this version of künefe. Maura flavors the syrup with a brilliant cardamom-spiked champagne, and she tops the warm, crispy cheesecake with a dollop of mascarpone cheese and crushed, toasted pistachios.

⌒ᴠ SERVES 12 ᴧ⌒

½ package shredded phyllo (kadafi), about ½ pound

10 tablespoons butter, melted

2 tablespoons whole milk

½ pound fresh buffalo mozzarella, grated on the large holes of a box grater

⅛ teaspoon freshly grated nutmeg

½ cup whole green cardamom pods

1 (750 ml) bottle sparkling wine (champagne), such as Prosecco

Zest of 2 lemons

¼ cup freshly squeezed lemon juice (about 2 lemons)

1½ cups sugar

½ cup coarsely ground pistachios

8 tablespoons mascarpone cheese

1. Preheat the oven to 375°F.

2. Place the phyllo in a food processor and chop finely into ¼-inch shreds, so that it looks like shredded wheat cereal.

3. Place the shredded pastry into a medium mixing bowl and add the butter and milk, stirring to coat the phyllo. Line an 8-inch-square heavy baking dish with half of this mixture.

4. Mix the mozzarella and nutmeg in a small mixing bowl. Spread this mixture onto the phyllo. Top with the remaining shredded mixture. Press the mixture with your hands, so that it becomes compressed or even and packed down. Bake for 45 minutes.

5. Meanwhile, crush the cardamom by placing the pods in a plastic bag and pounding them lightly with a rolling pin until the pods open and you see the black, oily seeds.

6. Combine the crushed pods, wine, lemon zest, lemon juice, and sugar in a medium-large saucepan. Bring to a boil over high heat, stirring to dissolve the sugar.

7. Turn the heat to medium-low and simmer the mixture for about 40 minutes, until it is slightly thick and syrupy and is reduced by about ⅓ (so that you have 2 cups left). Strain through a fine sieve.

8. When the pastry comes out of the oven, ladle 2 cups of the syrup, little by little, over the *künefe* until it's soaked.

9. Cut the künefe into slices and serve it immediately while it is still warm. Sprinkle each slice with pistachios, spoon on a dollop of mascarpone cheese, and let guests add the remaining syrup if they want more sweetness.

Paopao Cocktail

This cocktail is one of my favorites on the fall/winter menu at Oleana. Just for fun, our wine director Theresa Paopao (pronounced "pow-pow") and I created it. Theresa has developed a wonderful wine program at Oleana, and this pear and cardamom combination is another winner. Sweet and fragrant, it's perfect before a meal and is also a delicious accompaniment when served with Fried Haloumi Cheese (page 10). I like to use Prosecco, a sparkling wine from northern Italy, because of its straightforward taste and generous bubbles. You can use any other inexpensive sparkling wine that you like, such as a Cava from Spain. I recommend saving good champagne to drink as is.

⌒ᴧ Makes 6 cocktails ᴧ⌒

8 cardamom pods

½ cup water

½ cup sugar

1 cup pear juice or pear purée (find an all-natural juice, such as Ceres brand)

1 teaspoon freshly squeezed lemon juice (about ¼ lemon)

1 bottle sparkling wine, such as Prosecco or Cava (750 ml)

1. Smash the cardamom pods using the bottom of a small, heavy saucepan or rolling pin. Make sure all of the pods are cracked open and most of the black seeds are crushed.

2. In a small saucepan over medium-high heat, bring the water and the sugar to a boil with the cardamom pods. Reduce the heat to low and simmer for 8 minutes, until the syrup has thickened slightly so that it clings to a spoon.

3. Add the pear juice and bring back to a boil over medium-high heat. Remove the syrup from the heat and cover. Let it stand for 30 minutes to infuse the cardamom flavor.

4. Using a fine sieve, strain the pear juice and cardamom syrup through the sieve, pushing it through with the back of a spoon or ladle, into a small container or bowl.

5. Stir in the lemon juice. Chill the syrup in the refrigerator for at least 30 minutes, until very cold.

6. Fill the champagne glasses with 4 tablespoons of pear syrup each. Top off with Prosecco and serve.

C-Licious: Orange-Coriander Sangria

Try this special sangria in midwinter when oranges are best. You can also make it with blood oranges. The coriander adds a rich, toasty, bright flavor.

~ᴧ Makes 6 cocktails ᴧ~

2 tablespoons plus 1 teaspoon coriander seeds

1 cup freshly squeezed orange juice

½ cup granulated sugar

1 tablespoon sugar in the raw or brown sugar

4 slices orange or blood orange for wetting glasses and for garnish

1 cup cognac or good brandy

2 cups non-oaky, floral white wine, such as a Spanish Verdejo or Muscadet from the Loire Valley or Portugal

4 cups ice

1 cup plain sparkling water

⅛ teaspoon orange-blossom water (optional)

1. In a small skillet over low heat, lightly toast all the coriander seeds for 6 to 8 minutes, constantly shaking the pan. The seeds will release some of their oils and you will be able to smell them. Remove 1 teaspoon and set aside.

2. Add the orange juice and granulated sugar to the small skillet with the 2 tablespoons coriander and bring to a boil over medium heat. Turn off the heat, cover, and let the mixture cool, allowing the coriander flavor to steep for about 15 minutes. The mixture should then cool completely for about ½ hour in the refrigerator.

3. Blend the cooled orange mixture in the blender for about 30 seconds on high speed. Strain the mixture through a fine sieve into a small pitcher or bowl. The syrup should be a deep orangey-amber color.

4. Grind the reserved teaspoon of coriander in a spice grinder until very fine. Mix it with the sugar in the raw and transfer it to a small bowl or saucer.

5. Wipe an orange slice around the rim of each glass, leaving the glass rim a little wet. Dust the rims of the glasses with the coriander and sugar by dipping them into the mixture.

6. Mix the syrup with the cognac and wine in a pitcher with the ice. Add a cup of sparkling water and the orange-blossom water. Pour into glasses.

7. Garnish each glass with orange slices and serve.

2

Saffron, Ginger, and Vanilla

These spices have very little in common individually, but they blend well together to create dishes that taste particularly Moroccan—a cuisine famous for sweet-savory combinations. Saffron lends an earthy flavor; ginger gives brightness, citrus, and spicy notes; and vanilla adds sweetness to the mix. Vanilla is typically used in sweet preparations but can balance out bold spices like saffron or ginger nicely.

These flavors, whether combined or on their own, create very different effects. Combined, they make rich, delicious broths for fish, meat, and vegetable stews. They also work well together with long braises of beef or lamb. Individually, they brighten or deepen fish, vegetables, soups, and meat dishes. Saffron blended with garlic creates a North African–influenced Spanish flavor that is particularly good with fish, shellfish, or rice dishes. Ginger is great blended with cumin or saffron or on its own as a spice for fish. For balance, vanilla should be blended with other ingredients–like earthy saffron or acidic tomato or tart tamarind–to add depth to fish, shellfish, and vegetable dishes.

SAFFRON

Saffron is the dried stigma (the female part of a flower, onto which pollen is deposited in fertilization) of a specific crocus that blooms in the fall. Its flavor is woody, bittersweet, and slightly honeylike. It must be used with a careful hand because it is strong; too much saffron can make a dish bitter. It's a spice with a beautiful orange, sunny color that bleeds into food; the threads need to be infused in liquid for saffron to make a dish glow. Often, recipes call for a pinch of saffron, which is generally about 12 or 15 threads. It is famously expensive, since it takes 100,000 flowers to produce about a pound of saffron.

There are many varieties of saffron and many saffron-producing countries, including Spain, Greece, Iran, India, and Tasmania. Spanish saffron is the most common, but I find Persian saffron to have a floral aroma that is better suited for Arabic cooking. You can find Persian saffron online at www.amazon.com in the gourmet section. There are different grades of saffron, and if you see the term *coupe* used, it means that the saffron is pure stigma. Sometimes, saffron is sold with another piece of the flower, called a style, attached to the stigma. This makes the saffron about 20 percent cheaper, since the saffron is not pure stigma, but the flavor should still be the same. This kind of saffron is referred to as *mancha* in Spain. Sometimes fake saffron, such as safflower petals, is sold at spice markets.

Saffron is often used in Spanish and North African cooking. It is one of the spices that, when combined with others–such as paprika, cumin, coriander, cinnamon, and ginger–gives North African food its signature taste. In Spain, saffron is most often combined with garlic, paprika, and citrus. Saffron lends its color and flavor to many stews, couscous broths, and the spice mix ras el hannout (page 16). Saffron is also the spice that colors many Indian rice dishes and makes risotto à la Milanese, bouillabaisse, and paella famous.

GINGER

Ginger is the bulb or rhizome of a very leafy, tropical plant. When used in fresh form, its flavor is lemony, sweet, and spicy. In powdered form, ginger tastes similar, but lacks the lemony tones. Ginger can range in spiciness, so it's best to smell or even taste a little before using it. If it's particularly strong, use a little less in your recipe.

Although it's most famous for flavoring Asian food, ginger is also found in Arabic cooking, particularly in North Africa, where it's often combined with spices like saffron, vanilla, coriander, and turmeric. These spice mixtures give a sweet-savory or sweet-sour quality to a dish.

Fresh ginger is particularly good with fish; because of its lemony quality, ginger softens the salty sea flavors. Dried ginger works well in sweet desserts and with squashes, and it also brightens the flavors of slow-cooked stews.

Ginger is cultivated in Africa, India, Australia, and Jamaica. Jamaican ginger has the most delicate flavor and aroma.

VANILLA

Vanilla, like saffron, is harvested from flowers. It comes from a particular kind of tropical orchid that grows in Mexico, Madagascar, Central America, Africa, and Hawaii. This orchid produces clusters of pods or beans, as well as flowers. A fresh vanilla bean is dark brown in color, moist to the touch, as pliable as a piece of licorice, and extremely fragrant. Vanilla smells sweet and has a slightly smoky, caramel taste.

I store vanilla beans in the refrigerator or freezer to keep them from drying out. Inside the pods are thousands of tiny, black, oily seeds, which you can remove by splitting the bean in half lengthwise and scraping the seeds out with the back of a small paring knife. You can then use the seeds for cooking or baking. The outer pod still has great fragrance. You can dry the pods by leaving them out in a cool, dry place for a day or in a gas oven overnight, with just the pilot light on. Then you can store the dried pods in a jar with sugar for at least a week to make vanilla sugar, or you can steep them for a month or so in alcohol–bourbon works particularly well–to make homemade vanilla extract.

Even though vanilla is widely known as a flavoring for sweets, cakes, and ice creams, its smoky, caramel quality also enhances shellfish. It works well with saffron, and it lends sweetness to the typical Arabic combination of savory flavors like cilantro and nuts. Vanilla gives a rich, caramel flavor to spiced broths; see the recipe for Spicy Fideos on page 47.

Avoid imitation vanilla, which is often made from chemicals and clove oil.

RECIPES WITH SAFFRON, GINGER, AND VANILLA

Sweet Potato Bisteeya

This is my version of *bisteeya*, inspired by the classic sweet/savory Moroccan pie made with chicken or squab, saffron, cinnamon, sugar, and nuts. Traditionally, bisteeya is made with *brik* pastry, which is a paper-thin crepe. Brik pastry is hard to find, so I substitute phyllo dough in its place. If you have access to Middle Eastern or eastern Mediterranean shops, look for "country-style" phyllo dough that is a little thicker than the regular brands. It's easier to handle and is just as flaky. If you do have access to *feuilles de brik* or brik pastry, you will need about 6 sheets.

This spiced-up sweet potato pie is perfect for the fall and winter and is delicious on its own with an arugula, watercress, or spinach salad. It also makes a good accompaniment to chicken, beef, or venison.

Makes one 10-inch pie to serve 6 to 8

2 pounds (about 4) sweet potatoes, peeled and cut in half crosswise

2 tablespoons butter

1 large onion, finely minced (about 2 cups)

⅛ teaspoon turmeric

Pinch of saffron (about 12 threads)

1 teaspoon grated fresh ginger

Salt to taste

¾ teaspoon freshly ground white pepper (or black pepper)

4 eggs, beaten

2 tablespoons freshly squeezed lemon juice (about ½ lemon)

¼ cup finely chopped fresh parsley (about ½ bunch)

¼ cup roughly chopped fresh cilantro (about 1 small bunch)

¾ cup pine nuts

¼ cup confectioners' sugar plus 1 tablespoon for dusting

2 teaspoons ground cinnamon

½ cup extra-virgin olive oil

1 pound phyllo dough (you will need only 9 sheets)

1. Preheat the oven to 350°F.

2. Place the sweet potatoes in a medium saucepan and cover them with water. Bring them to a boil over high heat. Lower the heat to medium and simmer for 20 to 25 minutes, until the potatoes are tender.

3. Meanwhile, in a medium sauté pan over medium heat, melt and brown the butter. Stir in the onion, turmeric, and saffron. Lower the heat to medium-low and cook for 4 to 5 minutes, stirring occasionally, until the onions are soft but not brown. Stir in the ginger and set aside.

4. Drain the potatoes, reserving ½ to ¾ cup of the cooking liquid.

5. In a food processor fitted with a metal blade, purée the potatoes until they are creamy and soft, adding the reserved cooking liquid.

Depending on the size of your food processor, you may need to purée them in two batches. Season the mixture with salt and pepper to taste. Add the eggs, lemon juice, and herbs and blend again until smooth. Scrape the mixture into a large mixing bowl, stir in the onion mixture, and season with a little more salt to taste. Set aside.

6. Place the pine nuts on a heavy baking sheet and toast them for 8 to 10 minutes in the oven, until golden brown. Cool.

7. Coarsely chop the pine nuts by hand or in a food processor fitted with a metal blade. Place in a small mixing bowl and stir in ¼ cup of confectioners' sugar and the cinnamon. Set aside.

8. Begin to assemble the bisteeya by brushing the bottom of a 9-inch pie pan with olive oil. Place one sheet of phyllo dough on the counter and

continued

7.

9.

9.

brush generously with oil. Sprinkle with about a tablespoon of the pine nut mixture. Top with another sheet of phyllo dough and brush generously with oil. Add a third sheet and brush with oil.

9. Place these layers in the pie pan, allowing the edges of pastry to hang over the sides. Repeat the same process with another three layers of phyllo dough (one with nuts and two with oil only) and place over the other sheets in the opposite direction, so that the edges of the pan are completely covered and you have 4 equal flaps to eventually fold over.

10. Fill the dough with the sweet potato mixture. Make one last layer of 3 by repeating the same process of nuts and layered sheets. Place the dough on top of the sweet potato filling and fold the overlaying edges over on top so that the pie is completely covered.

11. Brush the top with oil and sprinkle the remaining nuts on top.

12. Bake the pie for 40 to 45 minutes, until puffy and golden brown.

13. Cut the pie into slices and dust with more powdered sugar. Serve the bisteeya warm or at room temperature.

10.

11.

11.

SPICE: FLAVORS OF THE EASTERN MEDITERRANEAN

Grilled Mushroom Banderilla

Banderilla is Spanish for "little skewer," and the grilled mushrooms make a perfect *tapas* or snack. The mushrooms are first marinated in saffron, onion, and garlic, and then they are ready to grill.

Mushrooms' availability will vary, and it is best to use them when they are in season. Mushrooms are foraged in the fall, and this dish lends itself to that time of year. My two top choices for mushrooms for this recipe are chanterelles or hen of the woods. Their piney, herbal qualities go well with saffron. Otherwise, cultivated oyster mushrooms, which are now widely available, make a good substitute at other times of the year.

This dish is especially good when paired with Garlic and Almond Soup (page 338), another delicious fall treat. It also works well as tapas, served with toasted almonds, and is excellent with Celery Root Skordalia (page 341).

Try serving it with a chilled Fino sherry or a light-bodied, low-tannin red wine, like tempranillo from Rioja.

SERVES 4

½ pound chanterelle or hen of the woods mushrooms, or 12 oyster mushrooms	1 tablespoon tomato paste
	½ cup white wine
2 tablespoons extra-virgin olive oil	4 sprigs fresh thyme, leaves only, finely chopped (optional)
½ small white onion, finely minced	
1 rib celery, peeled and finely minced	Juice of ½ lemon
2 teaspoons finely minced garlic (about 2 cloves)	Salt and pepper to taste
	8 bamboo skewers
1 pinch (about 12 threads) saffron	

1. Clean the mushrooms with a towel and trim the dry, dirty stems. Avoid washing them if possible, because they absorb too much water.

2. In a medium skillet over medium-low heat, cook 1 tablespoon of the olive oil, the onion, celery, garlic, and saffron. Cook until the onions soften, 5 to 6 minutes. Do not brown the onions.

3. Stir in the tomato paste, wine, mushrooms, and thyme and simmer on low heat for about 15 minutes, until the wine and liquid that the mushrooms release while cooking has reduced and glazed the mushrooms. Stir in the remaining 1 tablespoon olive oil and the lemon juice. Season well with salt and pepper. Cool and set aside.

4. Prepare a charcoal grill (Grilling Tips, page 100).

5. While your grill is heating, divide the mushrooms evenly among the skewers: about 6 chanterelles or hen of the woods mushrooms, or 3 oyster mushrooms to a skewer.

6. You'll know that the grill is hot enough to use when the charcoal has turned from red and black to gray. Place the skewers on the edges of the grill, not directly over the fire, and sear the mushrooms for 3 to 4 minutes on each side. The mushrooms should be golden and crispy and smoky in flavor.

7. Serve the mushrooms warm.

Spicy Fideos with Chickpeas, Vanilla, and Saffron

Fideos is a Spanish pasta, made from little pieces of broken vermicelli, that is toasted and then cooked in a rich broth. The pasta absorbs the broth flavor and retains the starch, forming a creamy consistency.

Arabs brought fideos to Spain, along with the custom of toasting the pasta. Turks toast their ravioli, called *manti,* and add toasted vermicelli pieces to pilafs.

I once demonstrated how to make this dish at a conference in Rome, sponsored by Barilla Pasta and Oldways Preservation and Trust, called "Pasta Fights Back." The conference included doctors, scientists, nutritionists, and a handful of chefs, who were all trying to inform the media that dried pasta (made from durum wheat) is a good carbohydrate and not a bad one. In essence, we were attempting to stop the sweeping Atkins crash diet before we all get diseased, fatty livers. The audience was full of Italians, who gasped as I started to crush the vermicelli into little pieces. Italians never crush pasta, and they always boil it in plenty of water, to remove a lot of its starch. I demonstrated this way of cooking pasta as if it were rice in a pilaf. They were skeptical, but once they tried it, they loved it.

This little pasta dish is packed with flavor and is great with lots of cooked greens like Swiss chard or spinach. Traditionally, Spanish fideos is made with fish and is cooked in a highly flavored fish broth and then finished with a homemade garlic mayonnaise to make it extra creamy. Here's my vegetarian version, which is now a signature dish at Oleana. You can make the broth days ahead of time and freeze it.

Pair this vegetarian pasta dish with an Italian Barbera that is spicy, rich, and slightly smoky.

⌒ SERVES 10 ⌒

1½ cups dried chickpeas, soaked overnight

1 tablespoon salt plus more to taste

1 pound angel hair pasta coils,
  preferably De Cecco brand

1 tablespoon canola oil

1 large onion, roughly chopped

1 carrot, washed and roughly chopped

2 tablespoons peeled and smashed garlic
  (about 6 cloves)

1 bay leaf

1 teaspoon saffron

⅓ vanilla bean

1 teaspoon ground coriander

1 teaspoon fennel seeds, finely ground
  in a coffee grinder (see page 72)

4 ancho chilies, stemmed and most
  of the seeds removed (about 1 cup)

4 cups chopped, canned tomatoes with juice
  (28-ounce can)

1 tablespoon cocoa powder

8 cups water or vegetable stock

Pepper to taste

1 large bunch Swiss chard, washed, stems
  removed, and leaves very finely sliced
  (about ⅛ inch)

½ cup extra-virgin olive oil

¼ cup Lemon Aioli (page 50)

1. Preheat the oven to 375°F.

2. Strain the chickpeas, place them in a medium saucepan, and cover them with water to double or triple their volume. Place on high heat and bring them to a boil. Reduce the heat to medium-low and simmer for about 25 minutes, until very tender. Add a tablespoon of salt and let them sit.

3. Meanwhile, to make the fideos, crush the pasta coils with your hands into very small pieces (about ½ inch) over a large baking sheet. Spread the pieces out evenly on the sheet and then bake them for 10 to 12 minutes, until golden brown. Set aside.

4. In a large saucepan, heat the canola oil over medium heat and add the onion, carrot, garlic, bay leaf, saffron, vanilla bean, coriander, and fennel. Stir well so that all the ingredients are coated with oil and cook, stirring occasionally, for about 6 minutes, until the carrots and onion start to soften. Add the chilies, tomatoes, cocoa, and the water and bring the pot to a boil. Reduce the heat to medium-low and simmer for about 55 minutes, until the liquid has reduced by about a third. Remove the bay leaf and the vanilla bean. Scrape the vanilla bean lightly and add any black seeds back into the broth.

5. Purée the broth with a handheld emulsion blender or in small batches in a regular blender

until smooth. Strain through a fine sieve and season to taste with salt and pepper. You should have about 8 cups of well-seasoned, concentrated broth.

6. In a large sauté pan (about 11 inches) with deep sides, bring the broth to a simmer over medium-high heat, and add the chard leaves. Cook over low heat, until the chard wilts and starts to become tender, about 6 minutes.

7. Drain the chickpeas and add to the broth.

8. Reduce the heat to medium and add the fideos and ¼ cup of the olive oil. Cook for about 10 minutes, stirring occasionally, until the pasta absorbs all the broth.

9. Season with salt to taste.

10. Add 4 tablespoons of lemon aioli and stir until the mixture becomes creamy. If the fideos are really thick, stir in a little water. The mixture should have the consistency of macaroni and cheese before baking. It should be nice and creamy but thick enough to stay on the spoon when you eat it. Serve immediately.

3.

3.

Lemon Aioli

After you add this lemon aioli to the fideos, you'll have a lot left over. It's delicious served with roasted potatoes, raw or roasted vegetables, cold poached shrimp, or the Halibut Cakes on page 76 (substitute the aioli for the olive oil lemon sauce).

—⌐ MAKES 1 CUP ⌐—

---

2 egg yolks

1 teaspoon Dijon mustard

2 teaspoons finely chopped garlic (about 2 large cloves)

Zest of 2 lemons, preferably organic

1 tablespoon lemon juice

½ teaspoon salt

¾ cup canola oil

---

1. Using a food processor fitted with a metal blade, process the egg yolks, mustard, garlic, lemon zest, lemon juice, and salt until frothy, about 30 seconds.

2. With the machine running, slowly pour in the canola oil, little by little, until it becomes thick, like face cream.

3. Reseason with salt to taste.

☙ A Substitute for a Richer and Deeper Flavor

In place of the lemon zest in the aioli, take the zest of 2 oranges and dry them out in a low oven (200°F) for 15 to 20 minutes, until lightly toasted. For more information, see "Toasting Citrus Zest" on page 72. Cool and grind the toasted zest in a spice grinder. This zest adds a malty orange flavor that is absolutely fabulous with the fideos.

Egg-Lemon Soup with Saffron and Crab

This recipe is a twist on the classic Greek *avgolemono* or egg-lemon soup. It is rich and velvety–perfect for a cold day. I like to combine a bouillabaisse flavor like saffron to the lemony soup base. I'm partial to crab because I grew up eating so much of it in the Pacific Northwest, but you can also add or substitute lobster and shrimp to this dish if crab is not available or if you want to make a bigger meal. I like to use Spanish medium-grain or Arborio rice in this soup because it contains a little more starch than long-grain rice and helps to give the soup a silkier texture. If you need to substitute long-grain rice, add another half cup to the recipe. The fish broth that makes the base of this recipe is best when made the same day as the soup.

   Try this soup as a first course before serving a meat dish, such as Lamb Steak with Turkish Spices (page 166) or *Sarikopites* (page 83) for a light meal. It is delicious with a glass of chilled sake.

MAKES ABOUT 10 CUPS TO SERVE 8

3 pounds cod bones or any white fish bones, with heads removed	1 cup medium-bodied, non-oaky white wine, such as a dry Riesling
1 tablespoon canola or vegetable oil	1 cup medium-grain Spanish rice, or round rice such as Arborio
1 onion, peeled and roughly chopped	Salt and pepper to taste
2 bay leaves	6 egg yolks
2 cloves garlic, peeled and smashed	½ cup plus 1 tablespoon freshly squeezed lemon juice (about 2 large lemons)
2 ribs celery, roughly chopped	1 pound fresh lump crabmeat, either Maine or Dungeness
1½ teaspoons saffron	
½ teaspoon paprika	

1. Using a heavy knife or cleaver, chop the fish bones in 4-inch pieces so they fit easily in a large saucepan. Rinse the bones under cold water to remove most of the excess blood and drain them well.

2. In an 8-quart stockpot, heat the oil over medium-high heat and add the fish bones. Stir, using a pair of tongs, so that the fish bones are coated in the oil. Let them cook for 5 minutes, still stirring to draw more flavor out of the bones.

3. Add the onion, bay leaves, garlic, celery, saffron, and paprika. Add the wine and then cover the bones with water. Bring to a boil over high heat. Reduce heat to low and simmer for 20 minutes. Don't cook the broth any longer, or it will turn cloudy and off-flavored.

4. Strain the broth through a fine strainer into another 4-quart saucepan.

5. Add the rice and season lightly with salt and pepper. The liquid will concentrate when reduced.

6. Bring the mixture to a boil over high heat. Reduce the heat to low and simmer for 15 to 20 minutes, or until the rice is tender and cooked through.

7. About 15 minutes before serving, whisk the egg yolks and lemon juice in a small mixing bowl. Ladle 2 cups of hot soup into the egg mixture and whisk until combined. This will warm up the egg yolks and help to keep them from curdling when added to the rest of the soup.

8. Add the egg yolk mixture to the rest of the soup, whisking vigorously. Bring to a simmer over low heat and simmer for just a few minutes, to cook the yolks. Remove the soup from the stove.

9. Carefully blend the hot soup in small batches in a blender, or use a handheld emulsion blender, until smooth.

10. Using a small ladle or spoon, push the soup through a fine sieve to remove any bits of rice or egg yolk and to make the soup ultrasmooth. This step is optional but will achieve a worthwhile, very silky texture.

11. Bring the soup gently to a boil again over medium heat, reduce heat to low, and hold warm.

12. Place the crabmeat in a small bowl and sort through it with your fingers, removing any little bits of shell or cartilage. Squeeze out any excess water from the crab with your hands. Place the crab back into the bowl and season lightly with salt and pepper.

13. Spoon in ½ cup of the soup to gently warm the crab a little, and stir carefully to keep the large lump pieces intact.

14. Warm the bowls in the oven for a minute on low heat (250°F) or run very hot water over them, taking care to dry them well.

15. Divide the crab equally into 8 warm soup bowls. Ladle hot soup over the crabmeat and serve immediately.

Monkfish with Ginger, Crème Fraîche, and Seared Greens

Monkfish has a dense structure, like lobster, scallops, or tenderloins of pork or beef, so it can be cooked with powerful flavors such as ginger and is perfect for high-heat cooking and sweet fall flavors.

Try serving this dish with some roasted apples, figs, or peach slices. Brush some fresh-split figs or thick slices of apple or peach with extra-virgin olive oil, and then grill, or roast the fruit in a 350°F oven for 10 to 15 minutes, until tender.

Try a non-oaky chardonnay, such as chablis, with this dish.

⟿ SERVES 6 ⟿

2 pounds monkfish, skinned (ask your fishmonger to clean them for you)

Salt and pepper to taste

2 pounds green or red Swiss chard (about 4 small bunches)

2 tablespoons extra-virgin olive oil

2 tablespoons butter

4 tablespoons finely chopped garlic (about 8 cloves)

1 tablespoon peeled and grated fresh ginger

2 cups crème fraîche

4 tablespoons flour

½ cup vermouth or dry white wine

1 lemon, cut into 4 wedges for serving

1. Cut monkfish into 6 equal portions, each about 5 ounces, and sprinkle them with salt and pepper. Set them aside or refrigerate them while preparing the rest of the dish.

2. Trim the stalks from the Swiss chard and reserve them for another use or discard them. Wash the chard well and place it in a colander to drain.

3. Heat 1 tablespoon of the oil and 1 tablespoon of the butter in a large skillet or deep-sided pan with a fitted cover. When the butter begins to brown, add the garlic, stirring constantly, and cook until the garlic turns golden brown, about 2 minutes. Add the chard immediately and cover. Cook for about 8 minutes, until the chard

continued

is limp and becomes tender. Remove from the heat and season with salt and pepper. Stir in the ginger and crème fraiche and reseason if needed. Keep warm.

4. In another large skillet or sauté pan over high heat, heat the remaining 1 tablespoon oil and butter, until the butter starts to brown. Dredge the fish in the flour and shake off any excess. Fry the fish until it is golden brown both sides, about 5 minutes a side. If the fish is very thick, turn the heat down and cover the pan to brown it more slowly and cook it all the way through.

5. Add the vermouth to the pan and let it cook down to almost nothing. This should take less than a minute and should glaze the fish, by pulling up any sugars that may be stuck to the bottom of the pan.

6. Remove the chard from the pan, leaving the juices in the pan, and smother the fish with it.

7. Bring the liquid from the chard to a simmer and cook on medium-low heat for about 5 minutes, until the sauce becomes thick enough to coat a spoon.

8. Pour the sauce over the fish and chard and serve with lemon.

AUTUMN GREENS MADE SWEETER

One of my greatest pleasures in being a chef is the close contact I have with some of the farmers who provide me with the best possible ingredients for my restaurant. One of my favorite farmers (besides my husband, Chris) is Eero Ruuttilla, from Nesenkeag Farm in Litchfield, New Hampshire. In addition to farming, Eero has a real gift for poetry, and he likes to include his descriptions of the earth's cycles with all of his communiqués every week via fax.

Autumn frost is deadly to a lot of vegetables. But when it frosts, many garden greens become sweeter. Here's a communiqué from Eero, explaining this phenomenon, in the late fall of 2002:

A couple of frosts last week signal that the farm season is entering its last phase—not the end, but definitely the beginning of a steady but slow wind down. No hard tears shed because of the frost; it was past due. With the exception of a couple of fantastic rows of haricots verts, the wimpy frost-susceptible crops were starting to look ratty—definitely showing the wear of overextending their stay in field. Many of the current field greens and roots have been waiting patiently for the frosts; now they get to show off some real color and flavor as the plant stress triggers the sugars and colors. More than an acre and a half of greens are still untouched—inching into their designated baby size. So please note that the frosts hardly end the season; they just mark the final phase of New England—grown field greens glory. You, my loyal customers, are now rewarded with incredible flavor and color!

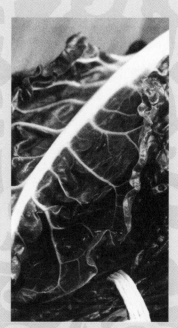

Persian Fried Chicken

The yogurt and saffron marinade in this recipe is a typical Persian seasoning for chicken kebobs. The yogurt acts as a tenderizer, so it's important to let the meat sit in the mixture for at least 3 hours. Flouring and frying chicken is not part of the Persian tradition, but I love these golden-hued, crispy, and moist chicken nuggets.

Drink a pale ale from England with this dish–one that's fruity, hoppy, earthy, malty, and buttery.

⌐∿ SERVES 4 ∿⌐

2 cups plain, whole milk yogurt	2 cups flour
½ teaspoon saffron	1 teaspoon paprika
1 tablespoon chopped garlic (about 3 cloves)	1 tablespoon dried spearmint
1½ pounds boneless, skinless chicken thighs (about 8 pieces)	Salt and black pepper to taste
	4 cups canola or vegetable oil
1 cup walnut pieces (almonds make a fine substitute)	4 lemon wedges

1. In a blender, purée the yogurt with a teaspoon of water and the saffron and garlic, until the mixture is smooth and bright yellow. Pour the marinade over the chicken thighs and mix well in a glass or stainless steel mixing bowl. Cover the chicken and let it sit in the refrigerator for at least 3 hours or overnight.

2. Preheat the oven to 350°F.

3. Spread the walnuts on a small baking sheet and toast them very lightly in the oven for about

6 minutes. The walnuts should be fragrant and oily but not dark brown, or they will taste bitter. Cool the walnuts and chop them finely by hand. Set aside.

4. In a small mixing bowl, combine the flour, paprika, mint, and a little salt and black pepper and set aside.

5. In a medium skillet (10 to 11 inches) with deep sides (that can hold 4 cups of oil so that it's ⅝ inch deep), heat the oil over medium heat to

350°F. Use a thermometer to check the temperature. Drain off the chicken marinade and discard, and then dredge the chicken thighs in the flour mixture and shake dry. Fry 4 pieces at a time, until they are golden brown on both sides, about 7 minutes, seasoning with a little more salt and pepper to taste. Remove the chicken using a slotted spoon or tongs and drain them on paper towels. You can keep them warm by lowering the oven to 200°F and leaving them there uncovered while the last four fry.

6. Serve the chicken immediately with lemon wedges to squeeze over the chicken and sprinkle with the walnuts. The chicken is wonderful on a bed of Mazy's Jeweled Rice (page 58) or with Rice Cakes (page 65).

Mazy's Jeweled Rice

This is a special-occasion rice, not for everyday meals. It takes some time to prepare.

Mazy Mozayeni worked with me for a little more than a year, and this recipe was inspired by a traditional Persian dish that his family made. Mazy's family used barberries instead of mulberries, which are harder to find without access to special shops. Dried mulberries look like little brown raspberries but taste like figs. They are used a lot in Turkish and eastern Mediterranean cooking, and they're fantastic in desserts or combined with nuts for pilaf, as in this recipe. You can find them at www.tohum.com.

Serve Mazy's Jeweled Rice with Persian Fried Chicken (page 56).

⌁ SERVES 8 ⌁

2 cups basmati rice	1 onion, finely diced
½ cup dried mulberries, or chopped dried figs	½ teaspoon saffron
¼ cup golden raisins	1½ teaspoons Persian Spice Mix (page 60)
1 large carrot, peeled	½ cup toasted pistachios
1 cup sugar	½ cup ground, toasted skinless almonds
Zest of 1 orange	Salt and pepper to taste
2 teaspoons butter	¼ cup extra-virgin olive oil

1. Soak the rice in cold water for about 1 hour. Drain in a colander or sieve.

2. Bring 8 cups of water to a boil in a large pot over high heat. (The rice needs plenty of water and room to cook.) Stir in the rice and cook uncovered, reducing the heat to medium-high, until just tender, for 10 to 12 minutes. Drain and rinse the rice under cold water until cool. Set aside in the rice-cooking pot.

3. While the rice is cooling, in a small mixing bowl soak the mulberries and golden raisins in hot water for 10 minutes or more, until plump.

4. Using a vegetable peeler, shave strips of carrot all the way down on all sides, stopping at the core. Set aside your pile of carrot ribbons.

5. Bring a small saucepan filled with 2 cups of water to a boil over high heat. Stir in the sugar and return the pan to a boil. Add the orange zest and carrot ribbons and return to a boil. Reduce the heat to low and simmer 8 to 10 minutes, until the carrots are soft and candied. Drain and roughly chop the strips.

6. Drain the mulberries and raisins and add to the chopped carrots.

7. Preheat the oven to 350°F.

8. In a medium sauté pan over medium heat, melt the butter and cook until it starts to brown. Stir in the onion, saffron, and spice mix. Cook on medium heat until the onions are soft, for about 6 minutes. Stir in the pistachios, almonds, and carrot mixture.

9. Fold this mixture into the rice and season with salt and pepper. Stir in the olive oil.

10. Place the rice in a roasting pan and bake for 20 to 30 minutes, until the rice is a little crispy around the edges and is hot. Serve immediately.

Persian Spice Mix

This spice mix reminds me of others from around the world: French four-spice (*quatre épice*), Chinese five-spice, and pumpkin pie spice from the United States. It is used to add aromatics to pilafs, stuffed rice, and bulgur dishes. I think it's also great sprinkled on cooked carrots, sweet potatoes, and squash. At Oleana, we use a similar spice blend, without the rose petals or nutmeg, on our Turkish-style steak tartare.

You can find dried rose petals at kalustyans.com.

─◆ MAKES ⅓ CUP ◆─

¼ cup dried rose petals, ground or pressed through a medium-size sieve	½ teaspoon ground cardamom (black seeds only)
¼ cup ground cinnamon	¾ teaspoon grated fresh nutmeg
2 teaspoons black pepper	¾ teaspoon ground coriander

Mix ingredients and store in an airtight container for up to 2 months.

UNDERSTANDING RIESLING AND GEWÜRZTRAMINER

Theresa Paopao, Wine Director at Oleana

There is plenty of confusion about Riesling and Gewürztraminer. Some think these wines are always sweet, so they won't go near them. Others who taste a dry Alsatian-style will insist that it's gone bad. Then, there are many adjectives which confuse matters even more. So to clarify:

Dry = not sweet at all

Off-dry = just the slightest hint of sweetness

Medium-dry = the sweetest wine to be enjoyed with a meal without overwhelming it

Spritz = a slight hint of effervescence

Seared Sea Scallops with Orange-Saffron Butter and Rice Cakes

I enjoy scallops when they are cooked only on one side, from the bottom up, until the pan side is golden brown. Scallops contain high levels of sugar and will brown beautifully, like no other fish or shellfish. In browning, the sugars are drawn out, and the scallop's flavor intensifies.

Orange saffron butter is fantastic on just about anything and really livens up simple dishes. It's a flavored butter or compound butter and will freeze very well. You can take a little out at a time and try using it with other dishes: in finishing a fish soup, for example, or to flavor a tomato sauce for pasta.

Drink a dry Gewürztraminer (see page 61) from Alsace with this dish.

⌒ SERVES 8 ⌒

---

1 teaspoon saffron

¼ cup dry vermouth

Zest of 1 orange and juice of half

Zest of 1 lemon and juice of half

2 sticks butter plus 4 teaspoons, softened to room temperature

2 teaspoons finely chopped garlic (about 2 cloves)

1 tablespoon chopped fresh parsley

½ teaspoon sweet paprika

2 teaspoons fennel seeds, ground finely in a coffee grinder (page 72)

1 teaspoon black pepper

Salt to taste

32 large, dry sea scallops (see note)

4 tablespoons canola oil

4.

4.

1. To make the orange-saffron butter, place the saffron in a small mixing bowl and add the vermouth. Let it steep for about 5 minutes. Add the orange and lemon zests and juices, the 2 sticks of butter, garlic, parsley, paprika, fennel, and black pepper. Mix to combine the ingredients and season with salt.

2. Lay a piece of plastic wrap out and spoon half of the flavored butter in an even layer. Fold the edges of the plastic wrap around the butter mound and twist the ends to form a small log. Repeat this process with the remaining butter and chill both logs.

3. Remove the foot or muscle from the side of the scallop (sometimes it has a little shell stuck to it). It is a little tough but is edible. I prefer to remove them.

4. In a medium sauté pan over medium-high heat, melt 1 teaspoon of the butter with 1 tablespoon of the oil until the butter starts to brown. Add 8 of the scallops and brown one side only, for 6 to 7 minutes, reducing the heat to medium if the scallops seem to brown too quickly or start to burn. The edges will turn from translucent to opaque, but the center on the top will remain a little translucent. Lift the scallops to check that they are brown with a golden crust and flip them over to cook the rare spot for 30 seconds.

5. Immediately remove the scallops from the heat and place them onto a platter. Dollop the scallops with 2 tablespoons of the orange-saffron butter and keep them warm by covering them with foil or by putting them into a small serving dish with a lid. The butter will melt from the heat of the scallops. *continued*

SAFFRON, GINGER, AND VANILLA

6. Wipe the sauté pan clean and repeat the searing process until all the scallops are cooked. It may be tempting to sear all the scallops at once, but the more crowded the pan is, the less likely you are to get a golden crust. Too many scallops cools the pan down, and they will start to steam instead of sear. If you have a very large pan, you can try to fit more scallops in at once, but leave about 1 inch between each. It's tempting to move the scallops around once they are in the pan, but don't do it. Allow them to attain a perfect sear.

7. Add 2 more tablespoons of orange-saffron butter to the scallops and stir to coat them.

8. Divide them evenly onto 8 plates and serve immediately with Rice Cakes (page 65) and Seared Greens (page 53).

❧ A Rule of Thumb for Searing

When browning, it is essential to sear your ingredients in a hot pan. To make sure your pan is hot enough, use 3 parts vegetable oil (do not use extra-virgin olive oil; it breaks down easily because it has a low temperature threshold) to 1 part butter. Add the oil and butter to the pan, and when the butter starts to brown, the pan will be hot enough to get a good, golden-brown searing color. Oil prevents the butter solids from burning, and the butter solids help to brown your ingredients. You're guaranteed a richer and more even color this way.

❧ Use Dry Scallops

Ask your fishmonger for dry scallops. A good fish market will carry only this kind. Sometimes lesser markets will sell sea scallops injected with water or saline to plump them up, making them more expensive per pound. These scallops won't brown well, as the water will release during cooking and cause the scallops to steam. Also, avoid using milky-looking scallops. During spring months, scallops start to spawn; it is during this time that they sometimes produce a cloudy liquid that makes them difficult to brown. I prefer not to wash scallops; however, if they are sandy, you must. Dry them well before cooking.

Rice Cakes

I love the sticky crust of a baked pilaf. I got frustrated that when I made pilaf in a big pot, there was never enough sticky crust to go around, so I came up with this recipe. By making individual rice cakes, everyone gets just the right amount of crust.

Yogurt and egg bind the rice in these little cakes. I sear them on the bottom side only so that they get golden and crispy, but the top stays soft.

MAKES 10 TO 12 MEDIUM RICE CAKES TO SERVE 5 TO 12

2 cups long-grain rice,
    such as jasmine or basmati

1 teaspoon salt plus more to taste

3 eggs

½ cup whole-milk plain yogurt,
    preferably Greek style

1 teaspoon salt plus more to taste

1 tablespoon canola or vegetable oil

1 teaspoon butter

1. Soak the rice for 20 minutes in warm water to cover. Add 1 teaspoon of the salt to remove some of the starch.

2. Bring 8 cups of water to a rolling boil over high heat.

3. Drain the rice and sprinkle it into the boiling water, little by little. Stir well.

4. Reduce the heat to medium and simmer the rice, stirring from time to time, for 6 minutes, until tender.

5. Drain the rice and allow it to cool for at least 20 minutes.

6. Preheat the oven to 350°F.

7. Meanwhile, in a medium mixing bowl, whisk the eggs with the yogurt until smooth and combined. Stir in the rice and season with salt to taste.

8. Heat a medium nonstick, ovenproof sauté pan over high heat, and add the oil and butter. When the butter browns, drop in four to six ½-cup scoops of rice and cook over medium heat until the bottoms brown, about 6 minutes. Repeat the process until all the rice cakes are cooked.

9. Place the pan in the oven and bake for 10 minutes. The bottoms of the rice cakes should have a beautiful crust and the tops should be soft. Serve immediately, with the crust side up, side by side with the Seared Sea Scallops (page 62).

Braised Beef Short Ribs with Vanilla-Glazed Carrots

These short ribs are a signature dish at Oleana. I created this recipe at Casablanca, the restaurant in Harvard Square where I cooked for five years before opening my own. I loved the ribs so much that I brought the recipe with me to Oleana

The ribs are like a decadent pot roast: they're soft, sweet, and tart from the tamarind, a Middle Eastern and Asian fruit that brightens a slowly braised dish.

With this dish, try a Carmenère from Chile, which is a sweet/savory wine with dark fruit, spicy flavors, and round tannins.

⟆ Serves 8 ⟅

---

8 beef short ribs, weighing about 6 to 8 pounds

4 tablespoons kosher salt

1 large onion, peeled and roughly chopped

1 whole carrot, peeled and roughly chopped

1 bay leaf

1 cup balsamic vinegar

1 cup medium-bodied, non-oaky white wine, such as a dry Riesling (see page 61)

½ cup packed brown sugar

1 tablespoon chopped garlic (about 3 cloves)

2 tablespoons tamarind paste (available in the Asian or Indian section of some grocery stores)

4 medium carrots, peeled

2 tablespoons butter

½ vanilla bean

Salt and pepper to taste

1 tablespoon freshly squeezed lemon juice (about ½ lemon)

---

1. Preheat the oven to 350°F.

2. Season each of the short ribs generously with the kosher salt. Lay them side by side in a large, heavy roasting pan.

3. Scatter the onion, chopped carrot, and the bay leaf over the ribs.

4. Combine the vinegar, wine, brown sugar, and garlic in a small mixing bowl and pour the

mixture over the short ribs. Place the tamarind in the same bowl and add 1 cup of hot water to dissolve it a little. Whisk the tamarind to loosen it and then add it and the liquid to the short ribs. There may be pulp and seeds from the tamarind, which you can strain out after cooking.

5. The liquid should come ¾ up the sides of the short ribs. Add more water if necessary.

6. Cover the pan tightly with foil and then again with a second layer of foil.

7. Place the pan in the oven and braise the short ribs for 3 to 3½ hours. Remove the foil and check that the short ribs fall apart when poked with a fork.

8. Remove the ribs carefully with tongs, place them onto a serving dish, cover, and set aside at room temperature.

9. Strain the liquid (you should catch any tamarind seeds or bits of garlic, onion, and carrot) through a fine strainer into a large container.

10. Chill the pitcher of liquid for at least 1 hour so the fat rises to the top. Remove the fat; it

should form a large, solid chunk at the top when cold.

11. While the braising liquid is cooling, slice the carrots slightly on the bias into ½-inch-thick ovals.

12. In a medium sauté pan over medium heat, melt the butter. Split the vanilla bean in half lengthwise and scrape the seeds with a knife into the melting butter. Add the carrots and ½ cup water. Season with salt and pepper.

13. Cook the carrots on medium heat until they soften and become lightly glazed, about 10 minutes. Add the lemon juice and stir. Reseason.

14. In a large, deep-sided sauté pan over high heat, bring the skimmed braising liquid to a boil and add the short ribs. Reduce the heat to medium-low and simmer the short ribs for 20 to 25 minutes, until they start to glaze in the sauce. The sauce will thicken after 15 minutes. Keep warm.

15. Roll the short ribs around in their sauce, using a pair of tongs, to make them a little more glazed and sticky. Place each short rib on a plate and spoon on a little extra sauce. Serve with glazed carrots.

Panforte

A cross between candy and cake, *panforte*, which means "firm bread," is a specialty of Siena and is excellent with coffee.

Many southern Italian sweets are Arab influenced. According to my friend and invaluable resource Cliff Wright, the traditional spices used in panforte–coriander seed, mace, cinnamon, cloves, and nutmeg–were all bought by Italian merchants in the great markets of Aleppo or Alexandria. It seems likely that the merchants encountered all kinds of Arabic sweets and that many culinary ideas passed to Italian cooks through them. The use of almonds, sugar, honey, and spices are markers of Arab influence, especially the sugar and almonds, because the Romans knew honey but not sugar.

At Oleana, Maura Kilpatrick creates her own version of this classic. It carries the use of spices on into the dessert course, with strong flavors of ginger, cinnamon, and clove.

Try serving this dish with a traditional Tuscan sweet wine, such as Vin Santo.

You will need a candy thermometer to make this recipe.

MAKES A 9-INCH ROUND FOR 16 SMALL PORTIONS

1 tablespoon soft butter	1 teaspoon black pepper
3 tablespoons cocoa powder	½ cup dried apricots
1 cup whole blanched almonds	½ cup candied ginger
1 cup whole blanched hazelnuts	½ cup dried figs
1 cup flour	½ cup candied orange
1 teaspoon ground cinnamon	½ cup currants
1 teaspoon ground ginger	1 cup sugar
¼ teaspoon ground cloves	⅔ cup honey
¼ teaspoon ground nutmeg	Confectioners' sugar

1. Preheat the oven to 350°F.

2. Butter a heavy 9-inch or springform pan and dust it lightly with some of the cocoa powder.

3. Toast the almonds and hazelnuts on a heavy baking sheet for 10 to 12 minutes, until golden brown. Cool and coarsely chop.

4. In a large bowl, combine the nuts with the flour, the rest of the cocoa powder, cinnamon, ground ginger, cloves, nutmeg, and pepper.

5. Chop the apricots, candied ginger, figs, orange, and currants into small pieces and combine with the nut mixture.

6. In a small saucepan, cook the sugar with the honey to 240°F on a candy thermometer. Immediately pour this mixture into the bowl with the rest of the ingredients and stir quickly to moisten. The mixture gets stiff very quickly and will become difficult to stir. Press the mixture evenly into the prepared pan. If the mixture gets too sticky, try wetting your fingers.

7. Lower the oven to 300°F and bake for 18 to 20 minutes, until it bubbles around the edges. It shouldn't brown.

8. When completely cooled, invert the panforte onto a serving plate or cutting board. Dust it generously with confectioners' sugar.

❧ 3 ❧

Sumac,
Citrus, and Fennel Seed

Tangy and bright, the flavors of sumac and citrus are interchangeable. Fennel seed, which is both savory and sweet, is a great companion and warms up citrus flavors. This spice group works best with fish, shellfish, and in salads. However, citrus notes and warm fennel flavor go well with almost anything.

SUMAC

Sumac is the edible round berry from a tree related to the mango. There are many species of sumac, and some of them are poisonous, so I do not recommend foraging for your own unless you are sure of the species.

Sumac berries grow in cone-shaped clusters and turn from dark pink to crimson as they ripen. The berries are about the size of a peppercorn, have a thin outer skin, and the flesh surrounds an extremely hard seed. Sumac is usually sold coarsely ground and slightly moist. Its aroma is fruity, and its flavor is tangy and somewhat salty, as sumac processors use salt to preserve it. Powdered sumac adds a beautiful purple color and a bright, lemony flavor to a dish. In fact, you can season food with sumac as you would lemon or vinegar. In the past, Arabic cooks used sumac when lemons were out of season or not available.

Sumac is excellent sprinkled on grilled fish, on chicken before roasting, on avocados, or in salads with cucumbers and tomatoes. I love it tossed with sliced raw onion and eaten with grilled meat. It's also excellent when mixed with other flavors like lime or orange and fennel (see Fish Spice, page 75). You can find sumac at www.tulumba.com, an online Turkish megastore.

CITRUS

All citrus fruits are used in Mediterranean cooking. Citrus is the flavor of the sun. It's in season in winter, just before Christmas.

In cooking school in Paris, I was taught to use lemon only to enhance the flavor of food. I learned that you should never be able to taste the lemon, unless you're making a lemon pie or lemon sauce. But this is not the Mediterranean way. Greeks buy lemons by the bushel, not by the piece. Lots of lemon, as well as garlic, makes Greek food taste

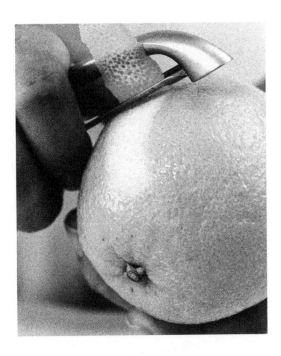

Greek. North Africans brine lemons to preserve them and then use them with grilled meats, in salads, and with vegetables. Sliced oranges are sprinkled with spices like cinnamon and paprika and combined with olives and cilantro. Sicilians use sour oranges in preserves and marmalades. Kumquats are baby oval oranges that are tart and sour but edible the whole way through; they are wonderful sliced thinly and eaten with salads or meats. There are many special varieties of tangerines and clementines; in southern France, they hollow out their clementines, fill them with sorbet, and sell them as fruit glacés. Spaniards and Sicilians use tart, black-red blood oranges in salads and gelatos. I have a fondness for these fruits, because my husband Chris proposed to me in a Sicilian blood-orange tree grove.

In most citrus fruits, the zest is sweet and contains natural oil, the pith is bitter, and the juice inside is tart.

Zesting Citrus

There are a few different ways to zest a lemon, orange, lime, or grapefruit. Some zesting tools have a handle and a blade with five or six small holes in them that strip the zest off the fruit. Other zesting tools are just small graters that shred the zest as it comes off. You can also use the finest gauge on a handheld box grater, or a vegetable peeler, being careful not to cut too deep into the pith. If you do take away a lot of pith during this process, you can remove it by placing a paring knife at a vertical angle between the pith and the rind and planing it off. Then you can chop, julienne, or mince the strips of zest.

Sectioning Citrus

Paul Ete, one of the chefs at La Varenne, explained sectioning an orange as follows. He described peeling an orange "a vif"–or skinning alive–and then trimming the top and bottom of the fruit by ¼ inch so that the fruit rests on a board without rocking and provides a cutting edge. Paul explained that an orange is like the world: you want to carefully follow its shape, starting at the North Pole and working down through the equator to the South Pole, removing the pith and the zest and leaving only the naked citrus. The fruit should maintain its original shape when finished, with no big dips or straight edges. Finally, using a small paring knife, you should cut in between each section inward at a slight angle to remove a perfect section without any membrane or pith attached. You should do this over a small bowl (to collect the juice) and follow all the way around the fruit, squeezing any excess juice over the cut sections.

Toasting Citrus Zest

One of my favorite flavors is toasted citrus zest, which adds a layer of caramel flavor to many of the dishes at Oleana. I even add a healthy pinch (or ¼ teaspoon) of toasted citrus zest to homemade mayonnaise with garlic and simple tomato sauces.

To make this delicious flavor addition, I peel the zest from a lime or orange and place it on a baking sheet in a gas oven overnight with just the pilot burning. I put a wooden spoon in the oven door to hold it ajar about an inch, creating a soft heat and allowing the air to flow. If you don't have a gas oven, you can dry the zest in 2 days in a cool, dry place and then toast it in a 200°F oven for a minute before grinding it in a blender to make a powder.

FENNEL SEED

Fennel can be eaten in many forms. The seed has a fresh, anise aroma and a flavor that evolves–

becoming warm, sweet, and slightly minty—and is best known for flavoring sweet Italian sausage. Pale green fennel seeds are cultivated from the sweet fennel plant in the fall, after it has flowered. Green fennel seeds are fresh, so the greener, the better.

The fronds (leaves) of the fennel plant look like wispy ferns and taste slightly sweet. They are good for flavoring light broths and soups and steamed fish and are also delicate enough to eat in salads.

Fennel bulbs are delicious sliced and eaten with coarse salt, plenty of black pepper, and extra-virgin olive oil.

Wild fennel is a different plant altogether and grows like a weed in warmer climates in Italy and California. It does not have a substantial edible bulb like sweet fennel does, and is harvested for its lively white flowers, which can be sprinkled on salads, ceviches, or broiled fish. Wild fennel has the flavor and aroma of fennel seed but with more intensity.

Fennel pollen is harvested from wild fennel flowers before they go to seed. The pollen is a golden-green dust that is rich and sweet, like honey. Fennel pollen is delicious sprinkled over raw Nantucket bay scallops which are eaten just like candy.

Sometimes fennel seed is confused with anise seed, which is from a different plant entirely. Anise seed has a much stronger flavor and is used to make licorice candies, pernod, pastis, ouzo, raki, and aquardiente.

I like to mix fennel with other spices, such as paprika, cumin, saffron, and cinnamon (see Moroccan Ras el Hannout, page 16) to flavor braised meats or Moroccan stews, to add to simple tomato-based pasta sauces for a layer of minty sweetness, and to sprinkle the whole seeds on pizza (Scallop Pizza, page 92), or onto homemade crackers (Crick-Cracks, page 176). Fennel is also a very important spice in making pickles (Nookie's Pickles, page 280).

RECIPES WITH SUMAC, CITRUS, AND FENNEL SEED

Fish Spice

There are many variations on spice blends. Knowing how to mix spices is somewhat more complicated than blending herbs: some spices require a heavy hand while others need only a pinch. Coriander, cumin, and dukkah (page 6) and za'atar (page 230) blends can be used very liberally. Saffron, cardamom, allspice, white pepper, nutmeg, cinnamon, allspice, and clove should be used more sparingly. Moreover, some blends work better with meats and others with fish. Stronger spices complement meat while acidic spices and dried herbs taste better with fish. Generally, all of the spice blends included in this book can be used with vegetables.

The citrus quality of this particular spice blend, which derives from either dried lime or orange and sumac, makes it perfect for fish. Toasting the zest gives it a caramel flavor. Sprinkle this fish spice on bluefish, squid, scallops, or shrimp after cooking.

MAKES A LITTLE MORE THAN ½ CUP

---

6 limes or 3 oranges

¼ cup sumac

¼ cup fennel seeds, ground finely in a coffee grinder (page 72)

1 teaspoon Aleppo chilies (see Resources, page 358)

---

1. Using a vegetable peeler, remove the zest of the limes or oranges without taking off too much pith. If you've got a lot of pith attached after stripping, remove it by using a small paring knife at a vertical angle to plane the pith off of the zest (see page 72).

2. Toast the citrus zest (see page 72).

3. Grind the zest in a blender or a coffee grinder and mix in the sumac, fennel seeds, and chilies.

4. Store the mix in an airtight container in a cool, dark place for up to 4 months, or in the freezer.

Halibut Cakes with Olive Oil–Lemon Sauce

Atlantic halibut is a large (50- to 100-pound) whitefish that is flaky and tender and has a rich, buttery flavor, even though it is lean. When halibut is not available, cod makes a good substitute. Atlantic cod, another lean whitefish, is firmer and more dense than halibut. The fish spice in this recipe perks up a simple fish-and-potato cake and adds bright flavors. It's great on any fish–including snapper, flounder, skate, monkfish, bluefish, striped bass, grouper, or salmon–but it's particularly delicious on whitefish.

The lemon–olive oil sauce is a favorite of mine, and I like it with any fish. Basically it's a lemon vinaigrette, blended until it emulsifies (a handheld emulsion blender would work well here). The sauce on its own is very lemony, and combined with the potato and whitefish, it's more elegant than the classic lemon wedge. You can also add some fresh oregano to the sauce and serve it with any grilled fish or squid.

These fish cakes pair nicely with a small glass of ouzo or Turkish raki before a meal. I learned the hard way that one must sip ouzo, merely to get it on the lips. It can be dangerous when consumed in large quantities. You can also try a white Rhone wine, such as a Rousanne or Marsanne, with this dish.

⟿ MAKES 8 LARGE FISH CAKES TO SERVE 8 ⟾

1 pound russet or Idaho potatoes
  (about 2 potatoes)

¾ cup plus 1 tablespoon extra-virgin olive oil

1 pound halibut fillet, boned and skinned

Salt and pepper to taste

1 tablespoon Fish Spice (page 75)

1 small white onion, finely chopped

1 teaspoon chopped garlic
  (about 1 large clove)

1 egg plus 1 egg yolk

¼ cup freshly squeezed lemon juice

½ teaspoon salt

1. Preheat the oven to 350°F.

2. Peel the potatoes and cut each into quarters. Place them in a medium saucepan covered with water over high heat and bring them to a boil. Lower the heat to medium and simmer the potatoes until they are very tender, about 10 minutes. Drain immediately.

3. Meanwhile, drizzle 2 tablespoons of the olive oil onto a heavy baking sheet and roll the fish fillet around in the oil, just to coat the baking sheet and the fish. Season the fish with salt and pepper.

4. Make sure the oiled fillet is skin-side down on the baking sheet, and sprinkle heavily with the fish spice. Bake until barely cooked through, for about 6 minutes.

5. In a small sauté pan, sauté the onion and garlic with 1 tablespoon of olive oil on medium-high heat. Cook for about 8 minutes, stirring from time to time, until the onions are softened and translucent. Set aside.

6. Using a small whisk, potato masher, or a fork, mash the potatoes. Do not worry if they are not really smooth. Season the potatoes with salt and pepper.

7. Stir in the onion, garlic, whole egg, egg yolk, and the fish fillet, being careful not to break the fish up too much. You want to bite into big, flaky chunks of fish. It gives the fish cakes more texture.

8. Place the lemon juice, ½ teaspoon of salt, and ½ cup of extra-virgin olive oil in the blender and blend until it thickens slightly.

9. Form the fish-and-potato mixture into 8 patties using a small ice cream scoop or a ½-cup measure.

10. Heat a large sauté pan with 1 tablespoon olive oil on medium heat. Brown 4 cakes at a time for about 4 minutes on each side. Wipe the pan clean and repeat the browning process with the remaining 1 tablespoon of olive oil. If the cakes absorb all of the oil, quickly add another tablespoon of oil after flipping the cake.

11. Serve immediately with a spoon of olive oil–lemon sauce and more fish spice sprinkled on top.

⚘ If the Sauce Separates

Try adding an ice cube and reblending the sauce. If it separates again, add ½ egg yolk to the blender and blend again. The sauce should coat the back of a spoon. You might find that the sauce becomes too thick, like mayonnaise; you can thin it out by adding a little water or more lemon juice.

Roasted Beets with Toasted Orange Aioli and Pine Nuts

I really enjoy the toasty, caramel flavor that the orange zest gives to the garlicky mayonnaise (*aioli*) in this recipe. The beets are a great way to start a meal as part of an antipasti or served with greens as a salad course.

There are many different beet varieties to discover nowadays. *Chioggia* (also called candy-striped) or golden beets work well in this recipe, as they are sweeter, milder, and more peppery than typical red beets. Both are heirloom beets (coming from old seed varieties that have been rediscovered), and they won't bleed much juice or stain your hands.

This recipe will trick guests who think they hate beets.

As a first course, serve this dish with an aromatic white wine, such as Viura, from Spain's Rioja region.

SERVES 4

---

6 small chioggia (candy-striped) or golden beets, the size of golf balls, with greens attached, if possible

½ cup pine nuts

1 tablespoon extra-virgin olive oil plus extra for drizzling

Salt and pepper to taste

1 cup toasted orange aioli (see the variation on Lemon Aioli, page 50)

1 sprig fresh oregano, leaves only, roughly chopped

Baby lettuces or your favorite salad greens

---

1. Preheat the oven to 400° F.

2. Cut the tops off of the beets and trim and discard any yellow or tough leaves. Trim off the stalks and wash the whole leaves well.

3. Trim about ¼ inch off the top and bottom of each beet so they stand without rolling around. Place them in a heavy roasting pan and drizzle them with 1 tablespoon of the olive oil and sprinkle them with salt and pepper. Cover them twice tightly with aluminum foil and place them in the oven.

4. Roast the beets for 30 to 40 minutes or until they are tender when pierced with a knife. They should be firm, but the knife should slide in easily. Cool and set aside.

5. Meanwhile, toast the pine nuts by placing them on a baking sheet in the oven for about 8 minutes, until they are golden brown. Cool and set aside.

6. Make the aioli.

7. Peel the beets with a small paring knife or by rubbing them with a paper towel to remove the skin.

8. Bring a small pot of water over high heat to a boil and drop in the clean beet greens. Add salt to taste. Reduce the heat to a simmer and cook the greens for about 4 minutes, until tender. Drain, cool, and set aside.

9. Smear some aioli to form a thin layer about ⅛ inch thick on the bottom of a large serving platter, using the back of a serving spoon.

10. Slice the beets in ¼-inch slices and arrange them over the aioli on the platter.

11. Chop the beet greens coarsely and season them with salt and pepper. If your beets came without greens, it's okay; the salad greens are sufficient. Sprinkle the beet greens and pine nuts over the beets and season with salt and pepper.

12. Sprinkle the oregano leaves over the top of the beets.

13. Drizzle a little olive oil on the top and serve the beets at room temperature with baby lettuces.

Endive and Apple Salad with Grapes, Sumac, and Pecan Labne

This salad is timely in the fall or winter, when delicate, local, fresh greens disappear after the frost. Look for tight, juicy heads of endive.

Labne is simply yogurt cheese. Yogurt contains a lot of water, and when you strain the water off, the yogurt becomes thick like ricotta cheese. You can buy labne at most Middle Eastern grocery stores, or you can make it yourself by mixing Greek yogurt with a little salt to taste and straining it overnight in the refrigerator in a colander or sieve lined with cheesecloth. The key to making your own labne is using yogurt that is high in butterfat, so whole-milk yogurt works best. If you use low-fat yogurt, the cheese will have a chalky mouth feel that you can eliminate with a splash of heavy cream, replacing the fat that is needed.

This labne recipe is inspired by my friend Maria Hatziiliades, the best home cook I know. Maria and her husband Max are from Thessaloniki, and I met her while her husband was building the restaurant space for Oleana. Max and Maria have taught me much about Greek food: one year they invited me to Athens to attend their daughter's wedding, and they took me on a several-day whirlwind tour of Greek cuisine. Max also now serves as Oleana's olive oil and ouzo supplier, filling boat containers of organic olive oil and pure organic ouzo and shipping them directly from Greece to the restaurant. Maria made this pecan labne for dinner one night and served it with mastic bread, which is made with the resin from the bark of a mastic tree.

Sprinkle the sumac over the salad at the last minute to make the color stand out. If mixed in with the rest of the ingredients, sumac turns everything purple.

Pair this dish with an off-dry chenin blanc, such as a Vouvray, that marries well with the sweetness of the grapes and apples and the bitterness of the endive.

⌒ᴠ Serves 6 ᴧ⌒

1 cup pecan pieces

2 small crisp eating apples, such as Fuji or Granny Smith, unpeeled

1 tablespoon chopped fresh parsley

1 tablespoon chopped fresh mint

1 tablespoon chopped fresh dill

1 tablespoon freshly squeezed lemon juice

3 tablespoons extra-virgin olive oil

Salt and pepper to taste

1 small bunch red seedless grapes (about ½ pound), stemmed and washed

2 teaspoons finely chopped garlic (about 2 cloves)

1½ cups labne

3 tablespoons ground zwieback crackers or plain melba toast

3 heads endive

1 teaspoon sumac

---

1. Preheat the oven to 350°F.

2. Toast the pecan pieces on a heavy baking sheet for about 6 minutes and until they are fragrant. Cool for at least 10 minutes.

3. Core the apples and slice them in very thin rounds, about ⅛ inch thick. Julienne them by slicing across the rings into very skinny sticks. If you own a mandoline slicer, you can use the julienne blade.

4. Place the apples in a small mixing bowl and toss them with the parsley, mint, and dill and 2 teaspoons of the lemon juice and 1 tablespoon of the olive oil. Season them lightly with salt and pepper.

5. Cut the grapes in half, figuring 4 to 5 grapes per person, and add them to the apple mixture.

6. Place the garlic and the remaining 1 teaspoon of lemon juice in a small mixing bowl and let stand for 5 minutes to soften the raw garlic flavor.

7. Add the labne, the remaining 2 tablespoons of olive oil, the zwieback crumbs, and season with salt and pepper, and stir.

8. Finely chop the lightly toasted pecans by hand or in a food processor, fitted with a metal blade. Reserve 1 tablespoon of the nuts for garnish and add the rest to the labne mixture.

9. Trim the bottom ends of the endive and remove the leaves, one by one. You will need to trim the bottom one more time to loosen the leaves. When you reach the heart or center of the endive and the leaves become very small and tight, set them aside.

continued

SUMAC, CITRUS, AND FENNEL SEED

10. Slice the endive hearts into thin rings and stir them into the apple mixture.

11. Assemble the salad by placing a quarter cup of labne on the bottom of each salad plate.

12. Using the back of a spoon, smooth the labne into a 2-inch circle. Arrange 5 endive spears on each plate, at a slight angle, sticking the bottom of the spears into the labne.

13. Spoon ½ tablespoon of the apple mixture over each endive spear. Sprinkle sumac and reserved pecan pieces over the salads and serve.

Sarikopites: Greek Pastries with Tuna, Fennel, and Kasseri Cheese

This recipe has a humorous origin, having to do with Sari Abul-Jubein, the owner of the Casablanca restaurant in Cambridge, where I headed up the kitchen for 5 years in the 1990s. Sari's great passions are food and travel. He taught me a lot about Arabic food (he is Palestinian, raised in Syria) and gave me many opportunities to travel and explore different Mediterranean cuisines.

Sari once returned from a trip to Crete and proudly handed me a recipe that included his first name in the title. Sarikopites are little pies, the shape of which are similar to sarikis, the traditional headdress of Cretan men. Cretans fill these pies with a local cheese and serve them for dessert with honey.

My version of sarikopites is not traditional but wonderful. I favor kasseri cheese, which is used in both Greece and Turkey and is made from sheep's or goat's milk. It has a creamy gold color, a mild flavor, and a firm texture–perfect for grating.

This dish is delicious paired with an intensely anise-flavored drink, such as ouzo, poured over ice, or Tsipouro from Crete.

⸺ Makes 8 pies to serve 8 ⸺

1 bulb fennel, stalks and outer tough layer removed

½ cup plus 1 tablespoon extra-virgin olive oil

1 small onion, minced

1 rib celery, peeled and minced

2 teaspoons finely chopped garlic (about 2 large cloves)

2 cups chopped fresh tuna (about 12 ounces)

¼ cup white wine

Salt and pepper to taste

½ cup chopped, pitted green olives

1 tablespoon chopped anchovies (about 4)

1 small bunch flat-leaf parsley, stems removed and chopped

1 cup grated kasseri cheese

¼ cup butter

1 pound phyllo dough (you'll need only 8 sheets)

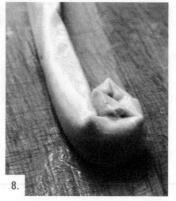

8.   8.   8.

1. Cut the fennel in half lengthwise and then in quarters. Remove the core by cutting at an angle with a knife. Wash and chop the fennel very finely by slicing it first and then dicing or mincing.

2. Heat 1 tablespoon of the olive oil in a large skillet over medium-high heat and sauté the onion, celery, and fennel until they are soft and translucent, about 5 minutes.

3. Stir in the garlic, tuna, and wine. Cook on low heat until the tuna is cooked through, for about 5 minutes. Season the tuna with a little salt and pepper. Keep in mind that the olives and anchovies will add salt as well.

4. Pour the tuna mixture into a strainer over a small mixing bowl to catch the juices. Cool for 10 minutes and chop very fine.

5. Place the tuna mixture in another small mixing bowl and stir in the olives, anchovies, parsley, and cheese.

6. In a small sauce pan, melt the butter and add the remaining ½ cup olive oil and any tuna juices.

7. Lay a piece of phyllo down with the longer side facing you, as if you are looking at a flag. Keep the phyllo covered with a damp cloth while you are working with each pie. Brush the phyllo sheet with a little of the butter-oil mixture.

8. Place about ⅓ cup of the tuna filling an inch from the bottom of the phyllo and spread it into a neat row, the long way. Roll it up as tightly as possible, so you have a long, thin coil. Brush the coil again with the butter-oil mixture, and holding one end, wrap it into a *sariki* or cinnamon roll shape. If the end wants to unravel, pin it with a toothpick or squish it tightly together with your hands.

9. Preheat the oven to 350°F.

10. Place the *sarikopite* on a heavy baking sheet and repeat the process with the rest of the phyllo and filling, making 8 pies.

11. Brush the top of the pies with the butter-oil mixture and bake for 25 to 30 minutes or until golden and crisp. Serve hot with a little glass of ouzo for sipping.

Serrano Ham with Blood-Orange and Fennel Salad

Versions of this dish have been on the menu at Oleana for years now, a light antipasti that bursts with flavor.

Serrano ham is a flavorful Spanish cured ham, available at specialty cheese shops or gourmet food stores. You can also order it online at www.formaggiokitchen.com; Formaggio Kitchen in Cambridge, Massachusetts, is one of my favorite local shops. Sliced Serrano ham can be wrapped well in plastic and frozen. Prosciutto is a fine substitute but has a milder flavor. In any case, it is crucial that the ham is sliced thinly enough so that any fat left around the edges will melt in your mouth. Ask your butcher to slice the ham as thinly as lightweight paper.

Blood oranges are in season from mid-December to early February. They are wonderfully tart and give bright acidity to the peppered fennel and salty ham. After you've sectioned the oranges, it's a treat to drink the juice. You can also freeze it to use in the C-licious Cocktail (page 37).

In November, this dish is wonderful with in-season persimmon instead of blood oranges. In the summer, I use peppery arugula mixed with the fennel. I like to season the fresh raw fennel with extra black pepper.

This antipasti is particularly delicious paired with a glass of delicate, dry Manzanilla sherry from Sanlúcar de Barrameda.

SERVES 6

2 bulbs fennel, stalks trimmed
and tough outer layer removed

Salt to taste

Fresh black pepper to taste

4 tablespoons extra-virgin olive oil

3 blood oranges, sectioned (see page 72)

12 fennel seeds

1 tablespoon chopped fresh parsley

12 green olives, pitted

12 very thin slices Serrano ham

1. Cut the fennel bulbs in half lengthwise and then in quarters. Remove the core by cutting it out at an angle. Slice the fennel as thinly as possible the long way and place in a medium mixing bowl.

2. Season the fennel with salt and plenty of cracked black pepper. Stir in the olive oil.

3. Toss in the orange sections, fennel seeds, parsley, and olives.

4. Place two slices of ham on each plate, side by side. Spoon ¼ cup of the orange mixture on the center of each slice of ham. Spread the mixture out evenly over the ham so that when your guests take each bite, they taste a little of everything. You can also roll the ham up and serve it as finger food or an hors d'oeuvre.

Chicken Egg-Lemon Soup with Grano and Sumac

This variation of the classic Greek egg-lemon soup called *avgolemono* is for lemon fans. It's one of my favorite soups; its smooth, velvety texture comforts me. See note on grano, page 88.

⌒ MAKES 8 CUPS ⌒

1 cup grano, soaked in water overnight

8 cups rich chicken stock, preferably homemade

½ cup plus 1 tablespoon freshly squeezed lemon juice (about 2¼ lemons)

4 egg yolks

Salt and freshly ground pepper to taste

½ teaspoon sumac

1. In a medium saucepan, bring 8 cups of water to a boil over high heat. Drain the soaked grano and add it, little by little, to the boiling water. Reduce the heat to medium-low and simmer the grano for 30 to 40 minutes until it is soft. Drain.

2. In a medium saucepan, bring the chicken broth to a boil and add half of the cooked grano (about 1¼ cups). Reduce the heat and simmer for about 10 minutes to concentrate the flavor of the broth and make the grano as tender as possible.

3. Allow the soup to cool down to a warm temperature, and then purée it in a blender until it is very smooth and thick enough to coat the back of a spoon. If the soup is very hot when you blend it, it may cause a suction in the blender and pop the top, so be careful to cool the soup.

4. Pour the purée back into the soup pot and add the remaining grano. Bring it to a boil on medium heat and reduce the heat again to a simmer.

5. Meanwhile, in a small mixing bowl, whisk together the lemon juice and egg yolks.

6. Ladle a cup of the hot chicken soup into the yolk mixture, whisking vigorously. Repeat with another cup of hot soup. Add the egg-lemon mixture to the pot, still whisking.

7. Bring the soup back to a simmer slowly, still on low heat, stirring constantly to prevent the egg yolks from curdling but allowing them to cook through and thicken the soup a little more.

continued

8. Season with salt and pepper and sprinkle each serving generously with sumac.

9. If you have bits of shredded chicken from a homemade chicken stock, you can stir in a cup or two of shredded meat. The grano will keep absorbing liquid (semolina is known for this), so this soup may get a lot thicker when left in the fridge overnight. You can thin it out with more chicken stock.

GRANO

Grano is whole durum wheat. I've become fond of grano since it was first introduced to me by Paula Wolfert, when she came to Boston in 1998 to cook with me after finishing her book, *The Cooking of the Eastern Mediterranean*. We created a meal from the recipes in her book, finishing with Turkish-inspired vanilla ice cream with grano and grape must, which is a molasses made from grapes. Grano, when cooked properly, plumps like little dumplings, and the dessert tastes like an amazingly creamy, caramely rice pudding.

As a culinary adviser to the Whole Grains Council, I've cooked with grano a lot lately in my quest to get more whole grains into America's diet. I work with Sunnyland Mills's Mike Orlando–who distributes grano, bulgur, and kamut all over the country–demonstrating to big companies such as Campbell's Soup, Pepperidge Farm, and Disney World how delicious these grains are.

I hope you will enjoy the wonderful texture and flavor that grano gives this soup and find other uses for it as well. Grano freezes well, so cook a big batch of it and freeze some. Try stirring it into your yogurt and eating it for breakfast with some honey like they do in Sicily. Or sprinkle it over ice cream as Paula Wolfert does in her book, and add some fruit sauce.

You can find grano at Corti Brothers (see Resources, page 358). To read more about grano online and for a list of places to find it near you, go to www.sunnylandmills.com.

Shrimp Brik with Pistachio and Grapefruit Charmoula

Brik is a savory deep-fried turnover from Morocco or Tunisia. Mine taste like spring rolls, enhanced with Moroccan spice. Traditionally, brik is made with feuille de brik or brik pastry: paper-thin crepes that are very difficult to find. Phyllo dough is a fine substitution. If you prefer to bake the pastry instead of frying it, that will work with phyllo but not brik.

In Moroccan cooking, charmoula refers to a condiment for fish, but it can be either a dry spice rub or–as in this recipe–a relish made with onion or shallot, cilantro, and spices. I gave this charmoula a twist, celebrating the grapefruit, which is in season in late November.

This dish is perfect with an Arneis from the Piedmonte region or a sauvignon blanc from the Loire Valley. Both are light white wines with grapefruit notes.

— MAKES 10 SPRING ROLLS TO SERVE 5 TO 10 AND 1 CUP CHARMOULA —

For the Brik

½ small head savoy cabbage, outer leaves and core removed, very thinly shredded (about 2 cups)

2 shallots, peeled and sliced very thin

2 tablespoons olive oil plus ⅓ cup for brushing phyllo

20 medium shrimp (about 1 pound), peeled, deveined, and chopped into small pieces

5 sheets phyllo dough (less than or 1 package) or 10 feuilles de brik

4 ounces rice vermicelli or cellophane noodles (pad Thai noodles)

10 tablespoons lightly toasted, ground pistachios (see page 91)

1 head Boston lettuce, leaves left whole, cleaned and dried

For the Charmoula

2 large pink grapefruits, sectioned (page 72)

4 shallots, peeled and minced

4 teaspoons finely minced garlic
(about 4 large cloves)

½ cup extra-virgin olive oil

1 teaspoon ground cumin

Salt to taste

2 tablespoons harissa (page 152)

1 large bunch cilantro, washed, sprigged,
and roughly chopped

For the Brik

1. In a small sauté pan over medium heat, sauté the cabbage and shallots in 2 tablespoons olive oil until soft and tender, about 5 minutes.

2. Add the shrimp to the sauté pan and stir to coat them with the shallot and cabbage mixture. Cook for about 4 minutes until the shrimp just start to turn pink. Remove from the heat immediately and season with salt and pepper.

3. Preheat the oven to 375°F. Soak the noodles in hot water until soft (about 10 minutes) and drain; set aside.

4. Cut 5 phyllo dough sheets in half widthwise. Stack the halves on top of each other and cover them with a damp towel. If you use feuilles de brik, follow the instructions on page 91.

5. Lay a sheet of phyllo on a board, orienting it toward you so that it is flag-shaped. Brush the phyllo sheet generously with olive oil and then put a heaping tablespoon of shrimp on the bottom third of the pastry. Pinch off some rice noodles (about ¼ cup) and lay the noodles over the shrimp mixture. Sprinkle the whole thing with 1 tablespoon of toasted pistachios. Fold in the sides and roll it up gently but as tightly as possible, like a cigar. Repeat this process so you have 10 rolls.

6. Place the rolls on a heavy baking sheet and bake them for 12 to 18 minutes, until they're golden brown and crispy.

7. Serve hot with grapefruit charmoula and torn pieces of Boston lettuce for wrapping and soaking up charmoula.

For the Charmoula

Combine all the ingredients in a small mixing bowl and check the seasoning.

❧ If Using Feuilles de Brik

1. Lay a sheet of brik on a work surface or board and place a heaping tablespoon of shrimp on the bottom third of the pastry. You don't need to brush brik with oil like you do with phyllo. Pinch off some rice noodles (about ¼ cup) and lay the noodles over the shrimp mixture.

2. Sprinkle the whole thing with 1 tablespoon of toasted pistachios. Fold in the sides and roll it up gently but as tightly as possible, like a cigar. Repeat this process so you have 10 rolls.

3. Heat a medium-large sauté pan over high heat and lightly coat the bottom of the pan with olive oil. After about 2 minutes, when the pan is hot, add the rolls, one at a time, placing them seam-side down and being careful not to crowd the pan. Depending on the size of your pan, you may need to fry 5 rolls at a time and repeat the process. Reduce the heat to medium and cook the rolls until they are golden brown on all sides, about 3 minutes per side. If the pan seems dry and the rolls aren't browning well, drizzle in a little more olive oil each time you turn them onto a new side.

4. Remove the rolls from the pan and place them onto a paper towel to drain off excess oil. Serve immediately, according to instructions in step 7 on page 90.

TOASTING NUTS

To make toasted nuts, such as almonds, peanuts, pine nuts, pistachios, and walnuts, toss whole, blanched or skinless nuts in a little extra-virgin olive oil and roast them in a 350°F oven until they are golden brown (8 to 10 minutes; pine nuts take only 5 to 6 minutes). You can also sauté them with olive oil over medium heat, constantly stirring until they start to pop and turn golden brown. Sprinkle the toasted nuts generously with salt, and serve them warm or at room temperature—not hot.

Scallop Pizza with Leeks and Fennel Seed

This recipe was very popular when I cooked at the Casablanca in Cambridge, Massachusetts. The sweet fennel pairs well with the scallops. The cream melts into the pizza dough as it cooks and makes the crust extra crispy. It's best when the pizza dough is homemade, but a fresh store-bought dough can work as well.

Serve this pizza with a rich and creamy white wine, such as a chardonnay from Italy.

MAKES TWO 12-INCH PIZZAS TO SERVE 4

---

2 cups heavy cream

½ cup white wine

Salt and pepper to taste

1 tablespoon olive oil plus a little extra to dress the arugula

3 large leeks, white part only, sliced and washed

½ teaspoon fennel seed

½ teaspoon nonflavored, whole-grain mustard, such as Maille

6 scallions, bottoms trimmed, cleaned and roughly chopped

2 teaspoons minced garlic (about 2 large cloves)

10 large dry sea scallops, muscles removed (see note, page 64)

1 recipe Manaaeesh dough (page 240)

About ½ cup flour for dusting

1 large bunch arugula

Squeeze of fresh lemon or 1 teaspoon sherry vinegar

---

1. In a 2- to 4-quart heavy saucepan, bring the cream and wine to a boil over high heat. Reduce the heat to medium-low and simmer for about 15 minutes, until the cream has reduced by one-third and is thick. Season the cream with salt and pepper and set aside.

2. Meanwhile, in a large sauté pan over medium-high heat, heat 1 tablespoon of the olive oil and sauté the leeks and fennel seed until the leeks are tender and soft, about 8 minutes. Be careful not to brown the leeks or they will become bitter. Season the leeks with salt and pepper.

3. Stir the leek mixture into the cream mixture and add the mustard, scallions, and garlic.

4. Turn a scallop on its side and split it down the middle so that you have 2 thin discs. Repeat with the remaining scallops so you have 20 pieces.

5. Preheat the oven to 400°F.

6. Divide the pizza dough into two, and roll each half into rounds as thin as possible (about ⅙ inch), dusting with a little flour as you go. Make sure the dough is room temperature and not cold.

7. Place each round on a pizza stone or heavy baking sheet.

8. Spoon half the leek mixture onto each pizza shell and spread it as evenly as possible in a thin layer. It should be very thin, as it is very rich, like butter.

9. Arrange 10 scallop slices on each shell and then season them with salt and pepper.

10. Place the pizzas in the oven and bake for 20 to 25 minutes, until the edges are crisp and browned and the top is bubbly.

11. Slice and serve hot with plenty of arugula, lightly dressed with lemon and olive oil.

Chicken Lamejun with Roasted Peaches, Pistachio, and Sumac

In Turkey, chicken lamejun would be shocking because it is always made with lamb or beef or vegetable paste. It is not made at home, but in the local flatbread bakery, where it's cooked over a wood fire. My version is not traditional, but it is simply delicious—especially as a light meal in the summertime.

I like to use lavash, which is a very thin bread, like a tortilla, for this recipe. Homemade pizza dough also works well (see the variation at the end of this recipe). You can find green or Jordanian za'atar at www.kalustyans.com; see page 230 for more about za'atar.

This lamejun can be eaten sliced in pieces like pizza or rolled up into a wrap with a dollop of yogurt. Peach season arrives at the end of the summer and continues into early September; see the Sweet Pepper Variation (below) when peaches are not in season.

This dish is wonderful with a glass of young Viognier from Condrieu in the Rhone Valley.

> MAKES 12 LAMEJUN TO SERVE 12 AS AN APPETIZER OR LIGHT MEAL

1 pound boneless, skinless chicken breasts	⅓ cup heavy cream
1 small Spanish onion, peeled and finely chopped	1 cup lightly toasted, finely ground pistachios (see page 91)
3 scallions, root end trimmed and finely chopped	4 rectangular pieces of lavash, about 18 inches long (or long rounds)
1 red bell pepper, minced	
1½ teaspoons sumac	1 tablespoon olive oil
¾ teaspoon za'atar	2 peaches, halved and pits removed
1 teaspoon salt	Salt and pepper to taste
1 egg white	1 cup thick Greek yogurt for garnish

LAMEJUN

Lamejun is a flatbread, like pizza, served in Turkey and Armenia, and made with spices, onion, and ground lamb that is finely chopped to a paste. I had my first lamejun with my friend Ayfer Unsal in her hometown of Gaziantep in southeastern Turkey. We watched the village bakers chop the meat by hand to make a paste with onions, parsley, and chilies. They smoothed a thin layer on the flatbread dough and then cooked it in a wood-fired oven, while Ayfer and I stood there, salivating with anticipation.

With lamejun, the thinner the dough and topping, the better—just like a good Neapolitan-style (thin crust) pizza. The meat is raw when it goes into the dough before baking, and the flatbread absorbs all the meat juices as it bakes.

I like to get lamejun from my favorite store in Watertown, Massachusetts: Sevan Bakery, owned by the Chavushian family. The Chavushians are from Istanbul, and they make wonderfully thin—like tortillas—beef lamejun that I buy frozen and keep in my freezer for late-night or quick snacks. They are so light but satisfying, especially with some good Greek yogurt and plenty of sumac sprinkled on top.

1. Place the chicken breasts, skinless side down, on a chopping board. Cut the breasts down the middle on one side of the thin cartilage that separates the breasts. Trim off the cartilage attached to the other breast and discard. Trim off any remaining pieces of cartilage or fat and cut into 2-inch chunks.

2. Use a food processor fitted with a metal blade to grind the chicken to a paste until it comes together in a ball and becomes smooth and thick, about 1 minute. The mixture must get smooth enough or it will crack and break up as it cooks into the lavash or pizza dough.

3. Using the pulse button on the food processor, incorporate the onion, scallions, red pepper, sumac, za'atar, salt, and egg white, until the vegetables and spices are thoroughly mixed into the paste, about six times on the pulse button.

4. Place into a small mixing bowl, stir in the cream and pistachios, and set aside.

5. Preheat the oven to 375°F.

6. Cut each lavash into 3 equal pieces, so you have six 5 × 6-inch rectangles. If your lavash is round or extra large, cut out six 5 × 6 or 5 × 7-inch rectangles. Set aside covered with plastic or tucked back inside the bag.

continued

7. Drizzle the olive oil onto a heavy baking sheet and place the peaches on the sheet with the cut side down. Season with salt and pepper. Roast the peaches in the oven for 12 minutes or until they are just soft and tender when poked with a knife. When cool, remove the skin using a paring knife. If the peaches are ripe and tender from being cooked, the skin should pull right off. Cut each peach half in 6 slices and set aside.

8. Place ⅓ cup of the chicken mixture onto each lavash and spread it as thinly as possible and as close to each corner as possible so the mixture coats the bread in an, even layer. If the mixture sticks to the spatula, dip the spatula into a little water or olive oil and continue spreading.

9. Place the lamejuns on a heavy baking sheet or pizza stone and bake them for about 12 minutes or until they are crisp and the chicken mixture is cooked through. (To create a unique lamejun shape, see presentation variation below.)

10. Top each lamejun with 2 slices of peach and a dollop of yogurt and serve hot.

🌿 Fresh Pizza Dough Variation

To are use fresh pizza dough in place of lavash, divide one recipe of manaaeesh dough (page 240) into 4 equal balls and roll them out, dusting with flour as you go, into thin rounds not thicker than ¼ inch. Preheat a gas grill to medium-high and par cook them for 3 minutes on each side. Then proceed with step 8 using ⅔ cup chicken mixture on each round. You can bake them in a preheated 425° F oven for 4 to 5 minutes on a heavy baking sheet or pizza stone.

🌿 Sweet Pepper Variation

When peaches are out of season, sweet peppers make a delicious variation to this recipe. Roast 2 bell peppers (see page 97). Top each baked lamejun with two strips of pepper.

🌿 Presentation Variation

If you've used lavash, place each lamejun in a 4- to 5-inch round casserole dish (such as a cazuela or a gratin dish), letting the sides hang over the top. Press the lamejun so that the middle is flat on the bottom. Drizzle each lamejun with 1 teaspoon of olive oil and bake for about 12 minutes until crisp and the chicken mixture is cooked through. Remove from the casserole dish, and you have a unique bowl-shaped lamejun. Continue with step 10.

ROASTING SWEET PEPPERS

Preheat the oven to 400°F and place red bell peppers on a lightly oiled heavy baking sheet. Roast the peppers for about 8 minutes or until they collapse. Remove them from the baking sheet and place them in a small bowl covered with plastic. Allow to steam for about 5 minutes, and then peel off the skin. Split the peppers in half lengthwise and remove the seeds and the stem. Cut each pepper into pieces and season the strips with salt and pepper to taste.

❧ To Roast Peppers Over an Open Flame

Place each pepper directly on the burner over a medium gas flame. Cook the peppers until their skin is completely black and charred and flakes off easily, for about 3 to 4 minutes on each side. Remove the peppers from the burner and place them in a small mixing bowl covered with plastic. Allow the peppers to steam for about 5 minutes, and then peel off the skin. Split the peppers in half lengthwise and remove the seeds and stem. Cut each pepper into pieces and season the pieces with salt and pepper to taste. Do not rinse the peppers to peel off the charred skin. Pull the black skin off using your fingers or scrape it with the back of a knife. Rinsing washes away natural oils and flavor.

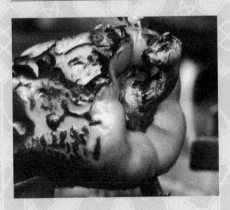
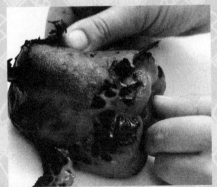

SUMAC, CİTRUS, AND FENNEL SEED

Beef Shish Kebobs with Sumac Onions and Parsley Butter

In Turkish, *shish* means skewer and *kebob* means grilled meat. This simple recipe introduces an addictive condiment for grilled meat: onions sliced very thinly and tossed with a generous amount of sumac. The sumac pickles the onion a few minutes after tossing. Sumac onions are the perfect pickle for all grilled meats.

Try to find fresh pita bread delivered daily to the market. It makes a difference. Good Middle Eastern markets receive bread daily. Look for the thinnest pita possible. If the bread seems a bit thick or a little stale, brush it with water and olive oil and soften it on the grill before cooking the shish kebob.

In Turkey, flatbreads serve a purpose. In the United States, we are served bread before our meal as though it's a snack while we wait for our food to arrive. In many Arabic countries, the bread is often skipped throughout the mezze course and is served where it is most important: with the meat course. The bread is placed on a platter or plate and topped with the meat after it is cooked, so that as the meat rests, the juices soak into the bread. Flatbreads like lavash or very thin pitas (or pides) dry out very quickly if left in the open air for a short amount of time. You can reconstitute dried-out flatbreads by spraying them with the fine mist from a pump water bottle or by rubbing them with wet hands.

I like to use sirloin for kebobs. A less expensive alternative is top round, but it is not quite as tender as sirloin. The parsley butter is a classic combination of garlic and parsley.

Serve these kebobs with a spicy and smoky French syrah from Cote Rotie or Hermitage in the Rhone Valley.

⟿ SERVES 6 ⟿

3 pounds sirloin strip, fat trimmed
and cut into twenty-four 1- to 1½-inch cubes

¼ cup extra-virgin olive oil

1 tablespoon dried Greek oregano,
preferably wild, crushed with
your fingers into powder

1 large bunch flat-leaf parsley,
stems removed, washed and dried

1½ sticks unsalted butter, softened
to room temperature

2 tablespoons smashed and chopped garlic
(6 to 8 cloves)

2 teaspoons salt plus more to taste

1 teaspoon black pepper
plus more to taste

2 small red onions, peeled, halved,
and cut into very thin long strips

1 heaping tablespoon sumac

6 metal skewers

Three 10-inch rounds pita bread,
cut in half

1. In a mixing bowl, toss the beef with the olive oil and oregano, and let it stand while you prepare a charcoal grill (see Grilling Tips, page 100) and make the butter.

2. Finely chop the parsley. Place it in a food processor, fitted with a metal blade, and process the parsley, butter, garlic, 2 teaspoons of the salt, and 1 teaspoon of the pepper until smooth. Place this mixture in a small bowl and set aside.

3. Place the onions in a small mixing bowl and toss with sumac. Let this rest for a few minutes, to give the sumac a chance to pickle the onion somewhat.

4. Using metal skewers, thread 4 cubes of marinated beef onto each and season with salt and pepper.

5. Over medium-high heat, grill each side of the beef for about 4 minutes until brown.

6. Remove the beef from the heat and place each skewer on a half of pita bread so that the pita bread catches the juice while it's resting.

7. Immediately, dollop each skewer with 1 tablespoon of the soft parsley butter so that it soaks into the meat and bread. You can freeze the extra butter or wrap it tightly in plastic wrap and store it in the refrigerator.

8. Remove the skewers and top the pita and beef with a generous amount of sumac onions.

GRILLING TIPS

I prefer to use natural lump charcoal when grilling. Natural charcoal is made from pure wood, with no chemical additives. I also like to throw some wet chips of apple, alder, or cherry wood on the grill to impart a sweet, pleasantly woody flavor. Gas grills are very convenient, but food cooked over a gas flame lacks the depth of flavor imparted from a wood fire. I also think that building and tending a natural charcoal fire is a wonderful ritual that enhances a meal.

Charcoal briquettes are convenient and available everywhere, but they are made from sawdust and scrap wood with starch binders and chemical additives, which produce oxygen for a longer and more even burn. The additives don't burn off and therefore can affect the flavor of your food.

Lighter fluid is also convenient. It usually burns off by the time you are ready to cook, so that the chemicals do not affect the food's flavor. However, I believe that I can taste the chemicals on food cooked over a fire started with lighter fluid. I prefer to start my grill fires in a metal chimney with a wooden handle. Good grilling chimneys are available at most hardware and kitchen stores.

Here's a recipe for a great grill fire. I like to build a two-level fire, with one side hotter than the other, which creates a "high" and a "low" flame. Remember that natural charcoal burns hotter and faster than briquettes. A good brand of natural lump charcoal is Nature's Own, which is available at most natural food and specialty kitchen stores. Or you can order your charcoal online at www.peopleswoods.com.

Grilling Supplies

Grill (my favorite is the Weber Kettle, 22.5 inch)

Natural lump charcoal

Chimney

Newspaper

Lighter

Good grill brush

Long tongs

---

1. Make sure the vents on your grill are open. Air feeds a fire.

2. Fill the bottom of your grill with charcoal (at least 4 inches high on one side and 2 inches high on the other) and set the chimney in the middle of the coals. The fire needs to be big enough in surface area to accommodate the amount of food you're cooking.

3. Fill the bottom of the chimney with one sheet of loosely crumpled newspaper and fill the top with charcoal.

4. Light the newspaper and allow it to burn. When the coals have caught fire, release them from the chimney and allow them to light the rest of the coals.

5. When the fire is at maximum heat, usually after about 20 minutes, the coals will be gray. Place the iron grill on top of the coals.

6. Once the grill gets hot, after about 5 minutes, brush it well with the grill brush to clean it.

7. Let the grill heat up for about 5 minutes more and then begin cooking. If you're grilling food with lots of marinade or fat, it may begin to smoke. Using your tongs, place food on the "low" side of the grill, and move it over to the "high" side when the smoke settles down.

❧ Turkish Alternative

An alternative to grilling directly over flame is to grill Turkish style: cooking skewered meat above the grill iron. To do this, roll up two long pieces of foil, about 12 inches long, depending on the width of your grill and how many skewers you're grilling. Place the foil rolls on the grill, parallel to each other, about an inch shorter apart than the skewers. Balance the ends of the skewers on top of the foil rolls, and spin the skewers as the meat cooks above the fire.

4

Allspice, Cinnamon, and Nutmeg

These three fragrant spices—which I sometimes refer to as "pumpkin pie seasonings"—blend well together and can be used almost interchangeably, as they lend similar warm, earthy, and sweet qualities to a dish. Cinnamon, however, may not always work as a substitute for allspice or nutmeg.

Allspice, cinnamon, and nutmeg are extremely strong and must be used carefully. They are delicious in dishes with squash and pumpkin, raw beef, stewed beef or lamb, and legumes like chickpeas. They perk up rice pilafs or rice stuffings and marry nicely with nuts or mushrooms. Because these spices add warmth, they work well in fall and winter preparations.

ALLSPICE

Allspice is the dried and cured, unripe berry from the tropical evergreen pimento tree. Some of the best allspice grows in Jamaica, where strict harvest laws and curing regulations keep the quality consistent. Its flavor is reminiscent of clove, cinnamon, and nutmeg; it gives pumpkin pie its unique taste, and it gives Jamaican jerk that distinct flavor. Allspice is also used in the Scandinavian preparation for pickled herring.

Combined with black pepper, allspice is great on red meat. In Arabic cooking, it flavors rice dishes, raw meat *köfte* (similar to the French steak tartare), vegetables, and chicken broths.

Use ground allspice, unless you are flavoring a broth or pickles and want to remove the berries. The allspice berry contains a lot of natural oil and can be revived easily if it has been sitting on a shelf too long. See tips for reviving spices on page 3.

CINNAMON

Cinnamon comes from the rolled, paper-thin layers of inner bark from a tropical evergreen tree related to the avocado and sassafras. The bark can be found ground or in whole quills or sticks, ranging from 3 inches to 3 feet. Although it grows wild in places such as the Seychelles and Indonesia, true cinnamon comes from Sri Lanka (formerly Ceylon), where they are serious about harvesting and sorting quality.

When the spice is ground, the perfume is sweet and pleasantly woody. Cinnamon is often confused with cassia, which grows mostly in Asia. Cassia's flavor is strong and slightly bitter, but pure cinnamon is not bitter at all. In England, it is illegal to sell cassia as cinnamon; in France the word *canele* means both cinnamon and cassia; in the United States, there are no restrictions on the labeling of cinnamon or cassia. You might find cassia labeled "baker's cinnamon."

Whole cinnamon is difficult to grind yourself, so I suggest keeping some ground cinnamon on hand. You can use whole cinnamon to flavor broths, ciders, hot chocolate, chutneys, and dishes in which the sticks are easy to remove before eating.

Like allspice and nutmeg, cinnamon flavors both sweet and savory preparations and lends its distinct taste to apple strudel and Mexican chocolate. It's combined with saffron in North African dishes and with garlic and lamb in Greek moussaka. A mixture of cinnamon, cumin, and allspice added to rice, sweet and hot peppers, and red meat makes for delicious dolmas, or stuffed grape leaves.

A good online source for true Ceylon cinnamon can be found at www.penzeys.com.

NUTMEG

Nutmeg has the strongest and sweetest flavor of the three spices in this chapter. It is the seed of a fruit from a tropical evergreen tree that grows in many hot-climate countries.

Nutmeg and mace are often confused. Mace is actually the placenta of the nutmeg. It has a lighter, subtler flavor and is much more expensive. A ripe nutmeg looks like a small nectarine but is very sour and almost inedible. When a nutmeg is broken apart, the mace is blood-red and turns dark orange after drying. The mace is removed from the nutmeg and then processed separately. It is rare to find the mace still attached to the nutmeg.

Although you can buy ground nutmeg, it is often stale, so I prefer to grate whole nutmeg. I use the tiny-gauge side of a box grater, which can also be used as a zester. You can also use the long, single-sided handheld graters that are used to grate Parmesan cheese. In any case, the grater's holes should be small enough to powder the nutmeg. Hold the nutmeg between your thumb and first three fingers, being careful to grate the nutmeg and not your fingers. Also, you can find grinders or mills made especially for whole nutmeg at kitchen shops and through online sources, such as www. amazon.com.

Nutmeg flavors eggnog, but it is also the perfect perk for the classic béchamel, Mornay, or white sauce. It adds a sweet, caramel fragrance to tomato-based pasta sauces (with or without meat), winter squashes, spinach, and cakes and pies.

PEELING AND SEEDING TOMATOES

Bring a medium saucepan of water to a boil over high heat. Meanwhile, cut off the tops of the tomatoes, and then score them with your knife by running a shallow slit from the top to the bottom. Add the tomatoes to the boiling water, and let them sit in the water for 45 seconds to 1 minute, or until the slits start to separate and the skin pulls away from the flesh. Drain the tomatoes immediately and plunge them into ice water or cool them under running cold water. Peel the skins off and cut the tomatoes in half. Remove as much seed as possible and squeeze them gently in your hand to drain off some of the water.

RECIPES WITH ALLSPICE, CINNAMON, AND NUTMEG

Squash Kibbeh with Brown Butter and Spiced Feta

This version of *kibbeh* (Arabic) or *köfte* (Turkish) is simple to make. The kibbeh is baked and steamed, which gives it the consistency of a dumpling: soft and pliable with a creamy center. I mold the kibbeh in a jumbo espresso cup, stuff it with spiced cheese, and then bake it in the oven just before serving. Then I invert the espresso cups to remove the kibbeh before serving. I love the spices in the feta combined with the brown butter and squash flavors.

The kibbeh is a wonderful accompaniment to rich red meat—such as beef sausage or rib eye or a gamy entrée like pheasant or venison. You can make the squash purée, kibbeh, and filling ahead of time (up to 3 days) and assemble and bake them right before serving.

I prefer red kuri squash for this recipe because it's dense and contains very little water. The goal here is to choose a squash that makes a very creamy purée. Butternut squash is a good substitute for red kuri, although the flavor is more delicate and the kibbeh will be softer.

I like the tall, thin shape that an espresso cup gives the kibbeh. But since Italian espresso cups usually only hold ¼ cup, I use jumbo espresso cups. Any ½-cup ramekin should work.

MAKES EIGHT ½-CUP SERVINGS

For the Squash Kibbeh

3 pounds squash, such as red kuri
   or butternut

Salt and pepper to taste

4 tablespoons butter

1 large onion, peeled and finely chopped

1 large green bell pepper, seeded
   and finely chopped

¼ cup extra-virgin olive oil

2 teaspoons sweet paprika

1 teaspoon Middle Eastern Five-Spice (page 109)

1½ cups fine bulgur

For the Spiced Feta Filling

½ pound feta cheese, preferably French sheep's milk or goat's milk, drained and roughly crumbled (page 349)

½ teaspoon Middle Eastern Five-Spice (page 109)

¼ teaspoon sumac

½ teaspoon Aleppo chilies (see Resources, page 358)

2 tablespoons finely chopped fresh parsley

Salt and pepper to taste

To Make the Squash Kibbeh

1. Cut the squash in half lengthwise, scrape out the seeds, and bake it, flesh-side down, on a lightly oiled heavy baking sheet for 30 to 40 minutes, until tender. When the squash is cool, remove the flesh from the skin with a large spoon, and purée it in a food processor fitted with a metal blade, until smooth and creamy. Season with salt and pepper. Reserve 2 cups of the purée for the recipe.

2. Make brown butter (page 108).

3. In a large saucepan or soup pan over medium-high heat, cook the onion and pepper in olive oil for 8 to 10 minutes, or until the onions are translucent and the peppers are soft.

4. Stir in the paprika and 1 teaspoon of the five-spice and stir to coat the onion mixture.

5. Stir in 2 cups of the squash purée and cook for about 5 minutes, until the squash is hot.

6. Reduce the heat to low and stir in the bulgur. Turn off the heat, cover, and let sit for 15 minutes. The mixture should be soft, like dough.

7. Season with salt and pepper, and stir in the brown butter.

To Make the Spiced Feta Filling

1. Place the crumbled feta in a mixing bowl and stir in ½ teaspoon five-spice, the sumac, Aleppo chilies, and parsley. Stir for a few minutes to make the mixture as creamy as possible, although chunks of feta will remain.

2. Season with salt and pepper (the feta may be salty enough, depending on the brand).

To Combine

1. Preheat the oven to 375°F.

2. Line up 8 jumbo espresso cups or any ½-cup ramekins. Fill each cup with ½ cup of kibbeh mixture. Then, using your forefinger, make a hole in the center of each cup so that you almost touch the bottom. The hole should be big enough to fit a few teaspoons of feta in the center. Some

continued

kibbeh will rise up over the cup, which is good, since you will use it to fold over the filling.

3. Using a teaspoon, fill each hole with 2 generous teaspoons of the feta mixture.

4. Seal the tops with the overlapping kibbeh. A few little holes may remain, but try to encapsulate the cheese filling as best you can.

5. Place the cups on a heavy baking sheet and bake for about 14 minutes, until they are hot.

6. Turn the kibbeh out of the cups and onto plates and serve with any leftover feta filling on the side. When you split the kibbeh open with a fork, the center should be warm, soft, and creamy.

❧ *Making Brown Butter*

To make brown butter, bring the butter to a boil in a heavy saucepan over medium heat, and then reduce the heat to medium-low. Simmer the butter for about 10 minutes, until it turns brown and smells like hazelnuts. The butter has just clarified—the solids have sunk to the bottom and the water has evaporated—and it can burn quickly (turning from brown to black), so you must watch it carefully after 6 minutes of simmering. As soon as you smell a toasted nut aroma, check the butter. Strain the clarified butter immediately through a fine sieve into a small bowl. Allow the butter to cool.

2.

3.

Middle Eastern Five-Spice

Many countries have a sweet spice mix like this Middle Eastern five-spice: the Chinese have a five-spice, the French have *quatre épice*, and in the United States, we have pumpkin pie spice mix. The combination of aromatic tropical evergreen seeds enhances meat, chicken, and rice dishes. It's also wonderful added to feta cheese (see Spiced Feta, page 107) and marinated mushrooms. Just use a pinch to lightly perfume a dish.

⁓ MAKES ABOUT ¼ CUP ⁓

---

2 tablespoons whole allspice

1 teaspoon whole cloves

1 tablespoon whole peppercorns

½ teaspoon freshly grated or ground nutmeg (see page 103)

1 tablespoon ground cinnamon

---

1. Using a coffee grinder or blender, grind the allspice, cloves, and peppercorns until fine. Transfer the ground spices to a small mixing bowl.

2. Stir in the nutmeg and cinnamon.

3. Store in an airtight container in a cool, dark place, such as a cupboard, for up to 4 months.

Chickpea and Potato Terrine Stuffed with Pine Nuts, Spinach, Onion, and Tahini

This is a variation of a traditional Armenian dish called *topic*, which I learned from my friend Armen Mehrabyan, who lives in Armenia and who grows herbs for Oleana's teas and prepares a special herb blend for one of our fish entrées. Topic is served in Turkey as well, and it tastes like exotic hummus. It's a chickpea and potato purée that's stuffed with onions, pine nuts, and spinach that have been spiced and mixed with tahini. The mixture is pressed into a terrine mold and then sliced, or you can wrap it up into a jelly roll, which I've included below as a variation. The terrine can be served at room temperature as a mezze, like antipasti or tapas.

I like to garnish the terrine with fresh chopped tomato and serve it as an appetizer. It livens up arugula, watercress, or other peppery greens that have been lightly dressed with lemon and olive oil. For a main course, I like to warm the terrine and serve it with duck or Braised Beef Short Ribs (page 66).

This recipe can be prepared ahead and then served the next day.

⌁ MAKES 1 TERRİNE OR LOAF PAN TO SERVE 6 TO 8 AS A FİRST COURSE ⌁

1 cup chickpeas, soaked overnight in 6 cups water	2 teaspoons finely chopped garlic (about 2 large cloves)
1 small baking potato, peeled and cut into quarters	3 tablespoons lightly toasted pine nuts (see page 91)
2 tablespoons butter	2 whole dried apricots, finely chopped
Salt and pepper to taste	1 tablespoon dried currants
1 large onion, peeled and finely chopped	1 teaspoon Middle Eastern Five-Spice (page 109)
4 tablespoons plus 1 teaspoon olive oil	1 tablespoon tahini plus extra for garnish
8 ounces stemmed spinach, washed and roughly chopped	3 plum tomatoes, peeled and seeded (see page 104)

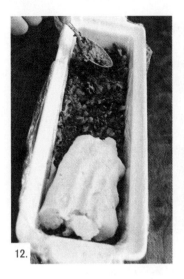

12.

13.

15.

1. Drain the chickpeas and place them in a medium saucepan with 6 cups of water. Bring them to a boil over high heat. Turn the heat to medium-low and simmer for about 25 minutes, until the chickpeas are tender and soft and can be squeezed easily with your fingers.

2. Meanwhile, in a small saucepan, place the potato, cover it with water, and bring it to a boil over high heat. Reduce the heat to medium-low and simmer for about 15 minutes, until soft.

3. Drain the chickpeas, reserving ¼ cup of the cooking water.

4. Drain the potato well in a colander and place it back in the pot. Mash the potato well with a fork. Stir in the butter and set aside. You should have about ¾ cup.

5. Using a food processor fitted with a metal blade, purée the chickpeas with 3 tablespoons of the reserved cooking liquid. If the mixture is very dry, add the remaining tablespoon of liquid and purée until smooth and creamy, about 1 minute. If you are making the jelly roll variation, as below, make sure to keep the mixture a bit on the dry side.

6. Add the mashed potato to the chickpea purée and process it by pulsing it 3 or 4 times, until it's incorporated. Season with salt and pepper. Spread the chickpea purée onto a baking sheet to cool for about 10 minutes. Cover it with plastic wrap and set it aside.

7. In a large sauté pan over medium-low heat, cook the onion in 4 tablespoons of the olive oil for 6 to 8 minutes, until the onion is soft and translucent.

continued

ALLSPICE, CINNAMON, AND NUTMEG

8. Stir in the spinach, adding half at a time, as there may be too much for you to add all at once. Cook for about 5 minutes, stirring until the spinach is soft and tender.

9. Stir in the garlic, pine nuts, dried fruit, and five-spice and cook for 2 minutes more, until you can smell the garlic.

10. Remove the spinach mixture from the heat and cool. Stir in the tahini and season with salt and pepper.

11. Begin to assemble the terrine by lining a terrine mold with plastic wrap. Tear a piece of plastic wrap two times the length of the terrine so that the edges will hang over the sides of the mold, and you can use them to cover the terrine after it's assembled. If you do not have a mold, you can make the terrine into a jelly roll, using plastic wrap (see variation, below).

12. Place half of the chickpea purée on the bottom of the terrine mold and spread it into an even layer. Make the next layer by adding the spinach filling and spreading it in an even layer. Top with the remaining chickpea purée and spread it in an even layer.

13. Cover the terrine with the plastic wrap hanging over the edges of the mold. Press down to pack the terrine. Leave it at room temperature for at least an hour before serving.

14. Chop the tomato as finely as possible. Place it in small bowl and add the remaining teaspoon of olive oil. Season with salt and pepper.

15. Turn out the chickpea terrine onto a plate and remove the plastic wrap. Slice the terrine into 1-inch-or-less slices and top with the tomato. Serve at room temperature. Drizzle a little extra tahini on top.

❧ Jelly Roll Variation

Spread the chickpea purée out on a long sheet of plastic wrap (at least 16 × 10 ½ inches), making a flat, smooth rectangle about ½ inch thick or less. Leaving at least an inch of space along the short edges of the plastic wrap and 3 inches alongside the long edges, spread the spinach filling along the bottom ¾ of the rectangle. Starting from the bottom, roll the chickpea purée around the filling into a jelly roll shape, using the plastic wrap to help you roll. Twist the ends of the plastic wrap and tighten them, so that you have a smooth shape. Serve at room temperature or slightly warm, cut into 1-inch slices. Top each slice with chopped tomato and drizzle on extra tahini.

Cranberry Beans Stewed with Tomato and Cinnamon

Cranberry beans are pink when fresh and brownish purple when dry. They are speckled, plump, and deliciously creamy. They're best if you can find them fresh in late summer, since they need no soaking, and they cook quickly and are buttery and dense. Dried beans make a good substitute, but you must soak them overnight. Soaking releases gas and softens them a little so they will cook more evenly. It's always best to discard the soaking water and cook them in fresh water.

Beans that are stewed with vegetables and spices and served at room temperature as a mezze are called *plaki* in Turkey and Armenia. There are many variations. This recipe makes a complete protein when complemented with rice and yogurt, and it's terrific served with warm goat cheese as a salad course or with grilled meat. The flavors are satisfying in all seasons.

⸺ MAKES 6 CUPS TO SERVE 4 TO 6 ⸺

4 cups fresh cranberry beans or 2 cups dried cranberry beans, soaked overnight in 6 cups water and drained

1 small Spanish onion, peeled and finely chopped

1 large carrot, peeled and finely chopped

1 green bell pepper, stem and seeds removed and finely chopped

1 rib celery, peeled and finely chopped

1 bay leaf

½ teaspoon ground cinnamon

2 tablespoons olive oil

4 teaspoons garlic, peeled, smashed, and minced (about 4 large cloves)

2 tablespoons tomato paste

10 plum tomatoes, peeled and seeded (see page 104)

Salt and pepper to taste

Juice of 1 lemon

1 tablespoon crushed, dried mint

1. Bring the beans to a boil with 8 cups of water in a medium saucepan over high heat. Reduce the heat to medium-low and simmer the beans for 35 to 40 minutes for dried beans or 20 to 25 minutes for fresh beans, until they are tender. Drain.

2. In a large, deep-sided sauté pan over medium-high heat, sauté the onion, carrot, green pepper, celery, bay leaf, and cinnamon in the olive oil, for about 10 minutes, stirring, until the onions are soft and translucent.

3. Stir in the garlic and tomato paste and add the tomatoes. Reduce the heat to medium-low and cook for 20 minutes, pressing down on the tomatoes and stirring occasionally, until the tomatoes are soft and jamlike.

4. Stir in the beans and simmer for another 15 minutes, until the sauce has thickened and coated the beans.

5. Season with salt and pepper and cool. Stir in the lemon juice and mint and serve warm, cold, or room temperature. The beans are even better the next day, as the flavors have time to marry.

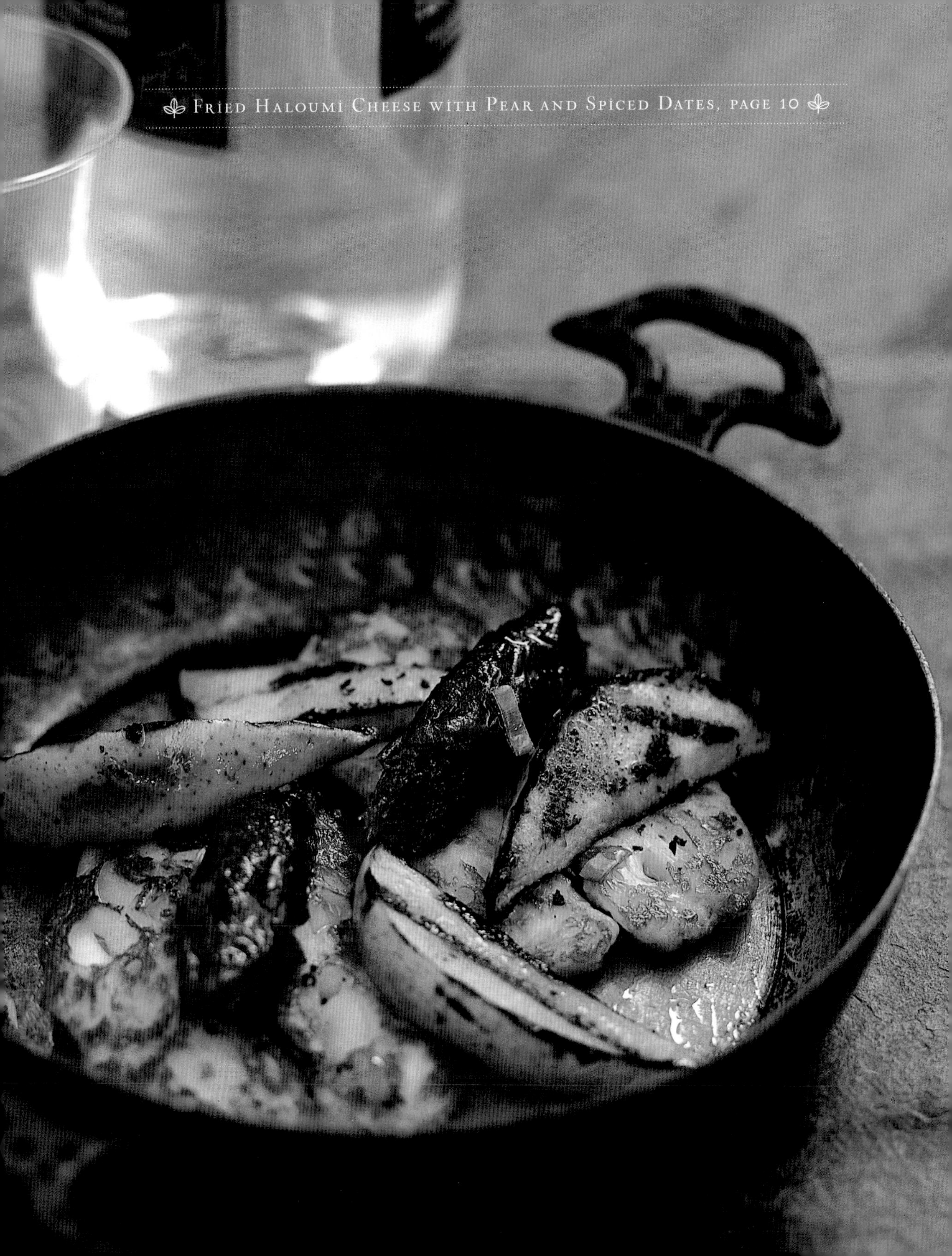

Fried Haloumi Cheese with Pear and Spiced Dates, page 10

Endive and Apple Salad with Grapes, Sumac, and Pecan Labne, page 80

KÜNEFE WITH CHAMPAGNE-CARDAMOM SYRUP, PAGE 34

GROUND BEEF AND PISTACHIO KEBOBS, PAGE 236

SQUASH KIBBEH WITH BROWN BUTTER
AND SPICED FETA, PAGE 106

POACHED NECTARINE STUFFED WITH NOUGAT GLACÉ, PAGE 316

Steak Tartare, Turkish Style, page 120

ROASTED CRISPY DUCK WITH TOMATO-SESAME JAM, PAGE 192

CRISPY LEMON CHICKEN WITH ZA'ATAR, PAGE 245

🌿 TROUT SPANAKOPITTA WITH AVOCADO AND SALMON ROE, PAGE 272 🌿

C-Licious: Orange-Coriander Sangria, and Serrano Ham with Blood-Orange and Fennel Salad, pages 37 and 85

Sweet Potato Bisteeya, page 42

VEAL TAGINE WITH MOROCCAN SPICES
AND ALMOND COUSCOUS, PAGE 162

Pumpkin Borek

Borek is a savory pie made with puff pastry, phyllo, or yufka dough and filled with vegetables, cheese, or meat. It's made throughout the eastern Mediterranean and Armenia, and I have even eaten Serbian borek. Turkish cheese borek is my favorite. Like a good lasagna or dumplings, the edges are thin and crispy and the filling is airy and soft.

When making borek, I prefer to use yufka dough, which is similar to a very thin flour tortilla. I find that puff pastry is too thick, and phyllo dough is too thin and crispy because of the cornstarch it contains. Yufka dough is available online at www.istanbulsupermarket.com.

Pumpkin borek is superb with a bitter green salad in the late fall, when pumpkins are in season. I like to use Long Island cheese pumpkins, an heirloom variety with dense, deep orange flesh.

This dish is outstanding paired with Bardalino, a light-bodied northern Italian red.

—⁓ MAKES ONE 10-INCH BOREK TO SERVE 8 ⁓—

1 cup milk

4 tablespoons butter, melted

½ onion, finely chopped (about ¾ cup)

2 teaspoons garlic, peeled, smashed, and minced (about 2 large cloves)

½ teaspoon Middle Eastern Five-Spice (page 109)

1 small sugar pumpkin or Long Island cheese pumpkin (weighing about 6 pounds)

1 tablespoon olive oil plus more for oiling sheet

Salt and pepper to taste

3 whole eggs

3½ large sheets of yufka dough, cut in half, making six 12-inch squares (see page 343)

3 balls fresh mozzarella (a little more than a pound)

3 egg yolks

¼ cup flour

1. Preheat the oven to 350°F.

2. To make the pumpkin purée, cut the pumpkin into large chunks and bake on a lightly oiled heavy baking sheet for 20 to 30 minutes, until tender.

3. When the pumpkin is cool, remove the skin and purée it in a food processor fitted with a metal blade, until smooth and creamy. Season with salt and pepper to taste.

4. Brush a 10-inch deep-sided baking dish with some melted butter.

5. In a small skillet over medium heat, cook the onion, garlic, and five-spice in olive oil for about 5 minutes, until the onion is translucent. Set aside.

6. Place the pumpkin purée, milk, and the onion mixture in a food processor fitted with a metal blade, and purée until smooth and creamy, 1 to 2 minutes. Season with salt and pepper.

7. Add the eggs and the rest of the melted butter and purée again, until smooth and creamy.

8. Lay a piece of yufka dough in a 10-inch pan so that the sides of the pastry reach up the sides of the pan. Tear the yufka that hangs over the edge of the pan off with your fingers, so that the yufka is even with the side of the dish. If you have smaller sheets of yufka, you can overlap them.

9. Spread ½ cup of the pumpkin filling over the yufka dough and then top it with another layer of yufka. Spread on another ½ cup of the pumpkin filling.

10. Break up one of the mozzarella balls and distribute it evenly over the pumpkin mixture and top with another layer of yufka. Spread on another ½-cup layer of pumpkin and cover with a layer of yufka.

11. Spread on another ½-cup layer of pumpkin mixture. Break up another ball of mozzarella and distribute it evenly over the pumpkin mixture, topping it off with another layer of yufka. Top the yufka with another ½-cup layer of pumpkin and any remaining mozzarella. Top this with another layer of yufka.

12. You will now have 5 layers of pumpkin and 3 layers with cheese.

13. Mix the remaining pumpkin (about ½ cup) with the egg yolks and flour and pour this mixture onto the top layer.

14. Cut into the borek, almost all the way to the bottom, making 8 even sections, so that the pumpkin and egg can soak into the cracks. Press on the pie with your hands to encourage absorption. Let the borek stand and soak for 20 minutes.

15. Bake for 40 to 45 minutes until the pie is puffy and golden brown on the top and serve warm.

Swiss Chard Dolmas with Ayfer's Rice

This recipe is inspired by my friend Ayfer Unsal, who introduced me to the glorious food of her hometown, Gaziantep, in the southeastern part of Turkey. The dried mint, the sweet and hot peppers, and the notes of allspice and cinnamon are the flavors of Gaziantep, famous for its lamb kebobs and baklavas. I became smitten with Ayfer and her friends; they make rice and Swiss chard that absolutely bursts with flavor.

I use a red pepper paste from Turkey that is similar to a concentrated tomato paste but is made with sweet and hot peppers. If you take the trouble to find it, it could become a staple condiment in your pantry. It's available in most Middle Eastern markets or online at www.tohum.com.

Serve these dolmas hot or at room temperature with lemon. Ayfer presents them with little sour plums, native to her area.

⤙ MAKES 20 DOLMAS TO SERVE 10 ⤚

¼ cup salt plus more to taste

20 to 25 leaves (about 3 bunches) green Swiss chard, washed and stems removed and reserved

⅓ cup olive oil plus 2 tablespoons for drizzling

1 cup finely chopped Swiss chard stems

2 small Spanish onions, peeled and finely chopped

4 teaspoons garlic, peeled, smashed, and minced (about 4 large cloves)

1½ teaspoons red pepper paste or ½ red bell pepper, stem and seeds removed and finely chopped

1 heaping tablespoon tomato paste

1 tablespoon dried mint

1 teaspoon Aleppo chilies

¾ teaspoon Middle Eastern-Five-Spice (page 109)

½ teaspoon ground cinnamon

2 cups medium-grain rice or Spanish rice (risotto is too starchy and long grain is not starchy enough)

Pepper to taste

Yogurt

1. In a large pot, bring 4 quarts of water to a boil over high heat. Add ¼ cup of salt, enough so that the water tastes salty.

2. Drop the Swiss chard leaves into the boiling water and bring the water back to a simmer. Simmer the chard for 2 minutes, stirring once to make sure all the leaves are cooking evenly. The leaves should be bright green and tender but not too soft or falling apart.

3. Drain the leaves and spread them out on a clean towel to cool and dry.

4. In a medium saucepan or a 10-inch skillet over medium-low heat, heat ⅓ cup of the olive oil and sauté ¾ cup of chopped chard stems with the onions, garlic, red pepper, tomato paste, mint, chilies, five-spice, and cinnamon for 5 minutes, stirring, until the onions are soft and translucent.

5. Add the rice and stir to coat it with the mixture.

6. Add 2 cups of water and bring it to a boil over high heat. Reduce the heat to low and simmer the rice, uncovered, for about 30 minutes, stirring every so often, until the water is absorbed and the rice is tender. Season to taste with salt and cool.

7. Preheat the oven to 350°F.

8. Scoop up ¼ cup of the rice mixture and roll it into a ball with the palms of your hands. Repeat this step until you've made balls with all of the rice.

9.

9.

9.

SPİCE: FLAVORS OF THE EASTERN MEDİTERRANEAN

9. Next, use a ramekin to shape each dolma. Place a chard leaf with the ribbed side up in the ramekin. Add a ball of rice and wrap the leaf around the rice. The leaf should cover the rice as completely as possible. If the rib of the chard leaf is too big and doesn't allow you to roll it easily, remove half of the rib with a small paring knife, carving it out in a V-shape, leaving the leaf on either side intact. If the leaf is too small to cover the rice completely, take part of another leaf and patch it together to make a piece large enough to roll. Invert the ramekin so that the dolma is seam-side down in a roasting pan. Repeat the process, making about 20 dolmas.

10. Add 1 cup of water to the pan. Drizzle in a tablespoon of olive oil and sprinkle the dolmas with salt and pepper to taste.

11. Cover the dolmas with foil and bake them for 40 minutes.

12. Serve the dolmas at room temperature or cold with yogurt on the side.

ALLSPİCE, CİNNAMON, AND NUTMEG

Steak Tartare, Turkish Style

This brightly flavored raw *köfte* is commonly eaten in the eastern Mediterranean and is often made with lamb instead of beef. Köfte is bulgur-based pâté or dough, and is known as *kibbeh* in Arabic. This dish is fantastic served on romaine lettuce leaves with roughly chopped mint and a squeeze of lemon.

Turkish-style tartare is lighter than French tartare because it's bound with fine bulgur instead of egg. Normally, to achieve a good consistency for steak tartare, you chop the meat and add an egg yolk, chopped shallots, lemon juice, cornichons, capers, mustard, salt, and pepper. You then stir the mixture until the egg coats the meat and creates a velvety texture. In Turkey, they forgo the egg and achieve the velvety texture by technique. They chop the beef by hand until it's fine enough to stick together, and then they stir in spices, onion, and fine bulgur and knead the tartare until it becomes creamy as its own protein begins to break down. Brilliantly, the bulgur absorbs the shallot juices and moisture from the meat and olive oil.

I love this dish best in the summertime, served with pickled green tomatoes (see Nookie's Pickles, page 280) and hot peppers. Use the best-quality beef possible.

This dish pairs well with a medium-bodied, earthy red wine with some spice to it, such as an Aglianico from Italy's Campagnia region or a Mourvedre from Provence.

SERVES 10 AS AN APPETIZER OR 6 AS A MAIN COURSE

1½ pounds sirloin or beef fillet, completely cleaned of fat and tissue

½ cup fine bulgur

3 large shallots, peeled and minced

4 teaspoons minced garlic (about 4 large cloves)

Juice of 2 lemons (about ½ cup)

1 heaping tablespoon Red Pepper Paste (see Resources, page 358) or ½ red bell pepper, roasted, seeded, and (see page 97) finely chopped to a paste

2 teaspoons Aleppo chilies

1 teaspoon Middle Eastern Five-Spice (page 109)

1 teaspoon ground cumin

1. Slice the sirloin into ¼-inch slices. Cut the slices into thin strips. Chop the strips into very small cubes, and further chop the cubes finely until they begin to stick together and become a little creamy. Cover with plastic wrap and chill for 20 minutes.

2. Place the bulgur in a small mixing bowl with ½ cup of very hot water. Stir to coat the bulgur with the water, and let it stand for 10 minutes.

3. Meanwhile, in a medium mixing bowl, combine the shallots, garlic, lemon juice, red pepper paste, chilies, five-spice, cumin, and cinnamon and add about 1½ teaspoons of the salt. Let stand for 5 minutes to soften the raw shallot and garlic flavor.

4. Stir in the olive oil, meat, bulgur, parsley, chopped mint, and dill.

5. Place the meat mixture in the mixing bowl of a KitchenAid mixer fitted with the paddle attachment and knead on medium-low speed for 2 to 3 minutes, just until the mixture becomes smooth and creamy and turns a slightly lighter color. If you're stirring the mixture by hand, do so for at least 4 to 5 minutes, to make a nice creamy consistency. Season well with salt and pepper.

continued

6. Chill the tartare for at least 20 minutes. You want to serve it nice and cold.

7. Chill a 10- to 12-inch plate for about 5 minutes in the refrigerator. Mound the tartare in the center of the plate. Fan some romaine leaves around half of the mound and pita chips around the other half. Use the pita and romaine to scoop up the tartare, and pass around little bowls of lemon wedges, mint leaves, and pickles to use as condiments. Top each bite with a little mint, pickle, and a squeeze of lemon.

TOASTED PITA BREAD CHIPS

1 10-inch pita bread

¼ cup olive oil

Salt and pepper to taste

1. Preheat the oven to 350°F.

2. Split the pita bread in half by tearing it with your hands, widthwise, so that you have two pockets. Open up each pocket and separate the halves so that you have 4 half-moon pieces. Roughly tear each half moon into 3 pieces.

3. Place the torn pita in a large mixing bowl and toss the pieces with the olive oil to lightly coat them. Season with salt and pepper.

4. Arrange the pita pieces on a baking sheet in an even layer so they can get uniformly crispy. It's okay if they overlap a little.

5. Bake for 8 to 10 minutes or until the pita chips are golden and crisp.

Halibut Cooked in Milk with Cinnamon, Fried Almonds, and Spinach

This is a variation on a dish that was described to me by my friend Gökcen Adar, a wonderful cook who lives in Istanbul. Gökcen cooks his fish in milk with lemon and capers. I decided to give this Greek technique an Arabic twist by using nuts, cinnamon, and orange, which was a risk, given that one rarely sees fish cooked with cinnamon. The risk paid off. People love this combination.

With this dish, try a rich rosé (see page 357) from the Chinon region of the Loire Valley. It is made entirely from cabernet franc, which lends mineral and herbaceous notes.

⌐⌐ SERVES 4 ⌐⌐

---

2 tablespoons extra-virgin olive oil

½ cup slivered almonds

Four 8-ounce halibut fillets or steaks

3 teaspoons plus ¼ cup kosher salt
  plus more to taste

1½ pounds fresh spinach,
  large stems removed, cleaned

2 cups milk

1 cup freshly squeezed orange juice
  (about 4 oranges)

1 teaspoon ground cinnamon

3 teaspoons garlic, finely minced
  (about 3 large cloves)

Lemon wedges

---

1. In a 6- to 7-inch skillet, heat the olive oil over medium heat. Add the almonds and toast them, stirring them with a fork for about 4 minutes, until they are golden brown. Lower the heat if necessary to avoid burning. Set aside. You don't need to drain off the oil unless it has burned.

2. Sprinkle the fish with 3 teaspoons of the salt and let it sit for at least 10 minutes (see note below).

3. Bring a 4-quart pot of water to a boil. Add ¼ cup of salt and the spinach and cook until the spinach is completely wilted, about a minute. Drain and place the spinach in a small bowl of ice water to cool quickly. Squeeze the spinach as dry as you can and set aside.

4. In a medium sauté pan with a lid (be sure the pan is large enough to hold the fish), mix the

milk, orange juice, cinnamon, and garlic. Bring the mixture to a boil over high heat, then reduce the heat to low and let it simmer until the milk separates.

5. Place the milk mixture in the blender and blend it until it becomes smooth again.

6. Return the mixture to the pan with the fish and spinach and simmer gently on low heat for 5 to 6 minutes. The fish is done when it is white throughout, with no opaqueness at its center. Cook for a few more minutes if the fish is thicker.

7. Check the seasoning, sprinkle with toasted almonds, and serve with lemon wedges.

❧ Salting Fish

My friend Max Hatziiliades, who built Oleana, taught me how to salt my fish ahead of time. Mediterranean fish is saltier than ours, and he likes to make his fish here taste like the fish back home, in Greece. Don't worry that your fish will be too salty if you salt it ahead of time. The fish just absorbs the salt throughout, which enhances the flavor.

Black Kale Malfati in Chestnut Soup with Moscato Wine

I ate some amazing spinach *malfati* in the winter of 2004 in a small restaurant in Siena, and it inspired me to create this recipe. *Malfatto* in Italian means "badly made," which possibly refers to the practice of using leftover ravioli filling to make these dumplings. Despite their name, these dumplings are absolutely delicious.

This is a great dish to serve after the first frost, when the kale is high in sugars (see Farmer Eero's note on page 55). The black kale in this recipe is deep green in color and tastes like a cross between broccoli and common kale. Other names for this kale include dinosaur kale, Tuscan black kale, and cavolo nero. You can also substitute regular kale, spinach, or chard for the black kale in this recipe if you like.

Moscato is the Italian word for the muscat grape. This wine brightens up the flavor of the earthy chestnut and helps pick up the sweet caramel flavor of the nutmeg. I like the moscatos from Pantelleria (an island off of Sicily) because they have a nice, dry finish. It's a natural pairing for this dish.

MAKES 8 MALFATİ TO SERVE 4

For the Chestnut Soup

4 cups chicken broth, preferably homemade

1 teaspoon soy sauce
(just for dark color, optional)

½ onion, finely chopped (about ½ cup)

1 rib celery, roughly chopped

2 cups peeled chestnuts (see note below)

½ cup heavy cream

Salt and pepper to taste

1 teaspoon freshly squeezed lemon juice

½ cup dry moscato wine, like that from Pantelleria in Sicily, or fino sherry

For the Malfati

1 cup ricotta cheese, strained over the sink
for about 10 minutes in a fine sieve

1 egg

⅛ teaspoon freshly grated or ground nutmeg
plus more for garnish

¼ cup freshly grated Parmesan cheese

1 teaspoon salt

¼ teaspoon pepper

½ cup flour plus more for dusting

4 cups chopped black kale, stems removed

1 tablespoon olive oil

To Start the Chestnut Soup

1. Bring the chicken stock, soy sauce, onion, celery, and chestnuts to a boil over medium-high heat. Reduce the heat to low and simmer for 20 minutes or until the chestnuts are soft and tender. Cool to a warm temperature.

To Make the Malfati

1. Place the ricotta in large mixing bowl and whisk for 2 to 3 minutes or until it is smooth and creamy with no lumps.

2. Add the egg and continue whisking until the egg is incorporated, for another 20 seconds.

3. Using a wooden spoon, stir in the nutmeg, Parmesan cheese, salt, and pepper. Add the ½ cup flour and continue to stir until it is incorporated. Chill.

4. Steam the kale by placing it with the olive oil and a tablespoon of water in a large sauté pan, fitted with a lid, over medium-low heat. Cook the kale until it's wilted and tender, about 8 minutes. Drain the kale well in a colander, and when it's cool enough to handle, squeeze a quarter of the kale at a time between your palms, pressing out as much water as possible. You should have about 1 cup of cooked kale. Stir the kale into the malfati mixture.

To Finish the Soup

1. Pour half the cooled chestnut mixture into a blender and blend with the cream until smooth and creamy.

2. Strain the chestnut and cream mixture through a fine sieve and season with salt and pepper. Purée the remaining soup and strain.

3. Place the chestnut and cream mixture back into a saucepan and warm over low heat.

4. Meanwhile, bring a large pot of water to a boil over high heat.

5. Divide the malfati mixture in half and then each half into half again, and then again, so that you have 8 equal pieces, approximately 1 inch around. Roll the pieces in flour to lightly coat the malfati.

6. Drop each piece, one at a time, into the boiling water. When the water starts to come back to a boil, after 4 to 5 minutes, the malfati should start to float to the top. Remove each malfati with a slotted spoon and place them in a shallow baking dish. Cover the malfati with foil to keep them warm.

7. Warm 4 large soup bowls in a low oven or by running really hot water over them.

8. Place two malfati in each bowl.

9. Stir the lemon juice and moscato into the soup and ladle it over the malfati to come halfway up the dumplings.

10. Garnish with a dash of freshly grated nutmeg and serve immediately.

❧ A Note on Chestnuts

It's very labor intensive to peel chestnuts. Unfortunately, most whole peeled chestnuts and chestnut purées are sweetened. I like to use flash-frozen peeled chestnuts from Italy. You can find them online at www.auiswisscatalogue.com.

❧ Spinach Variation

You can use spinach instead of kale in these malfati. Use twice as much chopped spinach (8 cups) because it cooks down and loses a lot more water than kale.

BAKLAVA

While visiting my friend Ayfer Unsal in her hometown of Gaziantep, in southeastern Turkey, I came to understand that making baklava is a serious and precise art. A baklava chef trains his entire life. The baklava shop Ayfer and I visited consisted of four floors. The top floor of the baklava shop employed young children (ages eight to fourteen), who were covered in so much cornstarch that their dark arms–and even their eyelashes–were dusted white. These were the beginning baklava chefs, and their job was to make the phyllo dough from scratch, rolling and rolling and stretching until the dough was as thin as parchment.

On the third floor, many men worked hard to assemble the baklava. They ground pistachios very finely with sugar and then layered them in between the homemade phyllo dough. They brushed the phyllo carefully with goat's milk butter, which had such a heady scent that I could smell it before I entered the room. Baklava is such a serious undertaking in this part of Turkey that they grow a special pistachio for use in the dessert, and it is not used for pilafs or snacking or anything else. These pistachios are as green as asparagus and smell like flowers, the way black walnuts do.

The second floor contained the oven, where the chef, who had trained his whole life, stood at the mouth of a very large, wood-fired oven. Only this chef could remove the pan of baklava from the oven at just the right moment and soak it with syrup. He told us that to be right, the baklava must "dance" (in other words, rise from the sides and bottom of the pan) when the syrup hits it. This way, just the right amount of syrup is absorbed–after being distributed in a fanatical evenness–to create the perfect sweetness and golden-brown, caramely top.

Ayfer and I finally reached the bottom floor of the shop, which housed the boutique where you could buy the baklava to take away or eat there with a cup of black tea. The shop was bustling with ladies, taking away beautifully packaged baklava. Very small boys–perhaps as young as six, and on track to become chefs–swept the floors and kept the shop clean. The pastry case was small but precious and you could buy baklava by the piece or by the whole, round, perfect pie.

The baklava at this particular shop was lighter, more perfumey, and less sweet than Greek versions I've tried, owing to the goat's milk butter, the special, flowery pistachios, and the amount of syrup used for soaking. The phyllo was thin, crisp, and perfectly caramelized and dissolved like sugar wafers in my mouth.

Black Walnut Baklava

There are great arguments about baklava: *my mom makes the best, my aunt makes the best, baklava is Greek, baklava is Armenian, baklava is Turkish,* and so on. But this is my favorite version: the one from Oleana, that our pastry chef Maura Kilpatrick has perfected over the years.

If you like sweet wine with your dessert, try to find a Greek dessert wine made from the muscat grape on the island of Samos. If you can't find that, a Moscatel de Malaga from Spain will be delicious.

MAKES ONE 8-INCH BAKLAVA OR ABOUT 16 PIECES

For the Baklava

8 ounces walnut halves (about 2½ cups)

5 ounces black walnuts pieces
   (about 1 cup; see note on page 131)

¾ cup sugar

2 tablespoons ground cinnamon

2 teaspoons freshly grated or ground nutmeg

2 sticks butter, melted

½ package phyllo dough

For the Syrup

1½ cups water

¾ cup sugar

½ cup honey

2 cinnamon sticks

5 to 6 whole cloves

2 teaspoons freshly squeezed
   lemon juice

To Make the Baklava

1. Toast both kinds of walnuts separately for about 8 minutes, or until lightly browned (see Toasting Nuts, page 91).

2. Coarsely chop the regular walnuts so they are similar in size to the black walnuts (black walnuts usually come in smaller pieces).

3. In a small mixing bowl, toss both kinds of walnuts with the sugar, cinnamon, and nutmeg.

4. Brush an 8-inch square pan (see note on the pan, below) with some melted butter.

5. Preheat the oven to 350°F.

6. Cut eighteen 8-inch squares of phyllo dough. Cover the squares with a towel to prevent them from drying out.

7. Lay a piece of phyllo in the bottom of the buttered pan and brush it generously with melted butter. Lay another layer of phyllo dough over this and brush it again, generously, with melted butter. Repeat this process until you have 8 buttered layers. Some pieces of the phyllo may need to be trimmed or patched.

8. Make a layer of nuts with ½ of the nut filling (about 1½ cups).

9. Top the nuts with 4 sheets of phyllo, brushing generously with butter between the layers.

10. Spread the remaining nut mixture onto the top buttered phyllo sheet.

11. Top the nuts off with 6 more layers of phyllo (with butter between the layers) to finish it.

12. Before baking, cut the baklava into four 4-inch square quarters. Then cut each on both diagonals into 4 more pieces.

13. Place the pan on a baking sheet and bake for about 45 minutes. The baklava will start to turn light golden brown. Lower the oven heat to 300°F and bake for 20 minutes more.

To Make the Syrup

1. While the baklava is baking, make the syrup by combining the water, sugar, honey, cinnamon sticks, and cloves in a small saucepan. Bring the mixture to a boil over high heat and then reduce the heat to medium. Stir to help dissolve the sugar, and continue cooking at a brisk simmer for about 20 minutes, until the syrup thickens and you have 1½ cups.

2. Stir in the lemon juice, and keep the syrup warm.

3. When the baklava comes out of the oven, pour the warm syrup evenly over the pan. Cool completely.

4. Cut through each marked piece and carefully lift from the pan. If you're not using a disposable pan, lift out a middle piece first with a narrow offset spatula; the other pieces will come out easily. See the note below about the pan.

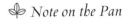 ## Note on Black Walnuts

At Oleana, we use black walnuts to make our baklava because their taste resembles that of the pistachios in Gaziantep, used to flavor their famous baklava. Black walnuts have a floral flavor that is stronger than regular walnuts. Eastern black walnuts are native to the central and eastern United States, and they are harder to find than regular walnuts. We found them on the Internet at www.black-walnuts.com. You can also substitute pistachios or regular walnuts in this recipe, but you would be cheating yourself out of the black walnut experience.

Note on the Pan

It is helpful to use an 8-inch disposable aluminum pan for baklava. This way, when it's time to remove the baklava, you can cut through one side of the pan, slicing through the corners, and flatten out the side. You can then slide the spatula under the first piece of baklava, and lift it easily out of the pan.

Poached Figs in Spiced Red Wine with Crème Fraîche Bavarian

Oleana's pastry chef Maura Kilpatrick created this spiced late-summer dessert. The red-wine syrup that the figs are poached in is delicious over ice cream as well, and any leftover syrup can be frozen and used later.

A Bavarian is a French custard set with gelatin. Because of the egg yolks, this custard is thicker and richer than a pudding that is thickened with cornstarch or flour.

Crème fraîche is a slightly tangy, slightly nutty, thickened cream. Traditionally made, it relies on good bacteria to ferment the cream and then it thickens naturally. It is widely available in Europe, but much less so in the United States, where almost all cream is pasteurized, and therefore needs to be fermented artificially. Vermont Butter and Cheese Company makes a delicious pasteurized crème fraîche that is widely distributed; you can find them online at www.vtbutterandcheeseco.com.

Fresh figs are in season from late June through mid-August, but you can still find them sporadically during the fall. You can use pears as a substitute for the figs (see variation at end of recipe), but don't use dried figs as a substitute for fresh figs, as they will be too heavy for the Bavarian.

Both the figs and the Bavarian are best if made a day before serving and can be made up to 2 days ahead.

For a nice, sweet wine match, try the fortified dessert wine from Banyuls in the south of France, made from grenache grapes.

SERVES 8 TO 10

For the Bavarian

1 teaspoon vegetable oil

1¾ cups milk

½ cup sugar

¼ cup mild honey
 (clover honey works well)

½ vanilla bean, split in half lengthwise

6 egg yolks

Ice cubes

1 tablespoon plus 1 teaspoon
 powdered gelatin

1 cup crème fraîche

¼ cup heavy cream

For the Poached Figs

4 cups fruity red wine, such as a
 ripe pinot noir from Oregon

1 cup sugar

½ cup honey

½ vanilla bean, split in half lengthwise

3 whole allspice berries

6 black peppercorns

One 3-inch strip orange zest
 (see Zesting Citrus, page 72)

15 to 20 fresh black mission figs,
 washed and stems removed

To Make the Bavarian

1. Prepare a 9 × 5-inch loaf pan (about 3 inches deep) by rubbing it with the vegetable oil. You can use a paper towel to distribute it evenly.

2. Tear a piece of plastic wrap big enough to line the whole pan, and press it in, smoothing the wrinkles.

3. Heat the milk in a small saucepan over medium-low heat, adding the sugar and honey.

4. Scrape the inside of the vanilla bean with the back of a small paring knife to remove the little black seeds or paste. Add the seeds to the milk mixture.

5. When the milk is hot and just under the boiling point, after about 4 minutes, turn the heat off and cover it with a lid or a baking sheet and let the flavors infuse into the milk for 30 minutes.

6. In a medium mixing bowl, whisk the egg yolks until they are smooth and creamy.

7. Stir the warm milk slowly into the eggs and return the mixture to the pan. Cook over medium-low heat, stirring constantly with a heatproof rubber spatula or wooden spoon, for about 5 minutes or until the mixture thickens slightly (to a sauce consistency) and coats the spatula or spoon.

continued

ALLSPICE, CINNAMON, AND NUTMEG

8. Strain the custard through a sieve into a medium bowl and set the bowl of custard over a larger bowl filled with ice. Stir for 3 minutes with the spatula, scraping the sides.

9. Sprinkle the gelatin into ¼ cup cold water and let it soften for 3 to 5 minutes.

10. In a very small saucepan, melt the gelatin over very low heat until it becomes liquid.

11. Stir the dissolved gelatin into the custard. Place the bowl in the refrigerator for 15 minutes, stirring it and scraping down the sides every 5 minutes. The mixture should thicken and cool completely.

12. Using an electric mixer with a whip attachment, whip the crème fraîche and heavy cream until it forms soft peaks. This should take less than a minute on high speed. You should be able to write your initial in the top of the cream and have it hold for a minute.

13. Gently whisk ⅓ of the heavy cream mixture into the custard, until it's incorporated. Add the rest of the heavy cream mixture and, using a rubber spatula, fold it into the custard (see Folding, page 135).

14. Pour the custard into the prepared loaf pan and cover with any overhanging plastic. The plastic will not completely cover the top of the custard.

15. Chill for at least 6 hours and preferably overnight.

To Make the Poached Figs

1. Combine all the ingredients except the figs in a medium saucepan.

2. Bring the mixture to a boil on high heat and reduce the heat to medium to achieve a brisk simmer. Simmer the syrup for 10 to 12 minutes to concentrate it and infuse the spices. Taste the liquid; if the syrup tastes good enough to drink at this point, then it's ready for you to add the fruit.

3. Drop the figs in the simmering syrup and continue to simmer for 8 minutes longer.

4. Remove the figs from the syrup, using a slotted spoon, and place them in a single layer on a platter or baking sheet. Cool.

5. Continue to simmer the syrup for another 10 to 12 minutes to thicken it slightly.

6. Cool the syrup completely, and then strain it through a fine sieve.

7. Slice the figs in half and toss them with the cooled spiced syrup. Chill, covered, overnight so that the figs absorb more flavor from the syrup.

8. Take the Bavarian out of the mold by uncovering the top plastic and inverting the pan onto a platter or small cutting board. Remove the plastic and slice the Bavarian into ½-inch pieces and place on small plates with 4 fig halves on top of each slice. Spoon a couple of tablespoons of the syrup over the figs and around the plate and serve.

❧ Pear Variation

To use pears in place of figs, increase the wine to 6 cups and increase the sugar to 4½ cups. Use 6 pears, peeled and sliced in half lengthwise. Remove the core with a melon baller and remove the fibrous string that runs from the core to the stem. Add the pears to the boiling liquid. Reduce the heat to medium-low, and simmer the pears with a heatproof dish placed on top of them to keep them submerged, until they are just tender, 20 to 25 minutes. They will take a bit longer if they are firm. Remove the pears from the syrup to cool and reduce the syrup as described in steps recipe above. Combine the cooled pears with the syrup and allow the pears to absorb more flavor from the syrup for at least 4 hour. Proceed with step 8, slicing the pear and distributing pieces onto each plate.

FOLDING

The point of folding is to allow you to mix the cream and the custard without deflating all the air that you just worked so hard to whip into the cream. The air bubbles are vital to keeping your dish light and airy.

It helps to initially take a third of the heavy cream and gently whisk it into the custard. You'll lose some of the bubbles, but it brings the consistency of both closer to each other, so they mix better.

Using a large rubber spatula, reach down through the center of the heavy cream to the bottom of the bowl and lift some of the custard up on top of the cream. As you turn your wrist to fold the custard on top of the cream, turn the bowl a few degrees. Then reach down to the bottom again and lift more of the custard up and over the cream. After 5 to 6 repetitions of folding and turning the bowl, the cream will be incorporated and the mixture will still be light and airy.

Persimmon Pudding Cake with Maple Sugar Crème Brûlée

This wonderful autumn dessert features persimmons, a fruit available mid-November through the end of January that is sweet and rich and slightly tangy. The persimmon purée makes the little cakes in this recipe deliciously moist, like banana bread or carrot cake. After baking, the cakes fall and leave a well to fill with everyone's favorite: crème brûlée.

There are many different kinds of persimmons, but they all fall into one of two categories: astringent and nonastringent. Astringent persimmons, like the hachiya variety, must be eaten when fully ripe, after they've become jelly soft. They make good pudding cakes, and the hachiya persimmon is preferred in this recipe. When not fully ripe, astringent persimmons taste like green bananas: their tartness makes you pucker and strips your mouth dry. A hachiya persimmon looks like a long or conical tomato with glossy, deep-orange skin, and tastes sweet and rich like a mango with a slight pearlike flavor.

Nonastringent varieties, such as the widely available fuyu, are still somewhat firm when fully ripe. They are delicious sliced and added to salads or eaten instead of melon with thinly sliced prosciutto in the winter. Fuyu persimmons look like bright gold tomatoes. They're best for slicing for salads and garnish but aren't for baking.

Persimmons ripen at room temperature within 3 to 4 days. If you can't wait that long, put them in the freezer, unwrapped, overnight. When they thaw, they're ready to use. Cut them in half and scoop out the pulp, discarding the skin. Purée the pulp in a food processor fitted with a metal blade, until smooth and creamy.

Maple sugar, also known as "Indian sugar," is a finely granulated sugar made from pure maple syrup. It's used as an alternative to brown sugar when baking or in coffee as a substitute for cane sugar. You can find it online at www.vermontcountrystore.com.

You can make both the custard and cakes a day ahead and assemble them just before serving. The custard can even be made up to 3 days ahead and won't suffer.

Drink a late-harvest Gewürztraminer (see page 61) with this dessert.

⟅ MAKES FOURTEEN 4-OUNCE (MUFFIN-SIZED) INDIVIDUAL CAKES ⟆
AND 2½ CUPS OF CRÈME BRÛLÉE

For the Persimmon Pudding Cake

7 tablespoons butter, melted

1 cup flour

½ teaspoon baking soda

½ teaspoon baking powder

1 teaspoon ground cinnamon

½ teaspoon ground allspice

¼ teaspoon ground cloves

¼ teaspoon salt

2 eggs

⅔ cup sugar, plus about ½ cup
for brûlée

1⅓ cups buttermilk

1⅓ cups persimmon purée, from about
3 jelly-soft ripe hachiya persimmons

1½ teaspoons grated orange zest
(about 1 orange)

1 tablespoon freshly squeezed orange juice
(about ½ orange)

For the Maple Sugar Crème Brûlée

2 cups heavy cream

½ cup maple sugar (or substitute ½ cup
sugar plus 1 teaspoon maple extract
or 1 tablespoon real maple syrup)

6 egg yolks

To Make the Pudding Cake

1. Preheat the oven to 350°F.

2. Lightly brush a medium muffin pan (that makes 4-ounce muffins) with about 2 tablespoons of the melted butter to prevent the cake batter from sticking.

3. Over a large mixing bowl, sift together the flour, baking soda, baking powder, cinnamon, allspice, cloves, and salt and set aside. If you don't have a flour sifter, you can use a medium sieve and shake the dry ingredients through it, into the bowl or onto a large piece of parchment paper (which can then be picked up and formed into a funnel to slide the flour mixture into the batter for step 6).

4. Using a handheld mixer or a KitchenAid mixer fitted with a paddle attachment, beat the eggs on medium speed for 1 minute, until they are broken and smooth like an omelet mixture. Slowly add the sugar and continue beating until the mixture is thick and pale yellow, for about 5 minutes.

5. Add the remaining 5 tablespoons of melted butter and mix for a few seconds until the butter is incorporated.

6. With the mixer on the slowest speed, add the flour mixture, little by little, until it forms a batter.

7. Pour in the buttermilk and mix another minute, until the batter is smooth.

continued

8. In a small bowl, combine the persimmon purée with the orange zest and juice, stirring with a spoon or whisk. Add this mixture to the cake batter, stirring for a minute, until combined.

9. Pour the batter into a medium pitcher or use a 4-ounce ladle to fill the muffin cups to the top with batter. If you have extra batter, butter one or two 4-ounce soufflé ramekins and fill them, just like the muffin tins, setting them on a small pie pan or cookie sheet to bake.

10. Bake the little cakes for 25 minutes. Insert a toothpick or a wooden skewer into the center of one of the cakes. If the skewer comes out clean, then the cakes are done. If a little wet batter clings to the skewer, then the cakes should bake for another 5 to 7 minutes. The cakes will rise when first baked and then sink as they cool, forming a well. They will be very moist and soft, like a cross between cake and pudding.

To Make the Crème Brûlée

1. Preheat the oven to 300°F.

2. Combine the cream and maple sugar in a small saucepan over medium heat. Maple sugar is very dry and the granules stick together, so you will have to keep whisking until it is dissolved, for a few minutes, over medium heat. Remove from the heat once the cream begins to simmer (after about 8 minutes). Set aside.

3. Place the egg yolks in a small mixing bowl and whisk them until they are broken and creamy, for about 1 minute. Slowly pour the hot maple cream into the yolks, little by little, whisking as you pour.

4. When the cream and eggs are incorporated, use a large spoon or a ladle to skim off any bubbles that form on top of the cream and discard.

2.

3.

3.

5. Strain the crème through a fine sieve, to remove any granules of sugar or bits of cooked egg, into a small (6- to 8-inch, round or square) ovenproof baking dish or soufflé dish. Use a large spoon or the back of the ladle to push the crème through. The crème should be 1 to 1½ inches high.

6. Place the dish in a baking or roasting pan that is slightly larger. Fill the larger pan with warm water so that it reaches ¾ of the way up the sides of the custard dish. This water bath will cook the custard more gently.

7. Bake for 55 minutes. The custard should be set around the sides and still loose in the middle when you gently shake the pan. Cover the pan with foil and bake another 15 minutes.

8. Remove the custard dish from the water bath and uncover it. Cool the crème for about 30 minutes, and then refrigerate it for at least 1 to 2 hours, until completely chilled.

To Serve the Cakes

1. Spoon about 2 tablespoons of the crème brûlée into the well of each persimmon cake, leveling the top with a spatula or the back edge of a knife. The cream should be smooth and even with the cake.

2. Coat the maple cream with a thin, even layer of granulated sugar, about a heaping teaspoon per cake.

3. Using a propane torch, quickly move the flame across the top of the cake to melt the sugar. Continue moving the flame back and forth for another minute, until the top becomes darkly golden, like caramel. Let it cool for a minute before serving so that the top hardens and crackles (the signature of crème brûlée). If you have any persimmons left over, you can serve them sliced on the side as a garnish.

❧ Note

Maple Sugar Crème Brûlée is delicious on its own. If you choose to make it separately from the persimmon pudding cakes, leave the baked custard in the pan and follow instructions for steps 2 and 3, above.

FAVORITE CHILIES
Aleppo, Urfa, and Paprika

My visits to Turkey and Spain opened up whole worlds of flavor to me, contained in the flesh of Aleppo, Urfa, and paprika chili peppers. Before my travels, I used widely available chilies, such as the jalapeño and habañero, which are just plain hot. But Mediterranean cuisine is not hot-spicy like Thai or Mexican food; the chilies used there do not overwhelm the taste of food, but rather heighten it. In my travels in this region, I discovered the varied and individually unique flavors of exotic chilies: bitter, leathery, earthy, chocolate, smoky, and sweet. I wandered the markets and ate in the restaurants, adding new chilies to my palette and slowly learning how to use them–just like other herbs and spices–to layer, tone, or brighten dishes.

Chilies contain natural oils, just as nuts do. Make sure the chilies you use are shiny. Shininess indicates that a chili has been dried properly and will be fresh and flavorful.

Like toasting nuts, toasting chilies releases their natural oils and perfume. You can lightly toast a whole dried chili by holding it with a pair of tongs a few inches over a gas flame for about a minute, until it steams and becomes more pliable, but being careful not to set it on fire. Store toasted peppers in an airtight container or in the freezer.

ALEPPO CHİLİES

Once you begin using these beautiful, coarsely ground chili flakes from northern Syria, you'll toss out your bottle of dried red pepper flakes meant for sprinkling on slices of cheese pizza. You can substitute Aleppo chilies to greatly enhance any recipe calling for dried red pepper flakes.

Aleppo chilies are used more for flavor than for heat; their flavor is deliciously deep with a cuminlike earthiness and a hint of sweetness. Chilies are celebrated in Aleppo–a city with a varied and plentiful gastronomy–but the food there is not typically spicy.

Aleppo chilies are especially oily and when fresh should look bright red and almost wet. You can substitute Aleppo chili pepper in recipes calling for paprika, but use slightly less Aleppo pepper, because it is hotter. And remember that paprika does have a unique flavor that may be important to certain dishes such as goulash. It's also fun to substitute Aleppo chilies for black pepper. It can be dangerous, though, if you love black pepper and use lots, so season with a cautious hand.

I sprinkle Aleppo chilies on green salads, feta cheese, tuna salad, cheese pizza, quesadillas, soup,

and potato salad. I recommend storing the chilies in your freezer, since freezing them keeps their oils from drying out. I always have a small bag of Aleppo chilies in my freezer as well as a little shakerful on my table.

Aleppo chilies are available at www.kalustyans. com. Maras chilies, which are nearly identical but come from Turkey, are available at www.formaggiokitchen.com.

URFA CHİLİES

My friend Ihsan Gurdhal introduced me to Urfa chilies. Ihsan is from Istanbul and owns one of my favorite stores in town: Formaggio Kitchen, in Cambridge, Massachusetts (see Ihsan's Doggy Eggs on page 218). To me, Formaggio Kitchen is like a toy store; I poke through fresh produce and wander the aisles when I need fun, new ingredients, and inspiration. Ihsan and his wife Valerie travel in search of great cheeses, olive oils, dried pastas, condiments, olives, and charcuterie. They are famous for their cheese-ripening room in the basement of Formaggio. I always leave Formaggio with lots more than I came for.

Ihsan is my local Turkish expert. He regales me with wonderful stories about his grandmother and her culinary experiences in the Ottoman palace she grew up in. One day I was in Formaggio when Ihsan had just received a shipment of Urfa chilies from Turkey. He told me to take them to try. From that day on, I was hooked.

Urfa chilies are dark red or purple-black and come from southeastern Turkey, near Syria, from the town of Urfa or Sanli Urfa, and they are very exciting to work with. In fact, they may be my favorite chili pepper. They are simultaneously bitter like coffee or chocolate and sweet like molasses, and they lend a wonderful, deep, smoky aroma to sauces. Like the Aleppo chili, the Urfa chili's heat is moderate but meaningful. And like the Aleppo, the Urfa has a high oil content and when fresh should look shiny and not at all dull. Urfa peppers are ground even more coarsely than Aleppo chilies. They freeze well and will keep in an airtight container for months.

When picked, Urfa peppers are dark purple in color, which deepens as they dry in the sun. After the chilies lay in the sun all day, the farmers wrap them up and leave them to sweat overnight. The chilies are then unwrapped and returned to the sun the next day. Over the course of a week, this process concentrates the chilies' color to near-black, and they develop their rich, earthy flavor and smoky aroma.

I sprinkle Urfa chili pepper on ceviche, Fried Haloumi Cheese (page 10), tomato sauces, scrambled eggs, eggplant, hot chocolate, and even on caramel popcorn (see Rosemary's Spicy Caramel Popcorn, page 170). They are also the perfect substitution for recipes calling for our native Ancho chilies.

Urfa chilies are available at www.kalustyans.com and at www.formaggiokitchen.com.

Paprika

Paprika chilies are unlike Urfa and Aleppo in that they are sweeter and warmer and have more caramel and bell-pepper flavors. Paprika complements many foods without dominating them and lends a rich color to dishes.

Paprika chilies vary in color from red to dark red to brown, depending on the type of plant, the climate, and the amount of red pigment in the pepper skin. They also vary in strength of heat and flavor styles–from bittersweet to smoky, semisweet to delicate, sweet to hot–and it can become complicated to choose. The heat of the chili depends on how much capsaicin (a compound found in the pepper's connecting tissues, placenta, and seeds) is left before processing. The mildest and sweetest paprika is made only with the flesh of the pepper; all traces of seed, stem, and connecting tissues are removed. The result is a silky paprika with no bitterness or aftertaste. Paprika chilies are always harvested ripe and resemble miniature sweet bell peppers. They are ground finer than Aleppo and Urfa chilies, but can be stored in the same way.

Spaniards use both sweet paprika and smoked paprika, but even sweet paprika is somewhat smoky. Spanish paprika is smokier and usually not as finely ground as Hungarian paprika, which has a delicate, sweet, and silky texture. It famously lends its flavor to goulash, the Hungarian veal or beef stew made with paprika and sour cream. The peppers grow all over the world, but paprika harvesting is a big industry with strict regulations in Spain, Hungary, and Israel.

I like to use a good paprika to lend rich color to chicken marinades and beef stews. It's fun to play with Spanish smoked paprika to make pan-fried or broiled steaks taste like they were grilled over charcoal and sweet red pepper sauces taste pleasantly woody and smoky.

For Hungarian-style paprika, try the különleges at www.penzeys.com. For Spanish-style paprika, try the sun-dried paprika in bittersweet or hot or the el ray smoked paprika (very smoky) at www.thespanishtable.com.

RECIPES WITH THREE FAVORITE CHILIES: ALEPPO, URFA, AND PAPRIKA

Smoky Eggplant Purée with Pine Nuts and Urfa Pepper

This eggplant preparation is heavenly: I love the combination of creamy, smoky, peppery, and nutty flavors. It's similar to the traditional Ottoman-style dish served in Turkey called "sultan's delight"–featuring creamy, smoky eggplant but minus the pine nuts–which is served with bits of stewed lamb.

Turkey contains many cuisines; Ottoman cuisine is the elaborate, refined cooking of Istanbul and the palaces. During the Ottoman Empire, the sultans hired extraordinary chefs, each specializing in one particular dish. Ottoman chefs concocted imaginative and sometimes bizarre-sounding recipes, including kebobs, minuscule ravioli, the priest fainted (stuffed eggplant), ladies' thighs (battered and fried meatballs with rice), and young girl's dream (2 scoops of chocolate ice cream with a banana sticking out of the middle). The feasts were served up on hand-hammered silver dishes, still used in the palaces today.

I was inspired to create this recipe after having tasted a similar dish in Cupia, a restaurant in the suburbs of Athens. The chefs at Cupia charred their eggplants over a wood fire and wrapped them in foil to steam until they collapsed. Then they removed the foil tableside, scraping the creamy white eggplant flesh into a bowl and mashing it with thick, garlicky mayonnaise and toasted pine nuts. The finished product, served with fresh pita right out of the wood-fired oven, was to die for.

My version is a cross between sultan's delight and the outstanding dish I sampled in Greece. I use yogurt instead of heavy mayonnaise, and I boil the eggplant to make preparation easier. I also use a little smoked salt to impart a wood-smoke flavor to the eggplant. You can find smoked salt at www.salttraders.com.

Smoky eggplant puree is a perfect side dish to the Grilled Skirt Steak on page 26 and is wonderful as a mezze with bread or greens. It's also great served with Braised Beef Short Ribs (page 66) and Spoon Lamb (page 22).

Always choose fresh, healthy eggplants that are firm and shiny. The light purple-skinned variety, or "neon" eggplant, works very well in this recipe, as the flesh is white and creamy, but they are hard to find. Chinese eggplant, which are long and thin and have a light purple color like the neon variety, are delicious too, but they yield less meat and so take more work to prepare. Regular dark-skinned "black bell" eggplants are also fine for this recipe.

⟞ MAKES ABOUT 2½ CUPS TO SERVE 4 TO 6 ⟝

2 eggplants (about 2 pounds), peeled and cut into 2-inch chunks

1 tablespoon salt plus more to taste

¼ cup whole-milk plain yogurt, preferably Greek style

1 teaspoon smoked salt

1 teaspoon finely minced garlic (about 1 large clove)

1 tablespoon freshly squeezed lemon juice (about ½ lemon)

2 tablespoons extra-virgin olive oil

½ cup toasted pine nuts (page 91)

2 teaspoons Urfa chilies plus a pinch for garnish

Pepper to taste

1. Bring a large saucepan (big enough to hold the chunks of peeled eggplant) of water to a boil, and cook the eggplant in the boiling water with the tablespoon of salt. Lower the heat to medium and continue on a brisk simmer. Cook for 15 to 20 minutes, until the eggplant is soft and translucent. Check by squeezing the eggplant with a pair of tongs. Drain well in a colander.

2. In a food processor fitted with a metal blade, purée the eggplant with the yogurt, smoked salt, garlic, lemon juice, and olive oil.

3. Place the eggplant mixture in a medium mixing bowl and stir in the pine nuts and Urfa chilies. Season with salt and pepper to taste.

4. Serve at room temperature or warm in small serving bowls, sprinkled with a pinch of Urfa chilies to show them off.

Chicken and Walnut Pâté with Smoky Paprika

I call this creamy chicken salad recipe pâté because it is similar in consistency to *rillettes*, which is a type of French pâté. Rillettes are made by cooking rabbit, duck, or pork slowly in a lot of fat until very tender; the meat is then shredded and mixed with enough cooking fat to form a paste, which is served on sliced bread. In this recipe, I use nuts, bread, and chicken poaching liquid to bind the chicken meat, for a creamy consistency without all the fat. Using nuts as a thickening agent is a sophisticated, heart-smart, healthful Arabic cooking technique (see also Turkish Tarator Sauce on page 353 and Garlic and Almond Soup on page 338).

This pâté recipe is a twist on Circassian chicken, a classic Ottoman dish. The Russians forced the Circassians out of their homeland in the North Caucasus Mountains in the 1860s, and 90 percent of these people fled to Turkey. Circassian women–renowned for their beauty and their cooking–were captured by or traded to the sultans and became part of the harem and cooking staff in the Turkish palaces.

The first time I prepared Circassian chicken was in 1999, when I was chef at the Casablanca restaurant in Harvard Square. Clifford Wright, the author of *A Mediterranean Feast* (a book that took him ten years to write and is my favorite reference on Mediterranean cooking), came into the kitchen and said, "No, it must be creamier." He helped me understand the proper texture. And then when I first met my friend Hamza Zeytinoglu, of Circassian descent and hailing from Istanbul,

he literally jumped for joy after I mentioned that I offered Circassian chicken on my menu at the Casablanca. Hamza came into the restaurant to try the dish and said, "No, it must be spicier."

So this recipe was perfected by the palates of both Cliff and Hamza. It's fun to play with any of the chilies in this chapter, altering the spiciness according to your preference.

Traditionally, cilantro is a main ingredient in Circassian chicken, but I like to use scallions instead, because I think the cilantro distracts from the beautiful flavor combination of smoky chilies and walnuts.

This recipe freezes very well.

Serve the pâté with a dry muscat from Portugal to make a perfect aperitif as a mezze course with homemade crackers (see recipe for Crick-Cracks, page 176).

MAKES 5 CUPS TO SERVE AT LEAST 10

1 whole free-range chicken (about 3 pounds)

1 cup dry white wine (if you are drinking the
  Portuguese Muscat, use that)

1 small carrot, cut in half

½ onion, peeled and cut in half

10 black peppercorns

4 whole allspice berries

2 bay leaves

Ice cubes

¼ pound French bread, most of the crust
  removed (about ½ baguette)

2 cups walnut pieces or halves

2 tablespoons finely chopped garlic
  (about 6 cloves)

½ cup walnut oil

Salt and pepper to taste

¼ cup sour cream

6 scallions, bottoms trimmed
  and finely chopped

1 teaspoon Aleppo chilies

1½ teaspoons smoked paprika

Crick-Cracks (page 176)
  or your favorite crackers

Condiments (pickled hot peppers,
  additional Aleppo chilies, whole radishes,
  romaine leaves)

1. Place the chicken in a large pot, add the wine and enough water to cover it. Add the carrot, onion, peppercorns, allspice, and bay leaves and bring them to a gentle boil over high heat. Turn the heat down to medium-low so that the pot just simmers; the chicken will be tough if the water boils too hard. Cover partially with a lid and poach for about 30 minutes. The leg should pull off the chicken easily when you tug at it with a pair of tongs.

2. Remove the chicken and place it on a baking sheet to cool. Continue cooking the liquid on low heat, simmering, until it reduces by half, 30 to 40 more minutes.

3. Strain the liquid through a fine sieve into a small, deep bowl.

4. Fill a medium mixing bowl with ice and add some cold water to create an ice bath. Set the bowl of broth in the bowl of ice and drop 2 ice cubes into the broth. This will help the fat rise to the top quicker and the liquid to cool so that it can be skimmed.

5. After the broth is cool, skim the fat off using a ladle or spoon in a circular motion. Discard the fat.

continued

6. When the chicken is cool enough to handle, discard the chicken skin and pull the meat off of the bones, using your fingers. Discard the bones.

7. Shred the meat so that it forms thin strands, like broken fettuccine. You can do this with your hands or pull the meat toward you in little pieces with a fork. The last alternative is to chop the meat coarsely with a knife, which is the quickest technique but doesn't allow for an extremely creamy *rillete* texture. Place the shredded chicken in a medium mixing bowl and set aside.

8. Soak the bread in a little more than ½ cup of the chicken broth for a few minutes, until soft. Stir the bread to coat it with the broth and allow it to soak evenly.

9. Using a food processor fitted with a metal blade, puree the walnuts with the garlic until they are ground to a paste.

10. Squeeze the bread dry with your hands and add it to the walnut paste in the food processor. Purée until the paste becomes homogeneous and creamy, stopping once to scrape the bowl. You will have a thick paste that forms a ball.

11. Scrape the mixture into a medium mixing bowl and whisk in about 1½ cups of the broth mixture to make a mayonnaise consistency.

12. Whisk in the walnut oil and season with salt and pepper.

13. Stir in the shredded chicken, sour cream, scallions, Aleppo chilies, and paprika. Add more broth to make the pâté creamier or more Aleppo chilies to make it spicier.

14. I like to serve this pâté in a crock or Luminarc jar–the French glass jar that has a flip-top lid with a rubber gasket–with a wooden spreader. Serve with crackers and condiments.

13.

14.

Whipped Feta with Sweet and Hot Peppers

At Oleana, we serve this addictive staple as a bread condiment, under the *prêt à manger* section of our menu. We dish it up in a little crock and sprinkle it with a pinch each of Aleppo and Urfa chilies and paprika to really show the peppers off.

This untraditional recipe is my interpretation of a typical hot pepper and feta spread eaten as a mezze in Greece. It's important to use a good creamy feta, such as a sheep's milk French feta, so that it will whip up very smoothly. For salads and more crumbly applications, Greek-style or cow's milk feta is fine. See page 349 for an explanation of different kinds of feta.

Serve this dish with manaaeesh (page 240) or with celery sticks, raw fennel sticks, or spears of endive as a salad course or snack.

⌁ MAKES 2 CUPS TO SERVE 4 TO 6 ⌁

---

1 pound sheep's or goat's milk French feta, drained and broken into rough ½-inch pieces or crumbled

2 medium red bell peppers, roasted, peeled, seeded, and roughly chopped (see page 97) and drained of excess juice

2 teaspoons Aleppo chilies plus a pinch for garnish

1 teaspoon Urfa chilies plus a pinch for garnish

½ teaspoon smoked Spanish paprika plus a pinch for garnish

1 teaspoon lemon juice

¼ cup olive oil

---

1. Place all the ingredients in a medium mixing bowl and combine them so that the sweet and hot peppers coat the cheese.

2. In a food processor fitted with a metal blade, purée the mixture for about 2 minutes, until very smooth and creamy. The mixture will be quite loose, but it will set when it's chilled in the refrigerator for about 30 minutes before serving.

3. Place the mixture in a crock and sprinkle it with a pinch of all three of the chilies to garnish and show them off.

Steamed Mussels with Leeks and Smoky Paprika

This dish has such Spanish flair that you'll think you've died and gone to Spain. It's fabulous with one of the first spring crops: wild leeks or ramps, which are more tender than regular leeks. Ramps taste much like scallions–only sweeter and feistier–and you can use them just like scallions or regular leeks. Look for ramps at local farmers' markets in the spring or at specialty shops that carry seasonal produce.

Focusing on the sweet flavors of the paprika, ramps, and mussels, this dish is simple but it also has some rich, smoky, buttery depth. To make an impression, use a special butter in this recipe, such as Plugra (available at Whole Foods Market or online at www.kellerscreamery.com) or any sweet, salty cultured butter. Cultured butter is made with natural bacteria which enhances its flavor and helps to bring out the sea in the mussels and the forest in the ramps. You can find cultured butter online at www.vtbutterandcheeseco.com.

If the mussels have beards on them, which wild mussels do, you will need to remove them. Pull the beard from the rounded end of the mussel toward the top, pointed end. Wild mussels also need to be scrubbed free of sand. In Boston, I buy Prince Edward Island mussels, which are farmed on poles. Since they don't touch the bottom of the ocean, they are sand-free.

After you've eaten the mussels, make sure to soak up the sauce with grilled or lightly toasted crusty bread. Drink an Alsatian Sylvaner, which has a smoky spice, an earthiness, and a hint of vanilla from the oak barrels.

SERVES 4 AS A FIRST COURSE

2 tablespoons European-style or cultured butter, such as Plugra

1 teaspoon olive oil

1 tablespoon minced garlic (about 3 cloves)

¾ cup white wine, such as European chardonnay or Spanish alberino

16 ramps, root ends trimmed and washed well, or 2 leeks, white part only, root ends trimmed, and cut into ½-inch rounds

1 tablespoon smoked Spanish paprika

½ teaspoon Aleppo chilies

32 mussels (about 2 pounds), washed well

1 tablespoon freshly squeezed lemon juice (about ½ lemon)

Salt or sea salt to taste (see note below)

1. In a large sauté pan over medium-high heat, melt 1 tablespoon of the butter with the olive oil. When the butter starts to brown, stir in the garlic and cook for 2 minutes, stirring until the garlic begins to release its aroma and becomes a little sticky.

2. Add the wine, ramps, paprika, and Aleppo chilies. Stir and continue to cook for 3 minutes until the wine reduces to ½ cup and the ramps start to soften and become limp.

3. Add the mussels to the pan and cover them with a tight-fitting lid or heavy baking sheet. Reduce the heat to medium and cook for 5 to 6 minutes, until the mussels open.

4. Stir in the remaining 1 tablespoon of butter and the lemon juice and season with very little salt (the mussels should be salty, so you won't need much).

5. Divide the mussels (8 per person) into 4 warm bowls (just out of the dishwasher or warmed for a minute in a 350°F oven). Divide the juices and leeks evenly among the bowls. Serve with fresh crusty bread, lightly grilled or freshly baked, to soak up the juices once the mussels are gone.

❧ A Note on Sea Salt

I prefer to use sea salt with all fish because it brings out its natural mineral sea flavors. See the salt discussion on page 25.

Harissa: North African Chili Paste

Harissa is a North African condiment or chili paste that gives a little zip to a dish. It's fun to use instead of cocktail sauce and is delicious whisked into broths or soups with as heavy a hand as you like. It's often used in *tagine* (a stew or long braise) to give the sauce a dark red, rusty color and a little or a lot of heat. There are many different versions of harissa: they can be smooth, coarse, extra hot, or very garlicky.

An Algerian chef named Michel Anik, whom I worked with at 8 Holyoke in Harvard Square, taught me to use sun-dried tomatoes as a sweet concentrated tomato element, which gives the harissa a consistency similar to a thick ketchup or jam.

⟳ MAKES 2 CUPS ⟲

1 cup ground Urfa chilies

2 teaspoons chopped garlic
(about 2 large cloves)

½ cup sun-dried tomatoes, soaked
in warm water for at least 1 hour

3 teaspoons kosher salt

1 cup water

1 tablespoon Moroccan Ras el Hannout
(page 16)

¼ cup olive oil

Combine all the ingredients in a blender and purée them on high speed until smooth, for about 3 minutes. The harissa should be as smooth as a thick ketchup. Store it in an airtight container in the refrigerator for a couple of weeks.

Muhammara: Red Pepper and Walnut Purée

This recipe is inspired by the many Armenian shops in Watertown, Massachusetts, outside Boston, which is home to the second largest Armenian population in the United States. I frequently visit Arax, a store owned by a Syrian man named Jack Bassmajian. His wife Elizabeth makes a delicious *muhammara*–a thick, spicy sauce that I love to snack on as an alternative to hummus or other bread spreads. It's also wonderful on grilled tuna.

Muhammara is simultaneously tart, spicy, sweet, salty, sour, and bitter, capturing every sensation on your palate. It is a deep rusty-red color; the word muhammara means "brick-colored" in Arabic. The warm, earthy chilies, sweet bell peppers, and bright pomegranate and citrus tones are truly flavors of the sun.

Pomegranate molasses is a syrupy reduction of pomegranate juice that has a unique, tart-sweet flavor and is a gorgeous, deep reddish-purple color. It's as thick as maple syrup and has both sweet and sour flavors that combine the best of balsamic vinegar with tart fruit. I often use it to add tartness to long-braised beef. You can find pomegranate molasses at Middle Eastern markets or online at www.zingermans.com.

Muhammara, a classic mezze, is found all over the eastern Mediterranean with many variations, especially on the nut that is used in thickening it. This is another demonstration of the Arabic technique of thickening sauces with nuts and/or bread (see Turkish Tarator Sauce on page 353 and Garlic and Almond Soup on page 338).

My interpretation of muhammara is wrapped in thin slices of roasted eggplant and can be passed as an hors d'oeuvre or served without the eggplant with crusty French bread or Toasted Pita Bread Chips (see page 122). Muhammara tastes even better on the second day, so I encourage you to make it in advance. You should roast the eggplant, however, just before serving it.

⟞ Makes about 2 cups to serve 8 as hors d'oeuvres ⟝

1 whole eggplant, peeled

¾ cup olive oil plus 1 tablespoon for garnish

2 large red bell peppers, (about 1 pound total), roasted and peeled (see page 97)

4 whole scallions, root ends trimmed and finely chopped (reserve 1 tablespoon for garnish)

1 teaspoon chopped garlic (about 1 large clove)

⅓ cup walnut halves, lightly toasted (page 91)

⅓ cup pine nuts, lightly toasted (page 91) plus 1 tablespoon for garnish

½ cup finely ground toasted bread crumbs (see page 156)

1 tablespoon freshly squeezed lemon juice (almost ½ lemon)

1 tablespoon pomegranate molasses

1 tablespoon Aleppo chilies plus ½ teaspoon for garnish

1 tablespoon Urfa chilies plus ½ teaspoon for garnish

1 teaspoon ground cumin

1 tablespoon yogurt

¾ teaspoon salt plus more to taste

1. Preheat the oven to 350°F.

2. Slice the eggplant lengthwise as thinly as you can (no thicker than ¼ inch), into 8 slices. Discard the rounded ends or roast for another use.

3. Place the eggplant slices on a heavy baking sheet and brush them generously using ½ cup of the olive oil or more (give or take a couple of tablespoons, depending on the size of the

eggplant) on both sides. The eggplant should absorb the oil and not look dry. Place the eggplant slices in the oven and roast them until soft, about 10 minutes. Set aside to cool.

4. Remove as many seeds from the red peppers as you can and place them in a small mixing bowl. Add the scallions, garlic, walnuts, pine nuts, bread crumbs, lemon juice, pomegranate molasses, Aleppo and Urfa chilies, cumin,

6.

7.

7.

yogurt, and the remaining ¼ cup of olive oil. Stir to combine.

5. Using a food processor fitted with a metal blade, purée the ingredients until smooth. Season to taste with salt.

6. Lay each eggplant slice down and place a heaping tablespoon of the pepper mixture at one end of the eggplant.

7. Roll up the eggplant, making a little bundle or roulade. Cut the roulade in half, making bite-size pieces. Serve at room temperature garnished with some toasted pine nuts or walnuts, chopped scallions, a drizzle of olive oil, and a squeeze of lemon. Sprinkle with more Aleppo and/or Urfa chilies if you like things spicier.

BREAD CRUMBS

A simple ingredient like bread crumbs can make a difference. I prefer to make my own or use a Japanese brand called Panko: the superhero of bread crumbs. Panko bread crumbs are made with flour, sugar, soybean and palm oils, yeast, and salt. A special baking method creates bread with little or no crust and a porous structure that results in a tender, yet crisp, texture. These bread crumbs are larger, flakier, and lighter than other brands, which is why I like them. I find that the seasonings in some Italian-style supermarket-brand bread crumbs overwhelm a dish and change its taste. Panko crumbs are unseasoned, so they remain neutral in recipes. You can find Panko bread crumbs at most Asian markets, and you can buy them online from specialty Asian food sites. For ½ cup of finely ground crumbs, start with 1 cup of Panko.

The next best thing is to make your own bread crumbs by toasting ½-inch slices of European-style bread (French baguettes work particularly well). Brush both sides of the bread slices with olive oil and then toast them for about 12 minutes in a 350°F oven, until golden and crisp. When they have cooled, grind them in a food processor fitted with a metal blade, until fine. You will need about 6 slices of French baguette to yield ½ cup of fine bread crumbs.

The last alternative, which is actually very good, is to find a good plain wheat cracker (not seasoned with cheddar cheese or herbs) or plain zwieback toast and grind them in a food processor fitted with a metal blade. One cup of coarsely crushed crackers or zwieback toasts will yield ½ cup of finely ground crumbs.

Salt Cod Fritters with Red Wine and Sweet Peppers

This recipe was created by my friend Rafael Maya–a fabulous cook I worked with at the Casablanca restaurant in Cambridge, Massachusetts. Raffi, as I call him, is from Colombia and cooks Mediterranean food with a gentle Latin hand. At the Casablanca, he was in charge of lunch service 6 days a week, and he made me these *bunuelos* (fritters) for breakfast when I came in every morning, serving them up piping hot with a lemon wedge. Raffi's fritters gave me great comfort and helped me get through the long days.

Raffi's fritters are cozy little pillows of fluffy salt cod and potato. He seasons them lightly with a *sofrito*–a basic seasoning for many recipes–using fresh chopped tomatoes, garlic, and scallions. I like my fritters with more zip, so Raffi altered his sofrito for me, adding chilies.

I like to serve Raffi's fritters with a red wine and red pepper stew, inspired by *marmitako*, which is a classic Basque fish stew. In this recipe, I use all of my favorite chilies, making a dish that is complicated, rich, earthy, and spicy. This warming stew is best in the winter, but the fritters are outstanding on their own in the summer, served with a little Lemon Aioli (page 50) or simply a lemon wedge. For a summer stew variation, substitute peeled and diced eggplant, chickpeas, or summer squash in place of the butternut or red kuri squash.

Salt cod is cured cod, and almost every culture throughout Europe eats it. The salt not only preserves the fish, but it also changes the texture, making it denser than regular cod. Salt cod is also richer in flavor because the salt draws out the water during the curing process. Salt cod needs to be soaked in cold water for 2 or 3 days (with the water changed two or three times each day) to draw out the salt. Some salt cod products are pre-soaked and will be so labeled. You can remove any cartilage, bone, or skin after soaking.

Salt cod is available in many Italian, Spanish, or Portuguese specialty markets, and you can also special-order it from your local fishmonger. You can find salt cod (also called *bacalao*) from www.thespanishtable.com; click on deli. You can make the braised vegetables and sauce up to 3 days ahead.

Serve this dish with medium-bodied Portuguese red wine from the Dao region.

MAKES 12 FRITTERS TO SERVE 4 AS A MAIN COURSE
OR 6 AS A FIRST COURSE

For the Fritters

1 pound salt cod, soaked at least 2 days
  in cold water and rinsed well

4 cups milk

1 bay leaf

1 pound russet or baking potatoes
  (about 2), peeled and quartered

3 egg yolks

Salt and black pepper to taste

1 teaspoon chopped garlic (about 1 large clove)

½ onion, finely chopped (about ¾ cup)

2 tomatoes, peeled, seeded,
  and finely chopped (see page 104)

1 teaspoon Aleppo chilies

1 tablespoon olive oil

3 scallions, root ends removed
  and finely chopped

2 eggs

1 cup heavy cream

4 cups canola oil or vegetable oil for frying

1 cup flour

1 tablespoon chopped fresh parsley, leaves only

For the Sauce

1 tablespoon plus 1 teaspoon butter

3 tablespoons olive oil

½ onion, peeled and roughly chopped

½ teaspoon fennel seed

2 teaspoons garlic (about 2 cloves),
  peeled and halved lengthwise

2 tablespoons Urfa chilies

2 teaspoons smoked Spanish paprika

1 cup medium-bodied red wine,
  such as a rioja or pinot noir

2 cups fresh plum tomatoes, quartered

2 cups fish fumet (page 161) or water

Salt and pepper to taste

1 large leek, root end trimmed and all dark
  green leaves trimmed

1 roasted red bell pepper (see page 97)

½ cup butternut or red kuri squash,
  peeled and diced into ½-inch cubes

To Make the Fritters

1. In a medium saucepan over medium heat, bring the salt cod to a boil with the milk and bay leaf. Reduce the heat to low and simmer the salt cod for about 15 minutes, until tender and flaky. Drain, reserving ½ cup of the milk. Discard the bay leaf.

2. Meanwhile, in another medium saucepan, cover the potatoes with cold water and bring them to a boil over medium-high heat. Reduce the heat to medium and simmer for about 20 minutes, until the potatoes are tender when squeezed with a pair of tongs or pierced with a fork. Drain well, by letting them sit in a colander for 5 minutes and allowing some steam to escape.

3. When they have stopped steaming, place the potatoes in a medium mixing bowl and mash them with a potato masher or whisk, removing large lumps and creating a rough purée.

4. Break up the salt cod into small pieces. Using your fingers, search for and remove small bones; this is a quick and easy process, and sometimes there aren't any bones at all. Using a rubber spatula, stir the salt cod into the potatoes, breaking it up more to incorporate it as much as possible. Stir in the egg yolks and the reserved ½ cup of salt cod milk. Season with salt and pepper.

5. Make the sofrito by sautéing the garlic, onion, tomatoes, and Aleppo chilies in 1 tablespoon olive oil in a medium sauté pan over medium-high heat, stirring for 10 to 12 minutes, until the onions soften and the mixture becomes a thick sauce or paste.

6. Stir the sofrito into the salt cod mixture and add the scallions. Cool for at least 15 minutes.

To Make the Sauce

1. In a large saucepan, melt 1 tablespoon of butter with 2 tablespoons of olive oil on medium-high heat. When the butter starts to brown, stir in the onion and fennel seed and cook, stirring for about 5 minutes, until the onion starts to soften. Stir in the garlic, Urfa chilies, and paprika to coat the onion. Add the wine, tomatoes, and fish fumet and bring to a boil. Reduce the heat to low and simmer the sauce for 35 minutes, until it has slightly thickened and becomes concentrated. Season with salt and pepper.

2. Allow the sauce to cool and purée it in a blender until smooth. Strain the sauce through a medium-fine sieve and into a bowl or large pitcher. Set aside. You should have about 8 cups of rich broth.

3. Split the leeks in half lengthwise and wash well, under cold water. Cut them into ½-inch slices and set aside. Remove the stem, ribs, and as many seeds as possible from the roasted pepper and cut into ½-inch pieces and set aside.

4. In a large sauté pan over medium-high heat, melt the remaining teaspoon of butter and tablespoon of olive oil. When the butter starts to brown, add the diced squash and stir to coat the squash with the oil and butter. Cook until the squash starts to brown on one of its sides, for about 6 minutes, and add the leeks. Season with salt and pepper and cook for another 3 to 4 minutes,

continued

stirring until the leeks begin to soften. Stir in the red peppers and add the tomato broth. Bring to a boil and lower heat to low. Simmer for 10 to 12 minutes until squash is tender. Season with salt and pepper.

5. In a small mixing bowl, using a whisk, beat the eggs and cream together with salt and pepper for about 1½ minutes, until the eggs are broken and incorporated into the cream, and it is smooth and liquid again.

6. In a large saucepan, or a tabletop deep-fryer, heat the canola oil to 350°F (using a thermometer).

7. Pour the flour onto a large plate or tray. Divide the salt cod mixture into 12 balls and roll them in a little flour, just enough to lightly coat the potato. Shake off any excess flour. Flatten the

balls a bit with the palm of your hand so that you have pillow shapes instead of round balls.

8. Drop each salt cod fritter into the cream mixture (4 to 5 at a time). Remove them one by one with a slotted spoon and carefully drop them into the hot oil. Fry for about 5 minutes, until golden brown. They will start to float on the top of the oil when they are almost done. Repeat with the remaining 4 to 5 fritters. Drain them on a paper towel and sprinkle them with salt to taste.

9. Ladle a little less than a cup of the pepper sauce into 4 large serving bowls. Top with 2 fritters, sprinkle each bowl with some parsley, and serve immediately. Offer yourself a glass of any leftover rioja or pinot noir used in making the sauce.

SPICE: FLAVORS OF THE EASTERN MEDITERRANEAN

FISH FUMET

3 pounds cod bones or bones from any
white fish, heads removed

1 tablespoon canola or vegetable oil

1 onion, peeled and roughly chopped

2 bay leaves

2 cloves garlic

2 ribs celery, roughly chopped

1 cup medium-bodied,
non-oaky white wine,
such as a dry Riesling

1. Chop the fish bones in 4-inch pieces so they fit easily in a large saucepot. Rinse the bones under cold water to remove any excess blood and drain them well.

2. In a large saucepot, heat the oil over medium-high heat and add the fish bones. Stir so that the fish bones are coated in the oil. Let them cook for 5 minutes, still stirring to draw more flavor out of the bones.

3. Add the onion, bay leaves, garlic, and celery. Add the wine and then cover the bones with 8 to 10 cups of water. Bring to a boil on high heat. Reduce heat to low and simmer for 20 minutes.

4. Strain the broth through a fine sieve into another large saucepot.

Veal Tagine with Moroccan Spices and Almond Couscous

Tagine means "stew" in North Africa, and on a cold winter night, this warm, hearty, exotic dish will transport you to Morocco. The chilies and saffron create earthy flavors that are perfectly balanced and brightened by the ginger and coriander.

There is an art to eating a tagine or couscous dish, adding liquid or rich broth to the stew and couscous, little by little, as it's consumed. If you immediately pour all the broth over the couscous, it swells too quickly, absorbing everything at once, and you won't be able to enjoy sauce with each bite of veal. Serve this dish with the broth in a little pitcher on the side, inviting your guests to add it to their couscous a little at a time. And if you like your food spicy, add extra harissa to the broth in the pitcher.

The long, slow cooking of tagine tenderizes less expensive cuts of veal, like the shoulder or shank. Long braises require twice as much salt as other cooking methods, which is why this recipe calls for so much salt.

This dish pairs well with dolcetto, from the Piedmonte region, which is a round wine, low in tannin and high in almond flavors and anise aromatics.

~ SERVES 4 TO 6 ~

6 tablespoons butter	1 tablespoon finely chopped garlic (about 3 large cloves)
4 tablespoons plus 2 teaspoons olive oil	Pinch of saffron
8 veal hind shanks, cut 1¾ inches thick or osso bucco style (see note, page 165)	1 teaspoon cinnamon or 1 cinnamon stick
⅓ cup salt	1 teaspoon whole coriander seed
2 cups white wine	4 cups chopped plum tomatoes (canned is okay)
1 large onion, peeled and roughly chopped	1 tablespoon freshly grated ginger
1 large carrot, peeled and roughly chopped	

1 cup harissa (see page 152)

Ice cubes

½ cup toasted whole blanched almonds
(see page 91) plus 2 tablespoons finely
chopped almonds for garnish

2 cups whole milk

1½ cups uncooked couscous

Salt and black pepper to taste

4 scallions, root ends trimmed
and finely chopped

1. Preheat the oven to 350°F.

2. Heat a large sauté pan over medium-high heat and melt 1 tablespoon of the butter with 2 tablespoons of the olive oil. Pat the veal shanks with paper towels to dry them. When the butter begins to brown, add 4 shanks to the pan and brown them on one side, for 4 to 5 minutes, creating a golden-brown crust. Season the meat generously with about a quarter of the ⅓ cup of salt. Turn the shanks over and brown the other side, seasoning with another quarter of the salt. Keep the heat high and turn on your fan, so your house won't get smoky.

3. Place the meat in a large roasting pan. Pour ½ cup of the white wine into the sauté pan to remove any sugars stuck to it (this also cleans the pan for you). Then, pour the wine over the 4 shanks in the roasting pan and wipe the sauté pan clean.

4. Repeat the browning process with the 4 remaining shanks, 2 tablespoons olive oil, 1 tablespoon butter, and remaining salt. It's important to brown the shanks a little at a time;

if the pan gets too crowded, the shanks won't brown well. When they're finished browning, add the shanks to the others in the roasting pan.

5. Deglaze and wipe out the sauté pan again, as in step 3. Heat the remaining 2 teaspoons of olive oil over medium-high heat, and stir in the onion and carrot. Cook them for 2 minutes, stirring, just to release some of their flavor.

6. Stir in the garlic and saffron and add another ½ cup of wine while the pan is still on the heat. Cook for about 2 minutes.

7. Remove the sauté pan from the heat and add the vegetable aromatics (onion, carrot, saffron, and garlic) to the roasting pan with the shanks. Add the remaining ½ cup wine, the cinnamon, coriander, tomatoes, ginger, and harissa to the roasting pan. If the liquid does not reach ½ or ¾ up the shanks, add extra water to adjust the level and cover with a tight-fitting lid or wrap twice with foil. You need to cover the pan tightly, so the liquid won't evaporate too quickly.

continued

163

8. Place the roasting pan in the oven and cook the shanks for 2 to 2½ hours, or until the meat pulls apart from the bone and tears easily with a fork.

9. Remove the shanks from the liquid in the roasting pan and place them onto a platter to let them rest. Cover them with foil.

10. In a small saucepan over medium heat, or in a microwave, melt the remaining 4 tablespoons of butter in ¾ cup of water.

11. Strain the liquid from the roasting pan through a fine sieve, into a medium mixing bowl or large pitcher, to remove the vegetables.

12. Place 8 ice cubes into the broth and stir. This will help cool the broth down quicker so that you can remove any fat that comes to the surface. Allow to cool for 1 hour in the refrigerator. If the broth seems too thick and more like a sauce, add 1 cup of water.

13. Meanwhile, in a blender, puree the toasted whole almonds with the milk for a minute, until the milk is smooth and the almonds are very fine, about 3 minutes. Strain the milk through a fine sieve into a small saucepan, to remove any little bits of almond. You should have milk that is infused with almond flavor but no almond bits. Heat the saucepan of almond milk over low heat; when it begins to simmer, remove it from the heat.

14. In a medium mixing bowl, stir the hot water and melted butter into the couscous until the couscous is coated. Let the couscous stand uncovered for 10 minutes.

15. Using a rubber spatula or large spoon, stir in 1½ cups of the hot almond milk into the couscous and let it stand uncovered for another 10 minutes. Stir again to fluff the couscous, seasoning with salt and pepper. The couscous should be tender–like tiny steamed dumplings with no crunch–but not sticky or lumpy. If the couscous is still a little dry, stir in another ¼ to ½ cup hot water. Once you've attained the desired consistency, you can use your hands or a fork to run through the couscous, breaking up any lumps.

16. About 30 minutes before serving, skim off any fat that has risen to the top of the broth, using a large spoon or ladle, in a circular motion. Pour the broth into a braising pan that can fit on a stove burner or in a large, deep-sided sauté pan big enough to hold the shanks, and bring it to a simmer on medium-high heat. Add the veal shanks to the broth and simmer for about 14 minutes, until tender and coated with broth.

17. Pack the couscous into large demitasse cups (big enough to hold ½ cup) or small ramekins. Heat them in the microwave for 2 minutes, until hot and steamed a final time. If no microwave is available, you can warm the ramekins up by placing them in a roasting pan

filled with water (so that the water reaches halfway up the ramekins) and then heating them for 10 minutes in a 300°F oven.

18. Froth the remaining almond milk in the blender on high speed for 30 seconds or use a handheld emulsion blender. You should have a foamy milk, almost as light as one for cappuccino.

19. Place 2 veal shanks next to each other on each dinner plate, setting them to one side.

20. Turn out the couscous by turning the ramekin upside down onto the plate and then lifting it away. Spoon 2 tablespoons of frothed almond milk over the couscous, and sprinkle the couscous with some chopped almonds. Sprinkle the shanks with the chopped scallions. Pour the remaining broth into a gravy boat or small pitcher to pass around the table.

❧ *Veal Shoulder Variation*

In place of the shanks, use 2 shoulder cuts, weighing about 2½ pounds each, making sure that they're boned, tied, and patted dry with paper towels. Follow the recipe as for cooking the veal shanks, but in step 2, brown two additional sides of meat, and eliminate 1 tablespoon of butter and 2 tablespoons of oil. The veal shoulders will take about 3 hours to cook. To serve, untie the shoulders by cutting the strings with a paring knife or scissors and slice the veal ½-inch thick. You can leave the meat in large slices or cut it into cubes.

Lamb Steak with Turkish Spices and Moussaka

This dish has become a signature at Oleana, and I think it's because it just tastes so Turkish. Plus, the recipe lets you enjoy the pleasure of eating lamb two different ways.

Moussaka is traditionally served as a heavy entrée, but I created this version as a side dish or light meal. I wanted the focus to be on the moussaka flavors—sweet cinnamon and spicy chilies—rather than heaviness.

Lamb top is a small roast cut from the top part of a leg of lamb. At Oleana, we trim the top and grind the trimmings to make our own ground lamb. You can have the butcher do this for you, or you can buy ground lamb separately.

This recipe is best when the lamb is marinated overnight. The marinade is all about the combination of peppers—sweet ones and hot ones—with Turkish signature spices like dried mint and oregano. Also, see page 100 for help with some grilling techniques; the smoky grilled flavors mixed with the spices make this dish unique, and roasting won't have the same effect.

Serve this with a full-bodied, tannic wine like an Amarone, or Nebbiolo from Barbaresco. If these wines seem too heavy in the summer, try a medium-bodied red, such as a Rhone blend.

SERVES 4 AS A MAIN COURSE

For the Lamb

1 lamb top (about 2 pounds)

2 tablespoons Aleppo chilies

2 tablespoons red pepper paste
(see Resources, page 358)
or 1 roasted red pepper, seeded,
and finely chopped (see page 97)

¼ cup tomato paste

½ cup canola oil

1 tablespoon chopped garlic (about 3 cloves)

1 tablespoon Turkish Baharat Spice Mix
(page 232)

For the Moussaka

3 tablespoons butter

1 tablespoon plus ½ cup olive oil

¾ pound ground lamb

Salt and pepper to taste

½ onion, peeled and finely chopped
  (about 1 cup)

1 teaspoon chopped garlic (about 1 large clove)

1 tablespoon tomato paste

1 teaspoon ground cinnamon

¼ cup golden raisins

1 cup peeled and seeded, finely chopped
  plum tomatoes (or drained chopped
  canned tomatoes)

⅓ cup chopped fresh parsley,
  leaves only

2 tablespoons chopped fresh mint,
  leaves only

2 small russet potatoes,
  peeled and cut into quarters

1 large eggplant, peeled and sliced lengthwise
  into ¼-inch slices, about 8 slices

2 tablespoons flour

1¼ cups milk, scalded

¼ teaspoon freshly grated nutmeg

½ cup yogurt plus additional for garnish
  (see page 331)

¾ cup grated kasseri cheese

1 tablespoon dried mint for garnish

To Make the Lamb

1. Cut the lamb top into four 6- to 8-ounce
   miniroasts or steaks.

2. In a medium mixing bowl, whisk together the
   Aleppo chilies, red pepper paste, ¼ cup of tomato
   paste, oil, 1 tablespoon garlic, and the baharat.
   Add the lamb steaks and stir to coat the meat.
   Chill overnight or let stand at room temperature
   for at least an hour. If chilled overnight, pull
   out 1 hour before grilling and let the meat and
   marinade come to room temperature.

To Make the Moussaka

1. Meanwhile, in a large sauté pan over high
   heat, melt 1 tablespoon of the butter with 1
   tablespoon of the olive oil. When the butter
   begins to brown, add the ground lamb and
   season with salt and pepper. Let the lamb brown
   on high heat, stirring and breaking it up with
   a spoon, for about 5 minutes. Add the onion, 1
   teaspoon garlic, 1 tablespoon of tomato paste,
   cinnamon, and raisins.

continued

2. Reduce the heat to medium-low and cook for 5 to 7 minutes, until the onions begin to soften. The lamb may release lots of natural juices while cooking; this is fine, because the mixture will thicken as it cooks.

3. Add the tomatoes and increase the heat to medium. Simmer for about 20 minutes, until the mixture is almost dry and becomes fluffy. The tomato water and juices will evaporate and the mixture will become a little glazy from the natural sugars of the raisins. Remove from the heat and set aside. Once it has cooled, stir in the parsley and fresh mint. Season again with salt and pepper.

4. Preheat the oven to 350°F.

5. Place the potatoes in a small saucepan and cover them with cold water. Boil over high heat until they are tender when squeezed with a pair of tongs or poked with a fork, about 15 minutes. Drain them in a colander for about 5 minutes, allowing some steam to evaporate.

6. Mash the potatoes with a fork, and season with salt and pepper.

7. Place the eggplant slices on a heavy baking sheet and brush them generously with the remaining ½ cup of olive oil or more (depending on the size of the eggplant) on both sides. The eggplant should absorb the oil and not look dry. Place the eggplant slices in the oven and roast them until soft, for 10 to 12 minutes. Set aside to cool.

8. Make a roux by melting the remaining 2 tablespoons of butter in a small saucepan on medium-low heat. When the butter starts to become bubbly, but before it browns, whisk in flour and cook for just a few minutes.

12.

12.

12.

SPICE: FLAVORS OF THE EASTERN MEDITERRANEAN

9. Whisk in the milk and cook for 5 minutes, or until the milk has thickened and the sauce is bubbly. Whisk in the nutmeg, ½ cup yogurt, and the cheese, and season with salt and pepper. You now have a Mornay sauce, Turkish-style.

10. If you want the sauce to be super-smooth with the ultimate coating consistency, blend it in a blender for 30 seconds or use a handheld emulsion blender to give it a little gloss

11. Prepare a charcoal grill (see Grilling Tips, page 100).

12. Meanwhile, spoon a tablespoon of the Mornay sauce into the bottom of a small soufflé dish or ramekin that can hold ¾ to 1 cup. Place 2 slices of eggplant criss-crossing in the bottom of the soufflé dish, so that the long ends hang over the side. Scoop ½ to ¾ cup of the lamb filling into the soufflé dish and fold the eggplant over

so that the lamb filling is bundled up by the eggplant. Pack on 2 to 4 tablespoons of potato purée and smear with the back of a spoon so that the surface is even and the moussaka is compact. Bake for 15 to 20 minutes or until bubbly.

13. Grill the lamb to medium rare (5 to 8 minutes on each side) and allow it to rest for 10 minutes before slicing.

14. Invert each hot moussaka onto a dinner plate and remove the ramekin. Spoon on another tablespoon of yogurt sauce and sprinkle the top with dried mint.

15. Slice each lamb steak into 4 pieces and arrange them to the side of the moussaka. Serve immediately.

Rosemary's Spicy Caramel Popcorn

I am lucky to have Rosemary Jason working with me in the kitchen at Oleana. A woman of all trades, Rosemary bakes, cooks, tests recipes–and brings in popcorn that no one can stop eating.

I love the salty and sweet or slightly spicy flavor combinations found in such favorites as almond ice cream, caramels made with sea salt, and chocolate-covered pretzels. Rosemary's popcorn recipe falls into the same category, and it is dangerously delicious.

Rosemary has perfected her popcorn recipe after trying out different flavor combinations and using Oleana's kitchen staff as her willing taste testers. The winning combination of caramel with Aleppo chilies is the hands-down favorite, and the runner-up is the lemon zest and star anise variation (see below). Star anise is an Asian pod spice with a sweet clove-fennel flavor.

Rosemary likes to use yellow popcorn because it pops up bigger and fluffier than white.

⟝ SERVES 4 ⟞

⅓ cup yellow popcorn

½ cup lightly toasted and salted pecan pieces (see page 91)

1½ cups granulated sugar

1½ tablespoons salt

2 tablespoons unsalted butter

¾ teaspoon baking soda

2½ teaspoons Aleppo chilies

1. Line a 10- to 15-inch baking sheet with parchment paper.

2. Prepare your popcorn. Pour the popcorn kernels into a small to medium brown paper lunch bag and roll the top of the bag down three or four turns. Microwave the popcorn for 2 minutes and 30 seconds on high (or use the microwave's "popcorn" setting). The popcorn is done when you can count to three between pops. There will be a few unpopped kernels, and popping time may vary depending on the brand of popcorn you use and your microwave. If you prefer, you can also use air-popped or stovetop-popped popcorn.

3. Pour the popcorn into a large mixing bowl and set aside. Remove any unpopped kernels and stir in the pecans.

4. Pour ½ cup of water into a deep 4-quart saucepan. Sprinkle the sugar and salt over the water and add the butter. Cook this caramel over medium-high heat without stirring until the bubbles start to turn light golden-amber on top and the edges start to turn golden amber, 8 to 10 minutes. The caramel will be a little darker under the bubbles. The caramel can overcook very quickly, which will make it dark and bitter, so it's important to pull it off the heat immediately and proceed to the next step.

5. Using a heatproof spatula, stir in the baking soda and Aleppo chilies. The baking soda will aerate the caramel and cause it to bubble furiously; be careful when stirring it in.

6. Immediately pour the caramel over the popcorn and nuts. Don't bother scraping the pot. Quickly toss the popcorn, nut, and caramel mixture with the spatula until the popcorn and nuts are well-coated.

7. Spread the popcorn out in a flat, even layer on the parchment-lined baking sheet and let it cool for 30 minutes. Break it apart and serve. The popcorn will keep up to 2 weeks in an airtight container or ziplock bag.

❧ Variation

Instead of using Aleppo chilies, substitute 1 teaspoon of finely grated lemon zest and 1 whole star anise pod, finely ground in your spice grinder. Try substituting Urfa pepper for Aleppo, too.

6
THREE SEEDS
Poppy, Nigella, and Sesame

The seeds in this chapter are a subtle group of flavorings, lending warm, nutty, and rich tones and texture to food. The seeds all have a high oil content, which is what makes them so rich, and toasting them draws out the oils that enhance their flavor. The seeds are great mixed or used separately in certain preparations. I love to make crackers and flatbreads mixing these three seeds, and sometimes I add smaller quantities of other seeds, such as fennel or cumin, to the mix.

Poppy seeds can be a little peppery; they combine well with sweet onions and enhance cheeses, fruits, and creamy dressings or sauces. Nigella seeds have a slight vegetal quality and are particularly good used simply on sliced radishes or cucumbers, in flavoring young cheeses, and on savory crackers. Sesame seeds are gorgeous with just about anything: on breads, sprinkled on cold vegetables like beets or spinach, in salads, with fish and duck, and mixed into tomato sauce. They also partner perfectly with honey. When sesame seeds are ground finely, they form a natural butter called tahini.

Poppy Seeds
Poppy seeds come from pink, white, or purple opium-producing poppy flowers, not the famously blood-red decorative variety. Once the seeds have formed, the flower contains no narcotic. The seeds are white or blue, and they taste almost identical in flavor, although the blue, which are larger in size, are also slightly more assertive. While white poppy seeds are more common in the Middle East and India (they are a key flavor of Indian vindaloo curry, for example), the blue seeds are more common in Europe and the United States.

Native to southeastern Europe and western Asia and cultivated in many countries, including Iran, Afghanistan, Holland, Turkey, and Canada, opium-producing poppies are grown on enormous plantations under strict supervision. The seeds are somewhat of a by-product of opium; poppy farmers take the green latex morphine capsules out of the plants before the seeds form and then leave the plants. Later, the farmers harvest the poppy seeds, treating them with heat or fumigation to stop further germination.

Poppy seeds give a toasty, nutty flavor to food—a flavor that intensifies if you lightly toast the seeds (see page 174). I love to sprinkle toasted poppy seeds over ricotta raviolis and salads, stir them into sautéed onions, and add them to crepe, pancake, waffle, and muffin batters. I also use them on pizzas

and tarts (see Caramelized Onion Tart, page 182), and then top that with crème fraiche and bits of smoky bacon. I also sprinkle them on breadsticks or rolls before baking and mix them with pastry to make homemade crackers (Crick-Cracks, page 176).

Because of their high oil content, poppy seeds should be frozen for up to a year to keep them fresh. You can also store them in a cool, dry place, but they can become rancid easily and may not last as long as other spices.

Most supermarkets carry blue poppy seeds; you can find the white variety in many Indian or Middle Eastern markets or online at www.penzeys.com.

Nigella Seeds
Grown mostly in Egypt, the Middle East, and India, nigella seeds come from a tall annual blue- or white-petalled flower that is a member of the buttercup family. The seeds—which decorate Turkish breads, crackers, and string cheese—are tiny and jet black and are often confused for black sesame seeds, but they are more teardrop-shaped and angular. People also incorrectly refer to nigella seeds as black cumin or black onion seeds.

Nigella seeds don't have much aroma, but their flavor is pleasantly sharp, nutty, peppery, and slightly vegetal, like celery. As with poppy seeds, it's best to toast them before using them in vinaigrettes and other dishes in which they won't be baked (see page 174).

In India, nigella seeds are combined with mustard, fennel, fenugreek, and cumin seeds to make a five-seed blend called panch phora, used to flavor fried potatoes. Some recipes for dukkah (page 6) include nigella seeds. I also like to use nigella seeds to flavor goat cheese with dried mint (page 229) and vinaigrette for fish (page 190).

Nigella seeds are quite stable and can last in a cool, dark place for up to a year. You can find them in many Indian and Middle Eastern markets or online at www.kalustyans.com.

SESAME SEEDS

Sesame seeds come from a 3- to 6-foot annual plant with white, pink, or lilac flowers that grow all the way down the stem. The flowers are followed by capsules that contain the seeds. When fully ripe, the capsules shatter with the slightest touch. The famous phrase "open sesame" in the tale of *Ali Baba and the Forty Thieves* has its roots in this phenomenon.

Before they are hulled, sesame seeds are golden brown or black and have a chewier texture and a sharper, nuttier flavor than the hulled white seeds. Hulled seeds have a very high oil content that you can feel with your hands, and they give off a faintly nutty aroma. Most of the world's sesame seeds are extracted for their oil, which is refined into sesame oil and tahini paste or a honey-sweet sesame butter called halvah.

When combined with chickpeas, sesame seeds make a complete protein, as in the Middle Eastern favorites falafel and hummus. Sesame seeds are a key ingredient in one of my favorite spice blends, called za'atar (page 230), and the Egyptian spice blend called dukkah (page 6). They're delicious on salads, cooked spinach, fish or scallops, flatbreads, with slow-simmered tomatoes (see Tomato-Sesame Jam, page 192), and even in ice cream.

You can store sesame seeds in a cool, dry place; they are best kept in the freezer, though, because they have a very high oil content, like poppy seeds.

TOASTING SESAME SEEDS

It's best to toast sesame seeds before sprinkling them over food. Sesame seeds take a little longer to toast than other spices, however. To toast them, heat a pan, just as you would for dry-roasting any spice, and shake the seeds around while heating them so they don't stick and burn. When they begin to hop around and show signs of tanning, tip them out of the pan and let them cool.

TOASTING POPPY AND NIGELLA SEEDS

Poppy and nigella seeds can be toasted to revive them if you suspect they're stale. See page 184, Reviving Spices and Seeds.

RECImPES WITH SEEDS

Crick-Cracks: Savory Turkish-Style Crackers

My friend Ayfer Unsal from Gaziantep, Turkey, introduced me to the savory treats she calls crick-cracks. Found in many different shapes–round rings, long and thin breadsticks, or flat–in bakeries throughout Turkey, they're traditionally eaten with afternoon tea, but I like to serve them as a cracker for spreads (such as the Whipped Feta on page 149, Creamy Parsnip Hummus on page 188, and the Hot Buttered Hummus with Basturma and Tomato on page 200). Turkish crick-cracks are sprinkled only with nigella seeds, but Oleana's pastry chef Maura Kilpatrick loads the restaurant's crick-cracks with all three seeds discussed in this chapter.

⌐⌐ MAKES 1 POUND OF CRACKERS TO SERVE UP TO 12 PEOPLE AS A SNACK ⌐⌐

1½ cups of flour plus ½ to ¾ cups
   for rolling out the dough

½ cup cornmeal

1 tablespoon sugar

1½ teaspoons salt

10 tablespoons cold, unsalted butter,
   cut into ½-inch cubes

¾ cup buttermilk

1 tablespoon sesame seeds

2 teaspoons poppy seeds

1 teaspoon nigella seeds

---

1. In the mixing bowl fitted for a standing mixer (such as a KitchenAid), combine the 1½ cups of the flour, the cornmeal, sugar, ½ teaspoon of the salt, and the butter.

2. Using the paddle attachment or an electric mixer, mix the ingredients on low speed until the butter breaks down into pea-sized pieces. Pour in the buttermilk and mix again until it is just combined. The dough will come together quickly and will be a little wet.

3. Wrap the dough in plastic, pressing it into a flat rectangle about an inch thick. Chill the dough for 3 hours or overnight.

4. Divide the dough into quarters. Lightly flour your rolling-out surface with about ¼ cup of

flour. Roll out the first quarter into a rectangle, approximately 12×15 inches. Don't worry about making the dough into the perfect size or shape; it's most important that it rolls out to be 1/16 inch thick or as thin as you can make it.

5. Line a heavy baking sheet with parchment paper.

6. Roll the dough over the rolling pin or fold it in half to pick it up and place it on the lined baking sheet. Place another sheet of paper on top of the rolled dough and roll out the remaining quarters of dough, layering them on the baking sheet, separated by parchment paper. This is an easy way to store the dough as it chills. Chill the rolled-out dough for at least an hour or overnight.

8.

7. Preheat the oven to 350°F.

8. Place 1 sheet of dough onto each of 4 heavy baking sheets, leaving them on the parchment paper. Dock the dough by pricking little holes into it with a fork; this keeps the dough from bubbling too much when it bakes and creates a cracker pattern.

9. Using a ruler and a pizza cutter or knife, cut the dough into 3-inch squares, leaving odd pieces on the ends. It's easier to leave those pieces to snack on after they're baked rather than reroll the scraps and repeat the process. The dough will get tough if rerolled.

10. In a small mixing bowl, combine the sesame seeds, poppy seeds, nigella seeds, and the remaining teaspoon of salt.

11. Using a pastry brush, moisten each sheet of cut crackers lightly with water and then sprinkle each evenly with the salted seed mixture.

12. Place the crackers in the oven and reduce the temperature to 325°F. Bake them for 8 minutes and rotate the pan. Continue baking the crackers for another 10 to 11 minutes or until lightly browned. If your oven can only hold two pans at a time, keep the other two chilled while you are baking the first two.

13. Cool the crick-cracks completely before serving. Store them in an airtight container for up to 5 days.

Shoushan's Homemade String Cheese with Nigella Seeds

Shoushan Stepanian is the sister of my good friend Vartan Nalbandian. She makes this string cheese for Oleana, and we serve it as a bread condiment alongside our Armenian Bean and Walnut Pâté (page 334) on the *prêt-à-manger* (ready to eat) menu. Shoushan's cheese is sweet and nutty, and the nigella seeds give it a subtle celery flavor.

The texture is fantastic: softer and silkier than commercial varieties and not nearly as salty. String cheese sold in Middle Eastern and Armenian stores is usually brined and can be very salty. When I've tried soaking that cheese in cold water to remove excess salt, the texture becomes mushy. Other commercial brands, found in grocery stores, are rubbery from stabilizers and overprocessing.

String cheese is easy to make, but it takes some practice to get it just right. For your first time, you'll want to order an extra pound of cheese to practice with. The practice batch may not look very appetizing, but it will taste delicious. You can also order a few pounds of cheese and make the string cheese in three batches. Kids love this recipe; they have so much fun stretching the cheese.

You need a good source for cheese curds. I get mine from www.todarobros-specialty-foods.com. You can buy it by the pound, and it usually arrives the next day. String cheese freezes very well, so you can make a big batch and keep it handy in the freezer.

MAKES 1 POUND OF STRING CHEESE OR 1 LARGE BRAID

1 pound mozzarella curd	1 tablespoon nigella seeds
2 teaspoons salt	

1. Cut the mozzarella curd into small pieces and place them in a Teflon pan. Add the salt and nigella seeds.

2. Heat the cheese on low, stirring, until it is melted thoroughly and there are no lumps left.

3. Remove the cheese from the heat and drain off the excess water in a colander.

4. While the cheese is still very warm but cool enough to handle, pick it up in a large lump and poke a hole in the center with your fingers, so that the cheese resembles a large doughnut.

5. You will need to work very quickly at this point because the cheese cools down rapidly once it has been stretched. You'll have about 3 minutes to stretch the cheese. Grab it with both hands and stretch it so that it forms a large loop. Stick your finger through each end of the loop, and very quickly start winding the two strands of the loop around each other, as if you were making a rope while winding. Keep stretching the cheese gently, almost to the breaking point. The more you stretch, the stringier the cheese will be. When finished, you should have a length of cheese that resembles a thick rope or a tightly wrung-out dish cloth.

6. Twist the ends of the cheese in opposite directions and intertwine the rope into a braid. Place one end through the loop of the other to lock it.

7. Set the cheese aside in the refrigerator or in a cool room for about an hour to dry thoroughly. Wrap the cheese in plastic wrap and refrigerate or freeze it; it will keep for a week in the refrigerator and up to 2 months in the freezer.

8. To serve the cheese, open the braid, cut one loop, and pull the cheese apart into thin strands. Serve with pita bread.

8.

8.

8.

POPPY, NIGELLA, AND SESAME

Spinach Bundles with Warm Goat Cheese

At Oleana, we list this dish as spinach dolmas and serve it as one of three mezze on a single plate, alongside Cranberry Beans Stewed with Tomato and Cinnamon (page 113) and Beet Tzatziki (page 252). I was originally inspired to create this dish because I wanted to offer three different mezze from the regions of Greece, Turkey, and Armenia, and showcase them harmoniously on one plate. These creamy, warm bundles are slightly nutty from the nigella seed, and the assertive, earthy mint complements the subtle cheese and is also perfect with the spinach. You can also substitute chard leaves for the spinach.

In this recipe, good goat cheese–creamy and delicate with some acidity, and that softens as it warms–is crucial. I like to use Laura Chenel from California or Westfield Farms Capri from Massachusetts, available at specialty shops. Both of these small companies raise goats specifically for making delicious goat cheese; they allow their goats to graze and eat what they would naturally. Neither farm uses gums or stabilizers like some commercial varieties.

As an appetizer course, this dish pairs wonderfully with a sauvignon blanc from Sancerre.

MAKES 6 LARGE BUNDLES USING 2-OUNCE RAMEKINS
OR 12 SMALL BUNDLES USING 1-OUNCE RAMEKINS

Salt to taste

Ice cubes

20 large, flat spinach leaves, washed
  (you will have extra for patching)

2 tablespoons extra-virgin olive oil

15 ounces soft goat cheese

1 tablespoon dried mint

2 teaspoons nigella seeds

Pepper to taste

---

1. Bring a small pan of water to a boil on high heat. Add salt.

2. Prepare a bowl with ice cubes and cold water for shocking and cooling the spinach down quickly.

3. Add the spinach leaves to the boiling water and cook them until they wilt and are soft; this takes less than 1 minute.

4. Drain the spinach into a small colander and then tip the leaves into the ice water, enhancing their green color. Let the spinach sit in the ice water for a couple of minutes, stirring to melt the ice.

5. Drain the spinach leaves in the colander again and squeeze them into a little ball. Pull the leaves apart and place them on a paper towel to drain more.

6. Preheat the oven to 350°F.

7. Brush the olive oil onto the insides of six 2-ounce ramekins.

8. Line each ramekin with two spinach leaves (smoothest side down), so that they completely line the ramekin and hang over the sides. Use a third leaf if two don't do the job. Place the ramekins on a small baking sheet.

9. In a small mixing bowl, combine the goat cheese, mint, and nigella seeds and mix well with a spatula or wooden spoon. Season with salt and pepper.

10. Fill each ramekin with 3 generous tablespoons of goat cheese and fold the spinach leaves over the cheese to make little bundles. Press down to pack them into shape.

11. Bake the bundles until the cheese is soft and melted, about 12 minutes.

12. Invert the ramekins onto plates and serve warm with cranberry bean salad, tzatziki, and/or Crick-Cracks (page 176) and a glass of ouzo or raki to slightly wet the lips between bites.

Caramelized Onion Tart with Poppy Seeds, Bacon, and Dates

This is a fun tart to serve as an appetizer or little hors d'oeuvres. The recipe has both Alsatian and Turkish origins; it's inspired by the famous *Flammekuchen*, an Alsatian pizza made with crème fraîche, smoked bacon, and onion. For Turkish flair, I use savory Crick-Crack dough (page 176) and add some poppy seeds to the onion mixture, finally sweetening and souring the flavors by adding date slivers to the bacon topping. The texture and nutty, earthy flavor of the poppy seeds make this tart one of my all-time favorites.

This dish pairs very well with an Alsatian pinot blanc. If you can find it, try Alsatian pinot auxerrois, a rich, ripe, spicy relative of pinot blanc that goes perfectly with the bacon and dates.

⁓ MAKES 6 TARTS TO SERVE 6 ⁓

6 regular slices smoked bacon or 3 thick-cut slices	2 teaspoons poppy seeds
2 tablespoons butter	2 to 3 sprigs thyme, leaves removed and finely chopped
1 tablespoon olive oil	½ recipe Crick-Crack dough (page 176)
2 medium onions, peeled and thinly sliced	Flour for dusting
2 tablespoons white wine	8 tablespoons (½ cup) crème fraîche
Salt and pepper to taste	3 dates, split in half and pits removed

10.

13.

13.

1. In a large 12-inch skillet, render the bacon over medium-low heat until crispy, cooking for about 5 minutes on each side. Drain the bacon on a paper towel and set aside. Pour the bacon fat into a heatproof container to discard later, after it cools completely.

2. Wipe the skillet, leaving some bacon fat behind.

3. Heat the butter and oil over medium-high heat, cooking until the butter begins to brown.

4. Add the onions, and increase the heat to high. Cook, shaking the pan from time to time, for about 7 minutes, until the onions become limp and translucent.

5. Reduce the heat to medium and continue to cook the onions while stirring, for about 15 minutes, until they are soft and are just beginning to brown. Stir in the wine and continue to cook for a few more minutes. Season with salt and pepper. Stir in the poppy seeds, crème fraiche, and thyme and set aside to cool.

6. Preheat the oven to 350°F.

7. Roll out the Crick-Crack dough, dusting with plenty of flour on both sides.

8. Keep rolling and dusting with just enough flour so the dough doesn't stick to the board or the pin, until the dough is ¼ to ⅛ inch thick.

9. Using a small glass bowl or round cutter with a 4- to 5-inch diameter, cut out 6 rounds. Reserve the scraps to make Crick-Cracks.

continued

10. Top each round of pastry with 2 tablespoons of the onion mixture, leaving 1 inch around the edge of pastry.

11. Cut each bacon strip into 4 pieces and tuck 4 pieces of bacon into each pile of onions. If you're using thick-cut bacon, you can cut it into smaller pieces and divide them equally among the tarts.

12. Cut each date half in two and tuck 2 pieces (a half date total) into each pile of onion.

13. Fold the edges of pastry up over the onions, in a free-form overlapping fashion. Each tart should be open in the center and ⅓ covered with the overlapping dough.

14. Place the tarts on a baking sheet and bake for 20 to 25 minutes, until golden brown. Serve warm with a nice glass of dry Alsatian Riesling as an hors d'oeuvre or with a green salad as an appetizer.

REVIVING SPICES AND SEEDS

If your spices have lost their oomph or you think your seeds might be stale, slowly and gently toast them on a low flame in a sauté pan for 3 to 4 minutes or until you can smell them and/or they begin to look oily. Shake or stir them constantly over the low flame; do not walk away from the pan. And remember that if you are toasting a spice powder such as curry or turmeric, it only takes a minute.

Toasting draws out the natural oils of seeds and spices and will perk them up considerably, but this technique doesn't work for dried herbs.

Spinach Falafel with Tahini Sauce and Pickled Pears

I created this nontraditional falafel–a very popular menu item at Oleana–as a light twist on traditional falafel, which I often find to be too heavy, especially as a side dish or mezze. When I was in the Turkish town of Gaziantep, I tasted ultralight and creamy hummus made with chickpea flour, and I was thus inspired to create a lighter, creamier, airier version of falafel, with all the typical falafel flavors. I like vegetables in my falafel–common in both Egyptian and Palestinian variations–so I load mine up with fresh, chopped spinach.

Serve this falafel on a rectangle of lavash bread with pickled pear, tahini sauce, and salad greens. Roll it up and eat as a sandwich for lunch.

At Oleana, we vary our pickles, depending on the season. In the summer, we use green tomato pickles. In the fall, we use turnip or pear pickles (see Nookie's Pickles, page 280).

The falafel batter will hold up to 3 days and freezes well. You can freeze the falafel in balls and fry them straight out of the freezer.

Falafel pairs wonderfully with a glass of pinot noir. Falaghina, an aromatic, rich white wine from Italy with piney and briny flavors, is also delicious with this dish.

⌁ MAKES 16 TO SERVE 4 TO 6 ⌁

½ small onion, peeled and finely chopped
    (½ to ¾ cup)

4 tablespoons extra-virgin olive oil

1½ teaspoons ground cumin

¼ teaspoon ground allspice

Ice cubes

¾ teaspoon salt plus more to taste

1 pound spinach leaves

1 cup milk

⅓ teaspoon black pepper plus more to taste

¾ cup chickpea flour (available at most
    Indian or Middle Eastern markets)

continued

¼ cup cooked (see page 111)
or canned chickpeas, drained

2 teaspoons lemon juice

4 to 6 cups canola oil for frying

¼ cup flour for dredging

2 rectangles lavash bread, cut into halves

½ cup tahini sauce (page 187)

Salad greens for garnish

½ recipe pickled pears or green tomatoes
(see Nookie's Pickles, page 280)

1. In a small sauté pan over medium-high heat, sauté the onion in 1 tablespoon of the olive oil. Add the cumin and allspice. Cook, stirring from time to time, for about 6 minutes, until the onions are soft and translucent. Reduce the heat to medium if the onions cook too quickly; they should not brown. Remove the onions from the heat and set aside.

2. Prepare a medium bowl of ice water.

3. Bring a medium saucepan of water to a boil and add salt to taste. Drop the spinach in and cook for 1 minute, until it becomes limp and dark green. Drain and drop the spinach in the ice water. Let the spinach sit in the ice water for a couple of minutes or until completely chilled.

4. Remove the spinach from the ice water, little by little, squeezing it dry in small amounts. Squeeze as much water as possible from the leaves (squeeze hard between the palms of your hands). You should have about 2 cups of blanched spinach.

5. Chop the spinach into small pieces and set aside.

6. In a medium saucepan, bring the milk to a boil (when it rises up in the pan) on high heat. Reduce the heat to medium and whisk in ¾ teaspoon of the salt and ⅓ teaspoon of the pepper. Taste the milk to make sure that it is seasoned well and add more salt and pepper to taste.

7. Slowly whisk in the chickpea flour, little by little, until it is so thick that you can't whisk it anymore. Switch to a wooden spoon and stir in the remaining 3 tablespoons of olive oil and keep stirring for another minute, until it is incorporated. Reduce the heat to very low and cook for about 12 minutes, stirring occasionally. Be careful not to get your face too close to the pan because it can bubble and spit, like polenta. When done, the edges should pull away from the sides of the pan and the mixture should be very thick.

8. In a large mixing bowl, combine the chickpeas, lemon juice, onion mixture, chickpea mixture, and chopped spinach. Stir until the ingredients are incorporated into the chickpea mixture, which is the binder for all the vegetables. Season with salt and pepper to taste.

9. Scrape the mixture onto a baking sheet or shallow roasting dish and chill for at least 2 hours or overnight.

10. Form the falafel into 15 to 16 balls, about 1½ in diameter.

11. Place the canola oil in a large, heavy saucepan or in a countertop fryer and heat to 350°F (use a thermometer if you don't have a countertop fryer).

12. Dredge each falafel ball in flour and carefully drop them, one by one, into the hot oil. Cook for about 4 minutes, until golden brown and hot inside. Remove the falafel from the oil and drain them on paper towels. Sprinkle the falafel lightly with salt.

13. Line a platter with the lavash bread and top them with the hot falafel. Spoon a couple of teaspoons of tahini sauce over the top of each falafel and garnish with just a few salad greens and enough pickled pear slices for everyone to have 1 or 2 with each falafel. Serve immediately, passing around extra tahini sauce and pickled pears.

TAHINI SAUCE

I prefer the dark-roasted variety of tahini from Tohum, available at www.tohum.com.

⌐ MAKES ½ CUP ⌐

¼ cup tahini

¼ cup extra-virgin olive oil

¾ teaspoons ground cumin

¾ teaspoon chopped garlic (about 1 clove)

1 teaspoon freshly squeezed lemon juice

Salt and pepper to taste

Place all the ingredients in a blender and blend until smooth. Season with salt and pepper. The tahini sauce will last for 3 to 5 days in the refrigerator.

POPPY, NIGELLA, AND SESAME

Creamy Parsnip Hummus with Parsley

Hummus versions abound, but most—except for some Turkish recipes—are made with chickpeas and tahini. *Hummus* means "chickpea" in Arabic, and it is taken very seriously in the Middle East, where people debate questions such as whether the chickpeas should be peeled before puréeing or whether chilling the tahini ruins its texture.

Sometimes I like to leave out the chickpeas and experiment with ingredients such as white beans, avocados (page 17), pumpkins, squash, and parsnips. This, of course, breaks the rules since technically hummus is not hummus without chickpeas. Oleana's customers, though, understand why I call this recipe hummus when they taste it. I purée parsnips in place of the chickpeas, but I flavor the dish with the traditional garlic, lemon, cumin, and tahini. The parsnip's texture is perfect for hummus: it is smooth and creamy, just like chickpeas, but has twice as much flavor.

In New England, parsnips are the first spring crop, even before spinach, nettles, or fiddleheads. Farmers like to harvest parsnips after they've "wintered over" because the freezing ground makes the sugars more intense. The sweetness of the parsnips paired with the bitter, nutty tahini and earthy cumin is just divine.

If I'm serving this dish to a group as a mezze, I mound the creamy parsnips onto a platter and make a well in the center, which I fill with tahini sauce, and then serve it with Crick-Cracks (page 176) or pita bread. This dish is also a wonderful accompaniment to the Beef Shish Kebobs with Sumac Onions and Parsley Butter on page 98; my guests pass the tahini sauce around the table like gravy at Thanksgiving.

I happen to like the dramatic visual contrast of the white parsnip purée holding the dark tahini sauce, but if this presentation seems too fussy to you, you can combine the tahini with the parsnips before serving.

If you serve parsnip hummus as an hors d'oeuvre, try pairing it with a Falanghina from Italy; the flavors in the wine have just enough bitterness to set off the tahini and sweet parsnip.

MAKES 4 CUPS TO SERVE 8 AS AN APPETIZER OR 4 AS PART OF A MEAL

1 pound parsnips (about 6 medium or 4 large), peeled and cut into 1-inch chunks

1 tablespoon chopped garlic (about 3 large cloves)

¼ cup freshly squeezed lemon juice

4 tablespoons butter, cut into small pieces

¼ cup extra-virgin olive oil

2 teaspoons ground cumin

Salt and pepper to taste

½ recipe tahini sauce (page 187)

2 tablespoons chopped fresh parsley

1. In a medium saucepan, cover the parsnips with water and bring them to a boil over high heat. Reduce the heat to medium and simmer the parsnips for about 20 minutes, until they are very tender when squeezed with a pair of tongs or pierced with a fork. Drain the parsnips in a colander, reserving 1 tablespoon of the cooking liquid or water.

2. Transfer the parsnips to the work bowl of a food processor fitted with a metal blade. Purée the parsnips with the reserved cooking liquid, garlic, lemon juice, butter, olive oil, and cumin until smooth and creamy, for about 3 minutes, stopping to scrape the sides of the bowl a couple of times.

3. Season the purée with salt and pepper. Spoon the purée into a serving bowl and cool it to room temperature, for about an hour.

4. Use the back of a large serving spoon to create a well in the center of the purée, big enough to hold about ½ cup. Spoon the tahini sauce into the center of the well. Garnish with parsley and serve.

Swordfish Kebobs with Nigella Seed Vinaigrette

I was inspired to create this recipe by traditional Circassian rice dishes and salads, which contain cilantro and coconut–unique in Turkish cooking. I was also inspired by the Black Sea region of Turkey, where marinated fish chunks are wrapped in grape leaves and then skewered and grilled.

In late summer, when swordfish is in season, these kebobs are wonderful served following Sliced Summer Tomatoes with Basil and Walnut Tabouleh (page 258) and accompanied with Rice Cakes (page 65) served with Seared Sea Scallops (page 62). To give the coconut vinaigrette a smoky flavor, I lightly oil the celery and grill it before chopping it and adding it to the vinaigrette.

It's preferable to use fresh grape leaves for this recipe, but jarred leaves are okay. You can find grape leaves at any Greek or Middle Eastern market or online at www.kalustyans.com.

This dish pairs nicely with a dry chenin blanc from Savennieres, a complex and full-bodied white wine with ever-changing flavors: herbaceous, mineral, floral, and citrus. You'll never tire of what this wine has to offer.

Serves 4

Four 6- to 8-inch skewers	2 ribs celery
2 pounds swordfish, boned and skinned	¼ teaspoon sugar
2 tablespoons freshly squeezed lemon juice (about 1 lemon)	2 teaspoons lemon zest (about 1 lemon)
4 tablespoons plus 2 teaspoons olive oil	4 tablespoons coconut milk
2 teaspoons dried oregano	1 tablespoon nigella seeds
1 teaspoon salt plus more to taste	Pepper to taste
12 grape leaves	¼ cup shredded unsweetened coconut, lightly toasted

SPICE: FLAVORS OF THE EASTERN MEDITERRANEAN

1. If you don't have metal skewers, soak bamboo skewers in warm water for 1 hour.

2. Slice the swordfish into 4 equal steaks, about ½-inch thick. Using a boning knife, trim off any blood line that may be left on the steaks (a dark red-brown color that the fishmonger may or may not remove). Cut each steak into three 1-inch-square nuggets.

3. In a medium mixing bowl, big enough to hold the swordfish pieces, combine 1 tablespoon of the lemon juice with 2 tablespoons of the olive oil. Add the oregano and 1 teaspoon of the salt and whisk until combined.

4. Add the swordfish and toss with your hands until the nuggets are well coated with the marinade.

5. Bring a small saucepan of water to a boil over high heat and drop in the grape leaves, one by one. Reduce the heat to medium-high and simmer the leaves for a minute to remove excess brine or soften them if they are fresh. Drain and cool.

6. Prepare a gas or charcoal grill (see Grilling Tips, page 100).

7. Trim the stems off the grape leaves by pinching them with your fingers or cutting them off with a small paring knife.

8. Place each grape leaf down on a cutting board with the ribbed side facing up and the smoothest side down. Place a nugget of swordfish on the bottom end or stem end of the grape leaf, ½ inch from the bottom of the leaf. Fold the sides over the swordfish and roll the swordfish up like a cigar, from the bottom toward the top.

9. When all the swordfish nuggets are wrapped, assemble them on the skewers by piercing through the sides of each bundle, spearing 3 wrapped chunks to a skewer. Leave about ¼ inch between each swordfish nugget so that the sides can cook thoroughly.

10. Using a vegetable peeler, peel the first layer of tough strings off of the outer side of each celery rib. Chop the celery into small pieces and set aside.

11. In a blender, make the vinaigrette by combining the remaining 1 tablespoon of lemon juice with the sugar, lemon zest, 2 tablespoons of the olive oil, the coconut milk, and celery, blending until the mixture is smooth and thick enough to coat a spoon.

12. Scrape the vinaigrette into a small mixing bowl and stir in the nigella seeds. Season with salt and pepper to taste.

13. Pour the remaining 2 teaspoons of olive oil onto a large plate or platter big enough to hold the swordfish skewers. Roll the 4 skewers around in the oil so that the wrapped swordfish nuggets are lightly coated.

14. Grill the skewers for 5 minutes on each side over a medium-high flame.

15. Place the wrapped swordfish on a clean platter, lined with extra grape leaves if you like. Spoon a tablespoon of vinaigrette over each skewer and sprinkle the coconut over each and serve. Pass around extra vinaigrette.

Roasted Crispy Duck with Tomato-Sesame Jam

The smell of a roasting duck drives me wild with anticipation, but I often find the consistency of roasted duck to be too rich. When I created this recipe, I was playing with condiments that would cut through the duck's richness. The North African spice tones, acidity of the tomato, spiciness of the ginger, and sweetness of the honey in this tomato-sesame jam do just that.

Duck is as easy to make as roasted chicken. I prefer Muscovy duck because the breast meat is larger than that of a Peking duck; when you roast the Muscovy duck whole, the breasts and legs cook in equal time. You can find Muscovy ducks at specialty meat or butcher shops or online at www.grimaud.com.

The tomato-sesame jam, inspired by the flavors of North Africa, is an excellent condiment for any roasted meat, including pork and rich fish, such as salmon. The idea is to cook the tomatoes as slowly as possible in olive oil over low heat so that they melt and become sticky, like jam or stewed fruit. The saffron, freshly grated ginger, and loads of sesame seeds add color, brightness, and texture. I serve this duck with Rice Cakes (page 65) and sautéed green beans, perfectly rounding out the meal.

Drink an Oregon pinot noir with this dish.

MAKES 1 DUCK TO SERVE 4, OR 2 WITH SOME LEFTOVERS

1 whole Muscovy duck (about 4 pounds)	Salt and pepper to taste
4 teaspoons salt	1 tablespoon honey
Black pepper to taste	1 tablespoon freshly squeezed lemon juice (about ¼ lemon)
1 lemon, cut into 8 slices	
2 tablespoons plus ½ cup extra-virgin olive oil	1 teaspoon freshly grated ginger
8 large plum tomatoes, peeled and seeded	⅓ cup toasted sesame seeds
1 pinch saffron (about 8 threads)	

1. Preheat the oven to 375°F.

2. Rinse the duck under cold water and pat very dry with paper towels.

3. Place the duck on a cutting surface with the breast side up and split it in half between the two breasts. Open the duck up, prying it open with your hands. Lay the duck flat with the rib side down, so that the skin side is facing up. Press on the duck legs with the palms of your hands so that you crack the bones a little, causing the duck to lay flat. Do the same with the breasts, making the duck as flat as possible. Trim off the tail part (it contains glands that are very bitter) and discard.

4. Trim the excess fat from the neck and discard it or reserve it for something else. Discard the liver, kidney, and neck meat or reserve it for something else.

5. Season the duck with 2 teaspoons of the salt and the black pepper. Turn the duck over and season the other side with the remaining 2 teaspoons of salt and more black pepper.

6. Place the duck skin side up into a very large roasting pan or heavy baking sheet with sides (the duck fat and juices will drip while roasting, so you need a pan that can catch the juices). The duck will be laying flat.

7. Tuck the lemon slices under the ribs in the empty cavity. It's okay if they rest between the duck and the roasting pan.

8. Rub the skin side of the duck with 2 tablespoons of the olive oil and place it in the oven to roast. Reduce the oven temperature to 350°F and roast the duck for 45 to 55 minutes, until the skin is crispy and the juices run clear from the leg when pierced. Remove the duck from the oven and allow it to rest for at least 15 minutes before carving and serving.

9. While the duck is roasting, make the jam. Simmer the tomatoes in a large sauté pan over low heat, adding the remaining ½ cup of olive oil, saffron, and salt and pepper and simmer for about 30 minutes until the tomatoes are very soft. Stir in the honey, lemon juice, ginger, and sesame seeds.

10. To carve the duck, remove the legs from the carcass and cut each leg into two between the joints of the thigh and bottom leg piece. Remove the breast meat from the carcass using your hands and a knife to pull the meat away from the bones. Trim off the wings. Slice each breast into 4 equal pieces. Discard or reserve the roasted bones for stock.

11. Skim off the fat that rises to the top of the roasting pan; you may have as much as 1 inch to remove. Place the roasting pan with the lemons over a medium flame and add ½ to 1 cup of water. Using a spoon, scrape the bits of stuck sugars from the bottom of the pan and bring the liquid to a simmer for just a minute.

12. Strain the liquid through a fine sieve and pour it back into the roasting pan. If the duck needs

continued

to be warmed before serving, you can place it in this glazy juice with the skin side up, so that the duck skin doesn't simmer in the sauce and get soggy. Heat the duck for about 5 minutes over medium-low heat.

13. Serve each guest 2 slices of breast meat and a half of a leg and pass around the bowl of tomato-sesame jam.

Roasted Red Peppers with Sesame Seed Vinaigrette

This recipe makes a delicious mezze served alongside Fried Haloumi Cheese with Pears and Spiced Dates (page 10) and a dry sherry such as Fino, or sparkling wine like the Paopao Cocktail (page 36).

The peppers are also great chopped into small pieces to make a relish for grilled fish; try mixing in some peeled and chopped grilled peaches in the late summer when peaches are at their best.

I recommend buying white sesame seeds and toasting them yourself for a richer flavor (see page 174).

SERVES 4

---

4 red bell peppers, roasted and peeled (see page 97)

3 tablespoons toasted sesame seeds

1 tablespoon red wine vinegar

2 tablespoons extra-virgin olive oil

1 tablespoon chopped fresh dill

½ teaspoon finely minced garlic (about ½ clove)

---

1. Cut each pepper into quarters, removing as many seeds as possible and scraping away any rib on the underside of each piece.

2. Place the peppers in a small glass mixing bowl and add the rest of the ingredients.

3. Stir to coat the peppers with the sesame seeds, vinegar, garlic, oil, and dill. Let the mixture sit at room temperature for at least 30 minutes (or up to 1½ hours) and serve.

7

GOLD AND BOLD
CURRY POWDER,
TURMERIC, AND FENUGREEK

The warm, bittersweet, earthy, golden spices in this chapter have similar qualities yet very different flavors, so using them interchangeably is not recommended. I chose to group the three spices together because turmeric and fenugreek are often found in curry powders. Here, "curry" refers to the spice blend and not the leaf or plant, which is also called curry.

Curry spices can brighten up soups or creamy preparations like whipped potatoes or sauces. They also add depth to beef or sausage meats and are wonderful with rich, oily shellfish, fishes, and chicken. Turmeric can be used in small quantities as a coloring agent to intensify the golden colors of corn or yellow tomato; its flavor is subtle enough to lend a background earth tone.

CURRY POWDER

Curry, which comes from the South Indian word *kari*, meaning "sauce," is a blend of sweet, hot, and earthy spices that can be mixed in hundreds of different proportions to complement meat, fish, and vegetables. Indian chefs do not use commercial curry powder and neither do Indian families; they grind and create their own blends containing as few as seven or as many as twenty spices. Commercial curry powder was invented and made popular by the British, who sought to replicate the taste of Indian food during the Raj.

Curry powders now spice food all over the world. In the Mediterranean and Portugal, curry is used with a light hand in combination with tomato and fresh herbs like cilantro. Jamaicans use curry powder in meat stews and potato breads. In England, they serve curried egg salad with their afternoon tea. The French whisk curry powder into crème fraîche to finish soups or sauce fish.

A typical Madras-style curry blend may include ground coriander to form the bright flavor base; turmeric for color and earthiness; ginger, black pepper, and chilies to give it zing; and cardamom and cinnamon to add sweetness. By adding different spices, you can change the balance of the curry: allspice or nutmeg will increase sweetness, cumin adds earthiness, mustard or additional chilies increase feistiness, and fennel or bay leaf impart fragrance and more brightness.

I find that curry powder can easily overwhelm the other flavors in a dish, so I like to use it with an extremely light hand and add just the slightest pinch that imparts fragrance. My favorite ways to use curry are with chopped fresh tuna in deviled eggs (page 203) and in tomato-based fish soups like the Portuguese Acorda (page 214). At home, I like to add a pinch to mayonnaise when making egg or chicken salad and to soft butter to eat on radishes fresh from the garden.

Curry powders vary in quality and strength: Madras can be hot, for example, but vindaloo is always very hot. The best curry powders are those you make yourself by toasting, grinding, and mixing spices by hand (see Make Your Own Curry Powder, page 209).

Some commercial brands that you can find in the grocery store—McCormick's, for example—are acceptable, but they can be chalky because the spices aren't toasted before grinding. To revive commercial curry powder, toast it for a few minutes in a skillet over low heat while shaking the pan until it gives off a fragrant oil.

I adore the subtlety of the sweet curry powder available at www.penzeys.com. All of the Madras curry powders at www.kalustyans.com are excellent, especially the India spice brand.

TURMERIC

Turmeric is the orange-yellow rhizome of a tropical plant—similar to ginger but with a rounder bulb—grown chiefly in India, China, and Indonesia. Powdered turmeric is bright yellow and has a distinct, earthy aroma and a pleasing sharp bitterness. It is used to give an earthy depth to curry powders and to color and flavor sauces, prepared mustard, pickles, relish, chutneys, and rice dishes as well as butter and cheese. Turmeric is used widely in North African cooking, as a fish condiment called Charmoula (page 205).

Although turmeric's bright yellow color is similar to saffron, the two should never be confused, as the flavors differ considerably: saffron is much stronger, acidic, and complicated. Turmeric is also used as a fabric dye, so be careful not to spill any on your clothes; the stains are hard to get out.

There are two main types of turmeric: Alleppey and Madras. Alleppey, which is deeper in color and more flavorful, is the type you'll find in the spice section of American supermarkets. If you want to try Madras turmeric, visit an Indian grocery store.

FENUGREEK

Fenugreek is an annual herb that is a member of the pea family. The seeds look like brown gravel, and they develop in horn-shaped pods that look like miniature broad beans. Fenugreek seeds are often toasted to release their nutty, burnt-sugar flavor, similar to maple syrup (imitation maple sugar is made from fenugreek). Toasting also highlights fenugreek's bitterness, a coffee or chocolate flavor that is desirable if used in the right proportion in a recipe. The leaves form long tendrils and have a similar flavor to the seeds but lack the underlying bitterness.

Fenugreek is distinctly bittersweet and adds a caramely richness without adding sugar. It's used in curry powders and in the preparation of eastern Mediterranean charcuterie. It flavors basturma, a pastrami-like dried cured beef that is made in almost every eastern Mediterranean country. It also flavors the *sujuk* (sausage) made by Greeks, Turks, and Armenians.

I've become addicted to adding fenugreek to my mashed potatoes (page 216) and homemade mayonnaise for French fries. A "white" platform showcases this spice's complicated flavors, so fenugreek also goes particularly well with white cheese, cauliflower, and white sauce. In this chapter, I prefer to use fenugreek leaves rather than seeds; I find the flavor to be warmer, grassier, and sweeter and the bitterness easier to control. Fenugreek has a very strong flavor, so use a careful hand. Too much of it—especially the ground seed—can make a dish bitter and inedible.

You can find fenugreek leaves at Indian markets or Middle Eastern stores, or you can get them online at www.kalustyans.com. To make fenugreek powder, push the leaves through a medium-fine sieve over a small mixing bowl, crushing them and removing bits of stem.

RECIPES WITH CURRY, TURMERIC, AND FENUGREEK

Hot Buttered Hummus with Basturma and Tomato

This recipe was inspired by my trip to Cappadocia, in the center of Turkey, where I saw the most incredible phallic natural rock formations. These "fairy chimneys" are volcanic deposits that have been sculpted by wind and rain. Cappadocia is also known for its *manti*–very small raviolis–and its kasseri cheese and thriving dairy farms. In Cappadocia, they make hummus without tahini, and they use butter instead of olive oil because of its quality and availability. I lighten this recipe by using half butter and half olive oil. The butter pairs well with the spicy beef, and the olive oil imparts the Mediterranean flavor.

Basturma is a dry-cured beef, meaning that rather than soaking in brine, it is rubbed with dry salt and spices, including fenugreek, chilies, and garlic. Armenians, Turks, Lebanese, and other eastern Mediterranean people eat basturma in paper-thin slices, much like prosciutto (the Italian dry-cured ham) or bresaola (the Italian dry-cured beef).

You can find basturma, also spelled *pastirma*, at a good Middle Eastern or Armenian market, but if you don't have one near you, try www.tulumba.com; my favorite brand is Ohanyan's pastirma. I prefer fatty basturma to lean because the texture is softer and the flavor is, of course, better. Most markets will slice basturma to order. When I slice it, I prefer to rub most of the spice mixture off with the back of a knife. The spice mixture is packed on for curing purposes, and there is no need for too much of it, since most of the flavor has already been imparted to the meat.

At Oleana, we serve this dish under the prêt-a-manger (ready to eat) portion of the menu, where we list several options for bread condiments before appetizers. We stuff each little ball of hummus with a butter nugget and then wrap each ball with basturma and bake until warm, serving them sprinkled with fresh chopped tomatoes, black olives, and scallions. Below I include another way of presenting the hummus–as a dip–which is more casual and perfect for cocktail parties.

I recommend plenty of French chardonnay with this dish. If you want to go red, try something earthy and peppery, like a Rhone-style wine or Chianti.

⌐ SERVES 8 AS AN APPETIZER ¬

SPICE: FLAVORS OF THE EASTERN MEDITERRANEAN

2 cups chickpeas, soaked overnight

1 stick butter, cut into small pieces,
plus 1½ tablespoons

½ cup extra-virgin olive oil

1 teaspoon finely chopped garlic
(about 1 large clove)

1 tablespoon freshly squeezed lemon juice
(about ½ lemon)

2 teaspoons ground cumin

Salt and pepper to taste

¼ pound or 16 thin slices basturma

2 teaspoons extra-virgin olive oil
or melted butter for garnish

2 plum tomatoes, peeled, seeded,
and finely chopped (see page 104)

8 pitted, dry-cured black olives

1 scallion, 1 inch green trimmed
from the top, washed, and finely chopped

Torn pieces of crusty French bread
or pita bread (cut into wedges, torn,
or left whole for guests to tear)

1. In a medium saucepan, cover the chickpeas in about 8 cups of fresh water. Bring them to a boil over medium-high heat. Reduce the heat to medium-low and simmer the chickpeas for at least 25 minutes, until very tender. Drain the chickpeas and reserve 1 tablespoon of the cooking liquid.

2. Before the chickpeas cool down, purée them in a food processor fitted with a metal blade, with the 1 stick of the butter, ½ cup olive oil, garlic, lemon juice, reserved cooking liquid, cumin, and salt and pepper, until very smooth and creamy. It may take 3 to 4 minutes, depending on how sharp your blade is.

3. Let the hummus sit at room temperature for 20 to 30 minutes and then cool it in the refrigerator for at least 45 minutes. This makes it easier to shape and stuff with butter.

4. Preheat the oven to 350° F.

5. Cut the 1½ tablespoons of butter into 8 equal, small cubes or rectangles.

6. Scoop the hummus into 16 balls, about 2 tablespoons each. Roll the hummus into nice rounds and put your finger in the bottom of each ball to make a pocket for the butter bit.

7. Stuff a butter bit into the bottom of each hummus ball and seal it by pushing the hummus around it. You may need to roll it between your hands again to reshape the ball. Press each ball a little so it flattens slightly.

8. Wrap a piece of basturma around each hummus ball and place them, with the seam side of the basturma down, onto a heavy baking sheet.

9. Bake for 8 to 10 minutes, until warm.

10. Drizzle a little of the remaining 2 teaspoons olive oil over each and then top each with tomatoes and an olive.

11. Sprinkle with scallions and serve immediately with the bread.

🌿 Dip Variation

After you've puréed the hummus, place it in a small round casserole or baking dish, but don't chill it. Using a rubber spatula, spread it in a smooth, even layer. Top the casserole with the chopped bits of butter and lay the slices of basturma in a round pinwheel pattern, laying each slice from the center to the edge. Each center slice may overlap a bit.

Bake for 8 to 12 minutes, until warm, and then sprinkle the top with chopped tomatoes, scallions, and olive. Serve as a dip with crusty French bread or pita bread.

Deviled Eggs with Tuna and Black Olives

These deviled eggs are a twist on traditional Spanish tapas. I was inspired by a trip to San Sebastian in the Basque country, where the tapas bars were full of fun, creative snacks: lots of grilled or toasted breads with artichoke or tomato toppings, miniature vegetable tarts, shrimps in garlic, and croquettes. And they stuffed their eggs with anchovies, olives, tuna, and sweet red peppers. If you haven't had a deviled egg for a while, it's time to try this recipe.

We serve these eggs under the *prêt-a-manger* section of Oleana's menu as a bread condiment and something to consider before an appetizer. If I ever took them off our menu, the customers would protest. They work perfectly for lunch with a green salad or as hors d'oeuvres at a cocktail party.

MAKES 16 PIECES TO SERVE 8 FOR LUNCH
OR 16 AS HORS D'OEUVRES

8 eggs

1 cup finely chopped fresh tuna
(about 8 ounces)

1 tablespoon extra-virgin olive oil
plus another 2 teaspoons for garnish

1 scallion, finely minced

½ cup peeled and minced celery

¼ teaspoon curry powder

Salt and pepper to taste

1 cup thick mayonnaise, preferably
homemade (see page 50 for Lemon Aioli
and leave out the garlic)

1 tablespoon chopped fresh parsley

1 teaspoon freshly squeezed lemon juice
(about ¼ lemon)

8 black olives, pitted
and finely chopped

1 plum tomato, halved, seeded,
and chopped

CURRY POWDER, TURMERIC, AND FENUGREEK

1. Carefully place the eggs in a medium saucepan and cover them with warm water by a couple of inches. Bring the water to a boil over medium-high heat, reduce the heat to medium-low, and simmer for 8 minutes.

2. Place the whole pan in the sink and run cold water over the eggs until they are cool, about 5 minutes. Drain the water off the eggs and set them aside.

3. In a medium sauté pan over medium-high heat, sauté the tuna in 1 tablespoon of the olive oil with the scallion, celery, curry powder, and salt and pepper until the tuna is just cooked, 3 to 4 minutes.

4. Drain the tuna mixture through a sieve to rid it of excess juices. Allow the tuna to cool for 10 minutes.

5. Finely chop the tuna mixture and refrigerate it while preparing the eggs.

6. Peel the eggs and slice them in half, lengthwise. Remove the yolk from each egg and place yolks into a small mixing bowl.

7. Cut a small sliver off of the bottom of each egg white so that the egg can sit on a plate or platter without wobbling. Add the egg-white slivers to the egg yolks.

8. Mash the egg yolks and slivers of whites with a fork until they are powdered and in fine pieces.

9. Stir in the tuna, mayonnaise, parsley, and lemon juice and season with salt and pepper.

10. Season each of the egg whites with a little salt and pepper and place a heaping spoonful of tuna into the center of each, dividing the tuna mixture evenly. Top each egg with a pinch of olive and tomato and drizzle them all with a little olive oil.

11. Serve with crusty French bread. You can prepare the eggs and tuna the day before and assemble and garnish them before serving.

Charmoula Spice for Grilled Fish

Charmoula is a North African condiment for fish. There are two kinds: one is a relish made with onion, herbs, and spices (see Grapefruit Charmoula on page 89) and the other is a dry spice rub. This recipe is a dry rub that works really well on salmon or other hearty fishes like swordfish, tuna, bluefish, or monkfish. Sprinkle each 6-ounce portion of fish with a teaspoon of charmoula before roasting or grilling and serve with lots of fresh lemon wedges.

↶ MAKES ABOUT ½ CUP ↷

2 teaspoons ground turmeric	2 tablespoons ground cumin
1 tablespoon ground white pepper	1 tablespoon sea salt
1 tablespoon ground ginger	2 tablespoons sweet paprika

Mix together all the ingredients and store in an airtight container up to 3 months in a cool, dry place, out of direct light.

Shrimp with Kasseri Cheese, Fennel, and Fenugreek Wrapped in Shredded Phyllo

Years ago, I had lunch at master chef Joel Robuchon's L'Atelier in Paris, where he served shrimp wrapped in shredded phyllo on a bed of greens dressed with Asian flavors. The presentation was so dramatic that I wanted to re-create it, adding some of my favorite Arabic flavors of fennel with bittersweet fenugreek and salty cheese, which pairs so well with shrimp.

In Greek, the shredded phyllo dough is called *kataifi*; it looks like shredded wheat and makes a dramatic presentation. You can find kataifi at most Middle Eastern markets, Greek markets, and at some specialty food stores.

Kasseri is a Turkish and Greek cheese, usually made from sheep's or goat's milk. It is mild flavored and has a creamy gold color and a firm, hard texture, making it perfect for grating. You can find it at any Greek market and many Middle Eastern markets or specialty cheese shops. Asiago makes a fine substitution if you have trouble finding kasseri.

The filling in this recipe is versatile and can be stuffed into crepes or puff pastry, added to scrambled eggs, or sprinkled over a pizza dough. The shrimp are excellent with salad greens and sliced tomatoes for dinner in the summertime or as hors d'oeuvres at a cocktail party.

This dish pairs well with a Grüner Vetliner from Austria.

⌁ MAKES 8 WRAPS TO SERVE 8 AS AN APPETIZER OR 4 AS A MEAL ⌁

1 tablespoon butter plus ¼ cup melted butter for brushing	2 fennel bulbs, top stalks and fronds removed
1 tablespoon olive oil plus ½ cup for brushing	1 tablespoon dried fenugreek leaves
2 small onions, peeled and thinly sliced	1 teaspoon finely chopped garlic (about 1 large clove)

1 teaspoon sweet paprika

Salt and pepper to taste

8 large shrimp, peeled and deveined
(about 10 per pound)

¼ cup dry white wine

1¾ cups grated kasseri cheese
(almost a pound)

1 tablespoon heavy cream

1 tablespoon chopped fresh parsley
plus a little extra for garnish

1 teaspoon freshly squeezed lemon juice
(about ¼ lemon)

½ package shredded phyllo dough
or kataifi

2 cups tomato sauce
with caramelized butter
(see Grilled Skirt Steak, page 26)

1. In a large sauté pan over medium-high heat, melt 1 tablespoon butter with 1 tablespoon olive oil until the butter begins to brown. Add the onions and cook for about 8 minutes, until they begin to soften and turn limp.

2. Meanwhile, cut the fennel bulbs in half lengthwise and remove the cores with a small paring knife, slicing around them in a V-shape and pulling them out. Remove the first outer layer of each bulb half and discard (this layer is a little tough and fibrous). Slice the fennel into thin strips, about the same size as the onions.

3. Add the fennel to the onions in the pan and continue to cook, stirring for about 6 minutes, until both vegetables become soft and translucent.

4. Meanwhile push the fenugreek leaves through a medium-fine sieve over a small bowl to remove bits of stem and to powder the leaves.

5. Reduce the heat to medium and add the garlic, fenugreek, and paprika and season with salt and pepper. Continue to cook for another 3 minutes.

6. Stir in the shrimp and wine and cook for 5 minutes, stirring, until the wine has evaporated and the shrimp are cooked through.

7. Remove the pan from the heat and place the shrimp mixture in medium mixing bowl. Stir in the cheese, cream, parsley, and lemon juice and season again with salt and pepper.

8. Preheat the oven to 350° F.

9. Cut the phyllo into eight 6-inch-long bundles and gather them into 1-inch-thick (or wide) ropes. Lay them down on a board and brush them generously with the ½ cup olive oil and the ¼ cup melted butter, coating them as well as you can.

continued

10.

10.

10. Place one shrimp on the bottom quarter of each rope of phyllo strands. Top the shrimp with a tablespoon of cheese and onion and roll the phyllo strands around the shrimp, covering it completely. Repeat this process with the remaining shrimp.

11. Place the shrimp wraps on a heavy baking sheet and bake them for 12 to 15 minutes, until golden brown and crispy.

12. Meanwhile, gently warm the tomato sauce on medium-low heat.

13. Serve each shrimp immediately with a couple of tablespoons of tomato sauce on the side, and sprinkle both with a little parsley.

Make Your Own Curry Powder

Start with this curry recipe as a base and add other spices to create your own signature blend. If you like your curry spicier, add more chilies. To sweeten it, add some allspice or fennel seed. To add more earthiness, try a little cumin.

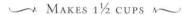 Makes 1½ cups ⌐

1 tablespoon dried fenugreek leaves

¼ cup coriander seeds,
   toasted (page 37),
   cooled, and ground

¼ cup plus 1 teaspoon ground turmeric

¼ cup ground dried ginger

3 tablespoons whole black
   peppercorns, ground

2 tablespoons Aleppo chilies

2 tablespoons cardamom seeds
   (not the pods; see page 3), ground

2 tablespoons ground cinnamon

1. Push the fenugreek leaves through a medium-fine sieve over a small bowl to remove bits of stem and to powder the leaves. You should have 1 tablespoon ground leaves.

2. Mix all the ingredients in a small mixing bowl until combined. Store in an airtight container in a cool, dry, and dark place for up to 3 months.

Golden Gazpacho with Condiments

In creating this recipe, I set out to give my guests the pure tomato experience of a refined Spanish gazpacho. It's worth it to wait all year until late summer to make this recipe, because that's when sungold tomatoes are in season. These tiny, yellow-gold cherry tomato hybrids are super sweet; eaten whole, they burst in your mouth like candy made from sunshine. They have a slightly nutty smell–almost like tobacco–on the calyx (the group of leaves that sits on the tomato like a little hat). I wash the tomatoes and put them in the blender whole, with a few of the calyxes on, because I think the fragrance adds to the gazpacho flavor. After puréeing the tomatoes with the other ingredients, I strain the soup through a fine sieve to remove bits of seed and skin; it's hard work, but this step creates the silkiest texture and purest tomato flavor.

This gazpacho must be served very cold, and guests can add condiments to the soup at their whim. They should first taste the concentrated flavor of tomato and then add toppings, little by little. For condiments, my favorites include minced fennel, bits of shredded Serrano ham or prosciutto, minced melon, crabmeat, Aleppo chilies, or minced onion. Just be sure to chop everything up as small as possible to maintain the elegance of the dish.

This gazpacho deserves a dry white port or Manzanilla sherry to go with it.

MAKES 4 CUPS TO SERVE 4

2 pints sungold tomatoes (about 6 cups)

½ cup fresh, plain bread crumbs or ½ a small pita bread, torn into ½-inch pieces

2 tablespoons Spanish sherry vinegar

¾ cup extra-virgin olive oil

¼ teaspoon turmeric

¼ teaspoon curry powder

1 tablespoon salt plus more to taste

Black pepper to taste

1 cup bottled sparkling mineral water

1 cup hand-torn crouton-size bread pieces

1 hard-boiled egg (see page 204)

1 red bell pepper, seeded, ribs removed, finely minced

6 chives, finely minced

1. Place the tomatoes, bread crumbs, vinegar, ½ cup of the olive oil, the turmeric, curry powder, 1 tablespoon salt, pepper, and sparkling water in a blender. Purée until smooth.

2. Strain the soup through a fine sieve or china cap (a very fine cone-shaped sieve) into a medium stainless steel or glass mixing bowl, pushing it through with the back of a small ladle or pestle. Discard the pulp and seeds and check the soup for seasoning. It should be a beautiful golden color. Chill in the refrigerator for at least one hour.

3. Chill 4 soup bowls for 20 minutes.

4. Preheat the oven to 350° F.

5. In a small bowl, toss the hand-torn bread in the remaining ¼ cup of olive oil and place them on a small, heavy baking sheet. Season with salt and pepper to taste. Bake for about 7 minutes, until golden brown and crispy. Cool and set aside.

6. Grate the hard-boiled egg with the finest side of a box grater so that you have little egg "jimmies." Place them in a small bowl and season them with salt and pepper to taste. Set aside and chill.

7. Ladle the soup into the 4 chilled soup bowls. Serve immediately with the egg, peppers, croutons, and chives, all passed around separately so that guests can add condiments with each bite.

Fanny's Fresh Pea and Two Potato Soup

At Oleana, Mother's Day is special: we depart from our regular Arabic/Mediterranean menu and prepare recipes I've collected from twelve wonderful mothers I know. The recipes are family-tested, comforting, and delicious. We serve this soup every year.

Fanny Ramirez, who created this recipe, is one of our honored mothers. She lives in Columbia and is the mother of one of Oleana's sous-chefs, Wilton Osorno. Fanny taught Wilton a lot about cooking and caring about food. She uses turmeric to make the soup golden and earthy and to give body to a soup base with or without meat. Little bits of tortilla or cooked egg float in the soup like hearty dumplings. This healthful soup can be served as a meal, and it's a great way to highlight different potatoes.

~ MAKES ABOUT 10 CUPS TO SERVE 8 ~

1 tablespoon butter

2 tablespoons plus 2 teaspoons olive oil

2 medium carrots, peeled, cut in half lengthwise, and diced into ½-inch cubes

2 ribs celery, peeled, sliced in half lengthwise, and diced into ½-inch cubes

1 large Spanish white onion, peeled and diced into ½-inch chunks

1 pinch saffron

1 teaspoon turmeric

½ teaspoon paprika, cayenne, or Aleppo chilies

2 medium baking potatoes (1 pound), peeled and diced into ½-inch cubes

5 small fingerling potatoes, washed and sliced into ¼-inch rounds

6 cups vegetable stock or chicken broth

Salt and pepper to taste

1½ cups freshly shucked peas

2 eggs, beaten until smooth

2 bunches cilantro, stems removed, washed, dried, and roughly chopped

1. In a large saucepan, heat the butter with 2 tablespoons of the olive oil over medium-high heat, until the butter begins to brown. Stir in the carrots, celery, onion, saffron, turmeric, and paprika. Stir and cook for about 5 minutes, until the vegetables are soft and the onions are translucent.

2. Stir in both kinds of potatoes and add the vegetable stock. Season with salt and pepper. Bring to a boil and reduce the heat to low. Simmer, uncovered, for about 20 minutes, until the potatoes are tender.

3. Stir in the peas and continue to simmer for about 8 minutes, until the peas are cooked and tender.

4. Meanwhile, in a medium nonstick sauté pan over medium-high heat, heat the remaining 2 teaspoons of olive oil until hot. Add the beaten egg little by little to the pan, stirring all the while, and cook until the egg is set, about 1 minute. You should have scrambled eggs.

5. Remove the eggs from the heat and slide them onto a chopping board. Chop them into ½-inch cubes, about the same size as the other vegetables.

6. Add the egg and cilantro to the soup just before serving. Serve this soup hot.

Acorda: Portuguese Bread Soup with Rock Shrimp

I discovered this unusual soup in Portugal when I was traveling with my business partner Gary Griffin, and my dear friend Ailsa Cooke, from Ailsa's house in the Piedmonte region of Italy through the south of France, over to the north of Spain, and on to Portugal. Gary and I wanted to do some research before we opened Oleana, so we were exploring Mediterranean recipes and design ideas. With Ailsa as our guide, we reveled in the Arabic-influenced foods we sampled: coffee-infused cream served with beef, heavy eggy flans, and subtle curries that enriched fish broths. And we ate many variations on the delicious, garlicky bread soup called *acorda*.

The toasted garlic gives this acorda its authentic flavor. The Spanish and Portuguese have a wonderful trick of toasting garlic: caramelizing it to lend a rich, nutty flavor to many dishes, including vinaigrettes. I also like to use this method of toasting garlic to add to sautéed greens like Swiss chard or spinach or with sherry vinaigrette, tossed into a hot escarole salad.

SERVES 6 AS A GREAT LUNCH OR VERY COMFORTING DINNER

1 tablespoon butter or olive oil

1 Spanish onion, peeled and finely chopped

1 rib celery, peeled and finely chopped

1 teaspoon curry powder

¼ teaspoon turmeric

1 bay leaf

4 cups chopped fresh plum tomatoes

4 cups water or fish fumet (page 161)

Salt and pepper to taste

½ French baguette, with the bottom crust removed, cut into ½-inch cubes (about 3 cups)

½ cup olive oil plus extra for garnish

2 tablespoons garlic, peeled and sliced paper-thin (about 6 cloves)

2 tablespoons chopped fresh cilantro

1 tablespoon chopped fresh parsley plus a little extra for garnish

1 teaspoon freshly squeezed lemon juice (about ¼ lemon)

2 pounds rock shrimp

2 eggs

1. In a 4-quart saucepan, melt the butter over medium heat and stir in the onion and celery. Cook for 3 minutes or until the vegetables begin to soften.

2. Add the curry powder, turmeric, and bay leaf and stir to coat the vegetables.

3. Add the tomatoes and water and turn the heat up to high. Bring to a boil and reduce the heat to low. Simmer for 20 to 25 minutes.

4. Cool the broth slightly and purée, using a handheld emulsion blender or a regular blender. Blend the soup until it's smooth, and then push it through a fine sieve, using the back of a small ladle, into a large mixing bowl. This removes undesirable bits of tomato skin, seeds, and bay leaf.

5. Place the broth back in the large soup pot and bring it back to a simmer on medium heat. Season with salt and pepper.

6. Place the bread cubes in a medium mixing bowl and set aside.

7. In a small sauté pan over medium heat, heat the olive oil with the slivers of garlic and cook, stirring constantly with a slotted spoon or a pair of tongs, until the garlic becomes golden brown and caramelized. As you are stirring, the garlic will release its natural sugars and stick to your spoon. After this point it will start to brown. Be careful to remove the garlic quickly from the heat once it has browned; garlic can burn easily and will taste very bitter.

8. Remove from the heat and pour the hot garlic and oil over the cubed bread. Season with salt and pepper and stir in the cilantro, parsley, and lemon juice.

9. Add the shrimp to the simmering broth and cook for 1 to 2 minutes, until the shrimp are pink and just cooked through.

10. Add the bread mixture to the soup and stir. Keep on very low heat.

11. In a small mixing bowl, whisk the eggs vigorously until they are smooth and broken up, as if you were preparing eggs for an omelet. Temper the eggs by ladling in 1 cup of the soup and mixing until the eggs are incorporated; you are bringing the eggs closer to the temperature of the soup so that they add creaminess without scrambling into bits. Stir the eggs into the pot and continue to stir until the soup becomes creamy. Remove the soup from the heat.

12. Warm your soup bowls by running them under hot tap water for a minute and then drying them off with a towel (you can also run them through a dishwasher cycle or heat them in a 200° F oven for 4 minutes).

13. Ladle the soup into warm bowls. Drizzle additional olive oil over the soup and sprinkle some chopped parsley on top. Serve immediately.

 Note

The soup separates after it's been sitting for a while, but a good strong stir with a spoon or whisk emulsifies it again.

Mashed Potatoes with Fenugreek

To me, the perfect mashed potato is light, creamy, buttery, and really smooth with no lumps. And there's a lot to consider when you're aiming for perfection.

First, the choice of potato: I like to use an Idaho or russet baking potato because they are starchy and dry and therefore stay fluffy after I add the butter and milk. Other kinds of potatoes–like new potatoes or fingerlings–can turn watery, mealy, or gummy.

Next, once cooked, be sure to dry your potatoes by putting them back on the heat for a few minutes on the lowest possible setting. This lets extra water evaporate and creates an extra fluffy mashed potato. When the potatoes stop steaming, they are ready for mashing.

These potatoes are "mashed" in name only. Since I like my potatoes without any lumps, I put them through a ricer or food mill; this produces the lightest and creamiest end result. Potatoes can turn quickly into a gluey mess if overprocessed or stirred too much, so never use a food processor or high-speed mixer.

Finally, consider the temperature of your dairy products. I like to melt the butter with the milk or cream before incorporation; the potatoes will absorb warm dairy faster, so you'll need to do less stirring.

If you do have lumps at the end, here's a good trick: buzz a handheld emulsion blender through the potatoes until the lumps are gone. But be quick or you'll end up with glue. An emulsion blender works better than a food processor because the blade pulls the ingredient in but doesn't push it out, so it purées more tightly and quickly.

Fenugreek is my favorite flavoring for mashed potatoes, especially with meats. When I serve these potatoes with fish, I add lemon zest or chopped preserved lemons to brighten the flavors to better suit fish.

These potatoes really spice up a Thanksgiving table. Try them with the Braised Beef Short Ribs on page 66.

—⌁ SERVES 4 GENEROUSLY AS A SIDE DISH ⌁—

4 baking potatoes (about 1¾ pounds)	1 cup whole milk or heavy cream
1 stick butter	2 teaspoons ground fenugreek leaves (see page 198)
2 teaspoons finely minced garlic (about 2 large cloves)	Salt and black pepper to taste

2.

4.

4.

1. Peel and cut each potato into 4 equal pieces. Place the potatoes in a large saucepan and cover them with warm water by 3 inches. Bring the potatoes to a boil over high heat and reduce the heat to medium-low. Simmer the potatoes for 18 to 20 minutes, until they are tender when poked with a fork or squeezed with a pair of tongs.

2. Drain the potatoes immediately into a colander and place them back into the saucepan over the lowest possible heat. Let them dry for 8 minutes or less. When the steam has stopped evaporating, they are ready to mash.

3. Meanwhile, melt the butter with the garlic, milk, and fenugreek over medium heat (about 5 minutes) and set aside.

4. Push the potatoes through a ricer or food mill over a large mixing bowl. Stir in the melted butter mixture and season well with salt and pepper.

5. Serve hot. You can reheat the potatoes gently over low heat, stirring constantly, or hold them warm in a low (150° F) oven. Stir to fluff before serving.

❧ Variation

Try substituting white pepper for black pepper for an earthier and more complementary flavor to the fenugreek. Freshly grated white pepper on buttery potato purée is divine!

Ihsan's Doggy Eggs

This recipe was inspired by my Turkish friend Ihsan Gurdhal. For a few summers, during the month of July, I shared a house near the beach with a group of friends including Ihsan and his wife Valerie.

The best days were those when Ihsan would get up early and make a breakfast dish that he called "doggy eggs" because he served them to us in a large, stainless-steel bowl that resembled a dog dish. Ihsan would bike up the street to fetch farm-fresh eggs from a roadside stand, where he'd drop his money into a tin can. When he returned, he'd prepare his signature breakfast. Everyone in the beach house got hooked on doggy eggs, and we'd beg Ihsan to make his breakfast treat. Eventually, we developed a sense of technique and teamwork: one person would toast, butter, and tear the bread into a giant mixing bowl, while Ihsan prepared the pancetta or basturma and poached the eggs.

The magic of doggy eggs is the way the bread soaks up the spicy basturma flavors and absorbs the runny, rich yolks from the poached eggs. Farm-fresh eggs make the best doggy eggs. You need to cook the basturma lightly, for if it cooks too long the spices will burn and become bitter.

Make your own vegetable juice (tomato, celery, and carrots pushed through a juice extractor) and serve it with lime over ice with this hearty breakfast that will last you all day at the beach.

—∧ SERVES 4 ∧—

---

4 slices country bread or sourdough, toasted and buttered

1 tablespoon chopped fresh chives or scallions

1 teaspoon olive oil or butter

8 paper-thin slices fatty basturma (see Resources, page 358)

1 teaspoon white vinegar

4 eggs, preferably fresh

Salt and plenty of freshly ground pepper to taste

---

1. Tear the toast into small bits by hand (about ¼ inch) into a large mixing bowl and add the chives. Set aside.

2. In a large sauté pan over medium-high heat, heat the olive oil until hot and add the basturma slices. Cook the basturma on one side only until it curls up a bit and the fat renders and melts. It should take 3 to 4 minutes. Don't let the basturma get dark or too crispy.

3. Scrape the basturma and any of its oils into the bowl with the torn toast.

4. Bring a small saucepan of water to a boil over high heat. Reduce the heat to medium-low so that it simmers. Add the vinegar.

5. Break 1 egg into a ramekin.

6. Using a large slotted spoon, stir the water in a circular pattern so that you create a spiral motion in the water, and drop the egg in. Add eggs this way, one by one. Stirring the water when you drop the eggs in forces the whites to stay close to the yolks and not scatter in shards. Let the eggs poach for 4 to 4½ minutes, until the white is set but the yolks are very runny.

7. Remove the eggs with a slotted spoon and drain them on a paper towel.

8. Drop the eggs into the mixing bowl and toss them with the toast and basturma, breaking them up a bit and stirring until the yolks are absorbed by the bread and the bread becomes swollen from the yolks. Add salt and pepper. Spoon into deep soup or doggy-sized bowls and serve immediately.

Homemade Sujuk

Sujuk, which means "sausage" in Arabic, is a delicious meat preparation spiced with fenugreek and chilies. In Muslim countries, sujuk is made with lamb or beef; Armenians and Greeks use beef that is sometimes combined with pork.

At Oleana, I had explored making homemade sujuk because I don't care for any of the commercially available brands. I find them to be too lean and dry. I spent years asking every Armenian and Greek person I knew how they made their sujuk. No one would share their secret. It seemed to be protected by the family!

So, after much trial and error, Cassie Kyriakides, who works in Oleana's kitchen with me, helped me develop a sujuk recipe that she now makes at her day job in the south end of Boston's Butcher Shop. We serve sujuk on our winter menu accompanied by Squash Kibbeh (page 106) and plenty of Sumac Onions (page 98).

If you have an electric mixer (such as a KitchenAid) with a sausage-making attachment and meat grinder, it is very easy to make fresh sausage. Hog casings, available online at www.sausagemaker.com, make long, thin, hot-dog-shaped sausages.

To make meatball-shaped handmade sausages, you can use caul fat, a weblike membrane from internal organs, to wrap parcels of sausage meat (called *crepinettes* in France) and either grill or fry them. The caul fat acts as a sausage skin and also bastes the meat as it cooks. It dissolves after slow cooking but is attractive enough in its own right. Making handmade sausages with caul fat is the easier of the two methods, but caul fat can be hard to come by. Pork caul fat, which is the best, should be available from most good butchers.

If you don't have a meat grinder attachment on your mixer, have your butcher grind the meat for you–and ask to have the meat frozen before grinding. Very cold sausage will have the best texture: if it's too warm when ground, the fat will whip into the meat and the sausage won't render properly. The flavor will still be wonderful, but the sausage will be soft and dry, since the fat will have escaped during the cooking process.

These delicious spicy sausages pair well with beer, especially India pale ale or a Belgian-style ale.

MAKES SIXTEEN 4-OUNCE SAUSAGES TO SERVE 8 AS A MAIN COURSE

2½ pounds pork shoulder	1½ teaspoons black pepper
½ pound beef chuck	1 tablespoon ground cumin
1 pound pork fatback	1 tablespoon paprika
¾ teaspoon ground allspice	1½ teaspoons sugar
¼ teaspoon cayenne pepper	¼ cup kosher salt
1½ teaspoons crushed fenugreek leaves (see page 198)	Hog casings for sixteen 6-inch sausages or 2 large pieces of caul fat plus a few extra for practice or to use as a taste test
1½ teaspoons ground fennel seed	

1. Cut the pork shoulder, beef, and fatback into 1-inch cubes and lay the cubes out on a large baking sheet.

2. Place the meat and fat in the freezer for 15 to 20 minutes, until the meat and fat are frosty but not frozen solid.

3. Using a meat grinder (or a meat-grinding attachment for a mixer) pass the pork and beef through the large die or grinding blade (the circular piece with holes) into a large mixing bowl. Then pass it through the small die or grinding blade. Finally, pass the fatback through the small die or grinding blade only.

4. Combine the ground meat and fatback with the spices, sugar, and salt and mix thoroughly.

5. Spread the mixture on a large metal baking sheet and freeze it again for about 15 minutes, until the mixture is frosty but not frozen solid.

6. Prepare the hog casings by rinsing the inside of each individual casing thoroughly to remove salt and excess particles. You can place the end of the casing on your faucet as though you were filling a water balloon and then let warm water (not hot or cold) rinse through each casing for about 3 minutes. After rinsing, let the casings soak in warm water for up to 10 minutes and drain.

7. Slip one end of each clean casing over the tip of the extruder attachment (for stuffing sausages) and feed the meat into a long sausage. Don't fill the skins too tightly or they'll burst when frying–even if you prick them with a fork. It may take two or three tries to get them just right, so make a few beforehand, for practice.

8. Twist the sausage every 6 inches to form individual sausages.

9. Hang the sausages up or lay them out in the refrigerator, uncovered, for 2 days to dry out a little and mature in flavor. This gives the meat a little time to cure. Once the meat has dried, it will shrink a bit so you'll have a better seal. You can then cut them off at the twists as needed or cut them and freeze half. *continued*

CURRY POWDER, TURMERIC, AND FENUGREEK

❧ Cooking Instructions for Sausage

Place a few sausages in a skillet over medium heat. Add water to cover the bottom of the pan. Cover and steam the sausages until they are plump and the liquid evaporates, about 5 to 6 minutes. Pierce the sausages with a fork or the point of a knife, and lower the heat to low. Brown the sausages slowly in their own juices for approximately 8 minutes. They are cooked thoroughly when pinkness disappears.

❧ Cassie's Important Tips

1. *Don't forget to test the sausage for proper seasoning and texture before stuffing it. Cook a small amount wrapped in plastic wrap in boiling water for about 6 minutes or until cooked through.*

2. *Casings are easier to work with when they have a little time to soak in warm water after they are washed.*

3. *When stuffing sausage, always keep one hand on the extruder, while pushing down the meat mixture with your other hand. You will have more control of the stuffing process if you feed a small amount of meat through, keeping the mixer on slow speed.*

Roast Chicken Stuffed with Basturma and Kasseri Cheese

Stuffing flavors under chicken skin before cooking turns a simple roasted chicken into something very special. Sometimes I use butter and lemon confit (slow-braised lemon slices in olive oil) as a stuffing, which makes the chicken rich and lemony. Sometimes I use herbs, garlic, and black truffles. Basturma and good kasseri cheese in this recipe make the stuffed chicken taste salty, nutty, and bittersweet with just the right amount of heat from the chilies on the basturma.

Kasseri is Greek- or Turkish-style grating cheese usually made from sheep's milk. It melts wonderfully and has a slightly nutty flavor. Use Gruyère or Asiago cheese as a substitution if you can't find kasseri at a local Greek or Middle Eastern market or specialty cheese shop.

I like to use whole, bone-in chicken breasts for a moister chicken. Serve this chicken with Rice Cakes (page 65) or Mashed Potatoes with Fenugreek (page 216) alongside it.

It's worth trying to find a Chateau Musar from the Bekka Valley in Lebanon to drink with this dish. Their unique, biodynamically cultivated reds are a blend of cinsault, carignan, and cabernet sauvignon that are grown in limestone. The result is a medium-bodied wine, full of rustic, earthy flavors that express Lebanon's terroir. See Theresa's note on biodynamic farming on page 225.

SERVES 4

2 whole bone-in chicken breasts
(skin on), split into 4 half-breasts

2 tablespoons chopped fresh parsley
plus a little extra for garnish

1⅓ cups grated kasseri cheese

12 paper-thin slices fatty basturma

Salt and pepper to taste

2 tablespoons butter

2 tablespoons olive oil

1 cup white wine

½ cup water or chicken broth

¼ cup freshly squeezed lemon juice
(about 1½ lemons)

1. Preheat the oven to 375° F.

2. Run your fingers underneath the skin of each chicken breast, loosening it up and creating a deep pocket between the skin and the meat for stuffing. Make sure that you don't poke all the way through to the other side of the skin.

3. In a small mixing bowl, combine the parsley and kasseri cheese.

4. Place 3 slices of basturma under the skin of each half breast, in as even a layer as possible.

5. Fill the rest of the skin pocket with about ⅓ cup of the kasseri cheese mixture, packing it down so that it's flat enough to sear on the skin side. Season the breasts on all sides with salt and pepper.

6. In a medium sauté pan over high heat, melt ½ tablespoon of butter with 1 tablespoon of oil, until the butter begins to brown. Add 2 of the chicken breast pieces, skin-side down, and cook for about 4 minutes on one side, until browned.

Remove the breasts from the sauté pan and place them in a heavy roasting pan, skin-side up.

7. Wipe the sauté pan clean and repeat the same process as in step 6 with the remaining 2 breast pieces, another tablespoon of olive oil, and ½ tablespoon of butter.

8. Place the stuffed breasts in the oven and roast them for 15 to 18 minutes, until cooked through. Allow them to rest for 8 minutes.

9. Remove the chicken pieces from the roasting pan and place them on a carving board. Put the roasting pan on the stove over medium-high heat. Add the wine, water, and lemon juice to the roasting pan and simmer, scraping the bottom of the pan until you remove the sugars; this makes a thin gravy or jus as well as a clean roasting pan.

10. Strain the liquid through a fine sieve into a sauté pan large enough to hold the 4 pieces of chicken and simmer until it's reduced by half, about 4 minutes. You should have about ½ cup to ¾ cup of jus.

11. Whisk in the remaining tablespoon of butter and season with salt and pepper.

12. Remove the chicken meat from the breast bone by inserting a knife where the bone meets the flesh to loosen it; then, using your fingers to remove the ribs and bone, pull it off completely. (The little rib bones make an excellent chicken broth.)

13. Place the boned, stuffed breasts in the large sauté pan with the sauce and heat them over medium-low heat until warm, about 6 minutes. The sauce will thicken a little more and glaze the undersides of the chicken.

14. Spoon extra sauce over the top of each breast and sprinkle with chopped parsley. Serve immediately.

✿ *Presentation Variation*

At Oleana, we split the chicken in half and debone it, and then we stuff the skin of each chicken half and tuck it into a flat ball shape. We cook the chicken in a heavy cast-iron pan, under a brick; this flattens it and marbles the dark meat into the white. This process makes for a dramatic presentation and ultracrispy skin. See Crispy Lemon Chicken with Za'atar on page 245.

BIODYNAMIC FARMING

Theresa Paopao, Wine Director at Oleana

Biodynamic farming is a supercharged method of organic agriculture, centered on the philosophy that all living organisms are affected by two forms of energy: earthly and cosmic. Biodynamic farmers use special preparations of fertilizer and plan the growth cycle according to the natural rhythms of the solar and lunar phases. Wine made from such healthy and sustainable vineyards will produce grapes that are of optimum health and quality. Without artificial additives, the wine may best express its terroir, or the soil in which it is grown. Most biodynamic wines are certified through an international organization called Demeter, which can be found on the label of the wine bottle.

PART II

Herbs and Other Key Mediterranean Flavors

8

DRIED HERBS
Mint,
Oregano, and Za'atar

In my kitchen, there are only three dried herbs: oregano, mint, and za'atar. I don't like to use most dried herbs because the flavors can be too strong or taste dusty and old. I prefer my herbs fresh.

I included these three dried herbs in this book because, like many spices, they are robust, earthy, and peppery, and they lend warm tones to food. Besides, their flavors evoke the Mediterranean region like nothing else, and they are extremely versatile.

Dried mint, oregano, and za'atar have similar effects on dishes and can be used interchangeably in most cases. These herbs taste stronger, richer, and deeper when dried, and you will notice that in fresh form, they taste strikingly different from their dried counterparts.

All three spices work well with other bold flavors, such as olives; salty feta cheese; vegetable or chicken soups; summer vegetables such as tomatoes, cucumbers, and peppers; on flat breads; and with chicken, beef, lamb, or duck.

DRIED MINT

The flavor of dried mint is warm, earthy, and tea-like and adds a different quality to a dish than the light, refreshing taste of fresh mint. Along with oregano, mint is one of the key dried herbs that makes some Turkish rice dishes, grilled lamb, and beef kebobs taste "Turkish."

There are many different kinds of mint, but spearmint is the most useful for cooking purposes because it doesn't dominate other flavors in a dish. Spearmint is usually the variety used in dried mint. Peppermint has a stronger flavor and tastes somewhat medicinal; it's better used for sweets. The Egyptian mint, which is a spearmint, available at www.kalustyans.com, is excellent; it's deeply herbal and smells like a cross between mint and oregano. Dried mint should look green and not dusty.

Mint is easy to grow—so easy, in fact, that it very quickly can take over your garden. To make your own dried mint, pull out the invasive stems, cut their roots, tie them up into bundles, and hang them upside down in a cool, dry place for a couple of weeks. You can also dry mint in a microwave by laying the leaves on paper towels and cooking them on high in intervals of 20 seconds; the mint is dried when the leaves are crisp to the touch.

Paula Wolfert, author of many Mediterranean cookbooks, heats olive oil gently and then adds sieved dried mint to it. When the mint hits the warm oil, it sizzles. She calls this "mint sizzle," and it's just wonderful drizzled on pastas or grilled meats.

One of my favorite recipes with dried mint is a yogurt soup that I make with toasted pasta or mini raviolis called *manti*. I sprinkle the soup generously with dried mint, and my husband Chris can't get enough of it. See Favorite Yogurt Soup on page 242 for a variation of this delicious and soothing soup using crushed, toasted pasta.

DRIED OREGANO

I finally understood the defining flavor of dried oregano while visiting the small Greek island of Hydra, a short trip from Athens. A man came down from the hillside carrying huge bags of wild oregano that he had foraged and dried himself, and I bought some and brought it home. The aroma was incredible: floral, tea-like, savory, vegetal, and sweet—all at once—and I've never been able to find oregano that compares to it since.

Dried oregano is key in making marinades for grilled meats, tomato-based sauces, and stews. I love to sprinkle it on Greek salads and feta cheese.

Oregano and marjoram are sometimes confused, but oregano is more robust and has rounder leaves. Oregano is peppery and sharp; its flavor is twice as strong as marjoram.

In my opinion, the best dried oregano is Greek, and they call it *rigani*, which means "wild." If you buy dried Greek oregano from a Greek market in bunches on the stems, strip the leaves off, and then follow instructions for sieving dried herbs on page 230.

DRIED HERBS: MINT, OREGANO, AND ZA'ATAR

Za'atar

Some sources maintain that the very green herb called za'atar is a type of thyme (*za'atar*, pronounced zah-tar, means "thyme" in Arabic); though some sources say it's Syrian hyssop (an herb very similar to oregano). Fresh za'atar in the Middle Eastern markets in Watertown, Massachusetts, looks more like summer savory, or a crossing of marjoram, oregano, and thyme. To further confuse matters, za'atar also refers to a blend of the green herb, sesame seeds, and other spices. You can also buy a jar of pickled za'atar that you can chop up and add to salads or soups (available at www.kalustyans.com).

Za'atar blends vary widely in color and spice flavors. For instance, the za'atar blends in Israel and Lebanon are similar to the Jordanian version, but they're not as vividly green. In Syria, the za'atar blends contain more sumac, and sometimes chilies or cumin are added.

You can find za'atar at all Middle Eastern markets, and you can try the different variations and choose your favorite. In this chapter, za'atar means the traditional Jordanian mix of sumac, sesame seeds, salt, and the essential bright green herb itself.

SIEVING DRIED HERBS

I push my dried herbs through a medium-fine sieve to powder the leaves and remove any bits of stem before I use them. Dried herbs store well in an airtight container in a cool, dark place for a couple of months.

RECIPES WITH DRIED MINT, DRIED OREGANO, AND ZA'ATAR

Turkish Baharat Spice Mix for Lamb

In Arabic, *baharat* has two meanings: it refers to this particular spice mix, and it also literally means "flowers and seeds" or more loosely translates to "herbs and spices." Many Arabic spice shops are simply called baharat.

Although it doesn't taste like it, baharat is like Indian curry: it's an exotic spice blend that is packed with diverse aromas–some peppery, some sweet, some pungent– but no one flavor dominates. And there are as many different blends of baharat as there are people who make it: the mixture varies from family to family. Baharat is not hot-spicy, but it conveys all the romantic fragrances and everything that spice is.

I love baharat on grilled mushrooms, in bulgur pilafs, in carrot salads mixed with pine nuts and currants, with cooked winter squash, in tomato sauces, in chickpea soup, and in lamb marinades. Here is Oleana's version of a typical baharat. You can also purchase a good one at www.kalustyans.com. I like their house brand. (See Lamb Steak with Turkish Spices on page 166.)

⌒ᴠ Makes ½ cup ᴠ⌒

---

1 tablespoon ground cinnamon

1 tablespoon ground nutmeg

1 tablespoon ground cumin

1 tablespoon ground coriander seed

2 tablespoons dried, sieved mint (page 230)

2 tablespoons dried, sieved oregano (page 230)

2 tablespoons ground black pepper

4 bay leaves, ground in a spice or coffee grinder

1 teaspoon ground fennel

1 teaspoon ground allspice

1 teaspoon ground cloves

1 tablespoon ground mustard seeds

In a small bowl, combine all the ingredients. Store this spice mixture in an airtight container out of direct light, for up to 2 months.

Kebob Spice Mix

The dried mint makes this spice mix taste very Turkish; it's excellent on any grilled meats, especially beef or lamb. At Oleana, we use it on sirloin, skirt, and rib-eye steaks as well as in ground lamb or beef kebobs, also called *köfte* (see the Ground Beef and Pistachio Kebobs on page 236). The combination of spices in this recipe will also work with any kind of dried bean; it's particularly tasty when added to black bean soup, bean chili, or any other bean soup. Use this spice mix generously.

— Makes ½ cup —

2 tablespoons ground cumin	1 tablespoon Aleppo chilies
2 tablespoons dried, sieved oregano	1 tablespoon black pepper
2 tablespoons dried, sieved mint (page 230)	

In a small bowl, combine all the spices. Store this spice mixture in an airtight container out of direct light, for up to 2 months.

Greek Salad with Winter Vegetables, Apple, and Barrel-Aged Feta Cheese

In Greece, the dish that Americans call Greek salad is called "village salad," and it's made with cucumbers, onions, peppers, olives, tomatoes, and feta. Rarely is any lettuce served.

The key to a great Greek salad lies in the feta and the kalamata olives. It's worth going out of your way to find barrel-aged feta; the barrel-aging process makes it firm but creamy with a nice strong flavor. French feta is creamier, and there are many choices (see page 349), so taste as many as you can and simply choose your favorite. And if you have access to a Greek market, beg them for barrel-aged feta.

Served with Chicken Egg-Lemon Soup (page 51) and some ouzo or raki to sip, this salad is so hearty that you can make a meal out of it. You can cook the cauliflower and Brussels sprouts up to a day ahead of time, but the squash is better cooked and eaten the same day.

SERVES 8 TO 10 AS A FIRST COURSE

1 small to medium buttercup squash
   (about 2 pounds)

2 tablespoons olive oil

1 tablespoon salt plus more to taste

Pepper to taste

Ice cubes

½ head cauliflower, cored and washed

Pinch of baking soda

8 Brussels sprouts, outer leaves trimmed
   and cut in half lengthwise

1 bulb fennel, quartered, cored, tough outer
   layer removed and cut into a ¼- to ½-inch dice

1 Granny Smith apple, cored and cut into
   a ¼- to ½-inch dice

16 kalamata olives, pitted

½ red onion, peeled and finely chopped

2½ tablespoons freshly squeezed lemon juice
   (about 1 large lemon)

4 tablespoons extra-virgin olive oil

2 teaspoons dried, sieved oregano
   (see page 230)

1 pound barrel-aged
   or French feta cheese

1. Preheat the oven to 350°F.

2. Cut the squash in half widthwise and use a small spoon to scoop out the seeds. Slice each half into quarters and then into eighths so that you have 8 wedges of squash. Toss the squash with the 2 tablespoons olive oil on a heavy baking sheet and season well with salt and pepper to taste. Roast the squash in the oven for about 25 minutes, until just tender. Set aside to cool.

3. Prepare a medium bowl of ice water.

4. Bring a 2-quart saucepan of water to a boil over high heat and season with 1 tablespoon of salt.

5. Using a small paring knife or your fingers, break the cauliflower into small florets. Add the cauliflower to the water and boil for 4 minutes, or until it is just tender.

6. Using a slotted spoon, remove the cauliflower from the water and drop it into the ice water. Let it chill for about 3 minutes, drain well, pat dry with paper towels, and set aside.

7. Prepare another medium bowl of ice water.

8. Add a pinch of baking soda to the pot of boiling water and drop the Brussels sprouts in. The baking soda helps keep the Brussels sprouts a nice bright green, but don't add more than a pinch, or they will turn out mushy. Cook them for about 5 minutes, or until they are just tender.

9. Drain the Brussels sprouts and place them in the bowl of ice water to chill for about 5 minutes. Drain well, pat dry with paper towels, and set aside.

10. When the squash is cool enough to handle, remove the skin by placing the wedges skin-side down on a cutting board and running a paring knife between the skin and the squash, staying as close to the skin as possible. Cut the squash into ½-inch chunks and place them in large mixing bowl. You should have about 1½ cups of diced squash.

11. Cut the cores off the Brussels sprouts and break the leaves up with your fingers. Add the leaves and the cauliflower to the mixing bowl with the squash.

12. Add the fennel and the apple to the rest of the vegetables. Stir to combine them and sprinkle the top with the olives.

13. Prepare the vinaigrette in a small mixing bowl: whisk together the onion, lemon juice, extra-virgin olive oil, and oregano. Season with salt and pepper. Let the mixture sit for at least 5 minutes to lightly pickle the onion (it will turn bright pink) before dressing the salad.

14. Toss the vegetables with the vinaigrette and season the salad with salt and pepper.

15. To serve, cut the feta into 8 equal slices. Spoon the salad into 8 salad bowls and top each salad with a slice of feta.

DRIED HERBS: MINT, OREGANO, AND ZA'ATAR

Ground Beef and Pistachio Kebobs

I learned how to make this dish when I visited Gaziantep, Turkey–famous for both its pistachios and kebobs. Not your average meatball, these kebobs are fun to make and packed full of flavor. Try making them with either lamb or beef, or a combination of both. Typical of Arabic cooking is the binding of meat with itself rather than using egg or bread crumbs the way we do for meatballs. The meat is kneaded until the proteins change, creating a creamy consistency that holds together well on a skewer. Egg whites are added not for binding purposes but to give the kebobs some volume and a lighter texture when cooked.

In Turkey, they cook these kebobs over the grill and not directly on it (see the foil propping method in Grilling Tips on page 100). This way, the meat becomes crispy on the outside and light and airy on the inside without getting charred. If you don't have metal skewers, you will want to soak bamboo skewers in water for at least 30 minutes before skewering and grilling.

You can remove the kebobs from the skewers and place them directly on the bread to rest; the bread will collect juices from the meat while your guests decide which condiments to sample. I like to serve the kebobs with thin slices of red onion tossed with sumac (Sumac Onions with Parsley Butter, page 98), Nookie's Pickles (page 280), thick Greek-style yogurt, fresh mint sprigs, pickled hot peppers, chopped fresh tomato, and romaine leaves. Pita or Greek flatbread, traditionally used for gyros, tastes best with this dish.

⌁ Serves 4 ⌁

1 pound ground beef or lamb
(85 percent lean)

2 teaspoons Kebob Spice Mix
(page 233)

1 teaspoon Aleppo chilies

1 roasted red bell pepper, finely chopped or
2 teaspoons of Turkish red pepper paste
(see Resources, page 358)

1 egg white

1 cup toasted and coarsely ground
pistachios (see page 91)

Salt to taste

8 skewers

Four 10-inch pitas, cut in half

1 cup red onions with sumac
(about 1 onion; page 71, optional)

1 cup Greek-style yogurt or
whole-milk plain yogurt

1 cup roughly chopped tomato
(about 1 large tomato)

1 cup roughly chopped romaine leaves
(about 4 large leaves)

1 cup Nookie's Pickles (page 280) optional

8 roughly chopped mint leaves

2.

1. Prepare a charcoal or gas grill (see Grilling Tips, page 100).

2. Knead the ground meat with the kebob spice, chilies, and red pepper in a standing mixer with a paddle attachment (such as a KitchenAid) on medium speed for 5 minutes, until the meat becomes creamy and a little sticky. If you don't have a standing mixer, use a food processor fitted with a metal blade, and carefully push the pulse button on and off until the meat becomes smooth. You can also do this by hand, but it will take much longer.

3. Add the egg white and pistachios and continue to knead the meat with the mixer until the mixture comes together again and resembles a wet dough.
continued

DRIED HERBS: MINT, OREGANO, AND ZA'ATAR

I like to pinch off some meat at this point and
cook it to test the seasoning. Add salt to taste.

4. Shape the meat into eight 2-ounce patties or
   short sausage shapes and press each patty into a
   skewer. Squeeze and shape the köfte into long,
   thin meatballs around the skewers. Set aside.

5. Grill the köfte for 3 to 4 minutes on each side,
   until golden brown and cooked through.

6. Rest the köfte on pita halves. Pass them around
   the table with bowls of sliced red onions
   sprinkled with sumac, yogurt, tomatoes,
   romaine, pickles, and mint leaves.

4.

SPICE: FLAVORS OF THE EASTERN MEDITERRANEAN

Warm Olives with Za'atar

The taste of za'atar makes you want more of it, so use it generously. Sprinkle it heavily over cheese, flatbreads, thick yogurt, and grilled chicken. My favorite za'atar comes from Jordan–it has the brightest flavor and the purest green color–but there are other delicious varieties from Syria and Lebanon as well.

I like to load za'atar onto niçoise olives and then gently warm them up to nibble on as a snack or before a meal. Although they aren't very meaty, these olives have a wonderfully fruity taste that will whet your appetite but won't fill you up.

⌒⌐ SERVES 8 ⌐⌒

---

4 tablespoons extra-virgin olive oil

¾ pound niçoise olives, drained

2 heaping tablespoons za'atar

---

1. Heat the olive oil in a skillet. Add the olives and gently warm them through over low heat.

2. Stir in the za'atar, transfer the olives to a bowl (preferably an olive dish with a lip or edge), and serve them with crusty bread.

Francisco's Manaaeesh (Flatbread with Za'atar)

Francisco Betancourt is a farmer and father of four from Colombia who is the tireless backbone of Oleana's kitchen. After he works at his day job in an Italian restaurant, Francisco comes into Oleana to wash the vegetables and greens, form the köfte (ground lamb kebobs), peel beets, cook mussels, peel and seed tomatoes, make dolmas, shuck peas, peel fava beans, plate desserts, and make manaaeesh.

Manaaeesh is a Lebanese name for a flatbread baked with generous amounts of olive oil, salt, and za'atar. It's not unlike a very thin focaccia. Francisco helped me perfect this recipe.

Manaaeesh is best made and served the same day. You can, however, make the dough a day before and let it rise–lightly oiled and covered with plastic–overnight in the refrigerator. The dough needs at least 4 hours to rise before baking, so it's not something that can be whipped up quickly.

Manaaeesh is a great bread to serve with meals and it's a centerpiece for many mezze-style dishes. It's wonderful alongside Whipped Feta (page 149), Armenian Bean and Walnut Pâté (page 334), Spicy Carrot Purée (page 6), or Hot Buttered Hummus (page 200).

⌁ MAKES ONE 10 × 12-INCH FLATBREAD ⌁

1 package (¼ ounce) active dry yeast	1 teaspoon salt
¾ cup warm water (110°F to 120°F)	4 tablespoons extra-virgin olive oil
¼ cup olive oil	4 tablespoons za'atar
2 cups flour	

1. In the work bowl of an electric mixer, whisk the yeast into the warm water and let the mixture stand for about 10 minutes, or until a gentle foam blooms across the surface. The water must be under 120° F or it will kill the yeast.

2. Whisk in the ¼ cup olive oil and add the flour and ½ teaspoon of the salt.

3. Using the mixer's dough hook or paddle, stir on low speed until the flour is combined and it

forms dough. Increase the speed to medium and knead the dough for 7 to 8 minutes, until the dough is still sticky to the touch but stays on the dough hook in one piece.

4. Lightly oil a large stainless or glass bowl and scoop the dough into it. Cover with plastic and chill for a minimum of 2 hours or overnight; the dough should double in volume.

5. About 2 hours before baking, place the dough and 2 tablespoons extra-virgin olive oil on a heavy baking sheet and cover it with plastic. Let it rest and rise again for 1½ hours at room temperature.

6. Preheat the oven to 375° F.

7. Press the dough onto the baking sheet–using your hands to stretch and pull it into the corners–into a flat 10 × 12-inch rectangle. Make dimples in the dough with your fingertips (this creates little pockets for the oil and za'atar to collect in) and brush the dough with the remaining 2 tablespoons extra-virgin olive oil.

8. Sprinkle the za'atar evenly over the dough, and then sprinkle the whole bread with the remaining ½ teaspoon of salt.

9. Let the dough rest for at least 20 to 30 more minutes, uncovered and at room temperature.

10. Bake for 15 minutes, until golden on the edges and cooked all the way through in the center. Serve warm.

7.

8.

Favorite Yogurt Soup with Toasted Pasta and Dried Mint

Inspired by the classic Armenian or Turkish yogurt soup, this recipe is my absolute favorite comfort food. It's very easy to make and incredibly delicious. It's also now on my husband's top 10 list.

I usually make this recipe with *manti*: tiny raviolis that can be smaller than cashew nuts and are filled with beef or veal and then toasted. In Turkey, the smaller the manti, the more honored the guest. I made manti in Turkey with a group of extremely skilled women, and it took the three of us half a day to prepare the dish. It is truly a labor of love. Now I buy my manti at my favorite Armenian shop: Sevan Bakery in Watertown, Massachusetts (see Resources, page 358), and I try to always have some on hand. At Sevan Bakery, six people gather to make the manti for the week. After toasting the raviolis, they freeze them. It's difficult to find manti in the United States, but if you can, you must try it.

For this recipe, crushed vermicelli works very well as a substitute for manti. I crush the vermicelli into very small pieces and toast them before adding them to the soup–a Turkish technique that doesn't take much time and imparts a rich layer of toasted flavor.

If it's spring and you're feeling fancy, you can also add morel mushrooms and chopped, sautéed ramps. I've also added spinach and even chunks of avocado to make this dish more substantial.

Yogurt soup is hard to pair with wine. Try a beer instead–like Efes Turkish pilsner.

MAKES ABOUT 12 CUPS TO SERVE 6 AS A MEAL OR 8 AS A FIRST COURSE

¼ pound De Cecco brand angel
  hair pasta coils (capelli d'angelo)
  or vermicelli

¼ cup extra-virgin olive oil

8 cups chicken broth,
  preferably homemade

Salt and pepper to taste

3 cups Greek-style yogurt
  or whole-milk plain yogurt

3 egg yolks

1 tablespoon flour

1 tablespoon dried mint

2 teaspoons sumac

1. In a medium mixing bowl, crush the coils of angel hair pasta with your hands, until they are broken into pieces ¼ to ½ inch long.

2. In a medium soup pot (3 quarts or more) over medium heat, warm the olive oil (don't turn up the heat too high or the oil will break down) and add the crushed pasta. Stir the pasta to coat it evenly with the oil and continue to stir for 3 to 4 minutes, until it is toasted and golden brown.

3. Add the chicken broth and increase the heat from medium to high. Bring the soup to a boil and reduce the heat to medium-low. Simmer the soup for 6 to 8 minutes, until the pasta is cooked. Season with salt and pepper.

4. In a medium mixing bowl, combine the yogurt, egg yolks, and flour.

5. Ladle 1 cup of the hot soup into the yogurt mixture, whisking until combined. This tempers the yogurt and egg so that it won't curdle when you add it to the soup. The flour also keeps the yogurt from curdling.

6. Add the yogurt mixture to the soup pot, whisking and continue to whisk on and off for about 5 minutes, until the soup starts to simmer.

7. Ladle the soup into bowls and sprinkle the top with dried mint and sumac. Serve hot.

DRIED HERBS: MINT, OREGANO, AND ZA'ATAR

DISCOVER GREEK WINES

Theresa Paopao, Wine Director at Oleana

Although the Greeks were one of the first civilizations to create wine, they are not the first to spring to mind for most people when choosing wine for dinner. The indigenous grape varieties have names that are not as easy to pronounce as merlot or chardonnay; assyrtiko, agiorgitiko, and xino-mavro don't exactly roll off the tongue. For some, retsina may be the first introduction to Greek wine made from savatiano, rhoditis, or assyrtiko and treated with pine resin—outside Greece, an acquired taste.

Here's a rundown on some of the more prominent Greek grapes.

Agiorgitiko (red) – also known as the grape of St. George, from the Nemea valley in the Peloponnesos, dark berry fruit flavors and oak aging give this wine New World appeal

Assyrtiko (white) – a white grape with high acidity; best known from Santorini

Malagousia (white) – a spicy, aromatic white, possibly related to malvasia

Mandelaria (red) – a very tannic grape from the island of Crete, which makes concentrated, powerful wines

Moscofilero (pink) – comparable to Muscat or Gewürztraminer, this grape makes white or rosé wines with delicate floral aromatics like rose petals

Rhoditis (white) – a spicy, Peloponnesian variety with low sugar and high acidity

Savatiano (white) – commonly used for retsina but also produces fruity, balanced wines

Xinomavro (red) – some think this grape may be related to nebbiolo. Highly acidic with red berry flavors with distinct savory qualities of truffles and leather. Look for Xinomavro from the Naousa region.

Crispy Lemon Chicken with Za'atar

This is an Oleana favorite, and my customers would protest if I took it off the menu. I developed this recipe in my quest to find a chicken recipe that's interesting enough to make people want to order it from the menu or to prepare as a special meal at home.

In the United States, chicken is so mass-produced and inexpensive that we consider it to be a boring, everyday protein. And the flavor isn't terribly exciting either, unless you can find a free-range bird. A chicken that roams freely, eating grass, bugs, nuts, seeds, dark wild greens, herbs, and fallen tree fruits will taste a whole lot better than a chicken that has spent its life in a tiny cage. Natural and organic chickens–often fed grains to fatten them up quickly–are a good alternative if you can't find free-range. "Natural" means the birds haven't been treated with antibiotics or been given steroids. The same is true for organic chickens, and in addition, the feed these birds eat is certified organic.

Deboning and tucking butter and herbs into a chicken and then cooking it under a brick is a classic Tuscan preparation that makes the skin crispy and tight–not flabby or soggy. The brick presses the chicken down to an equal thickness throughout, so the meat cooks evenly and retains its moisture. At Oleana, we debone half a chicken intact, and tuck some of the dark thigh meat around the white breast, which marbles the chicken and enriches the flavor.

If you're daunted about deboning the chicken yourself, your butcher can do it for you. Or you can buy the pieces separately and serve the breast and thigh pieces side by side, as in the variation below.

Don't be shy with the za'atar. Make sure you sprinkle each crispy chicken piece generously with this delicious spice mixture.

Serve this chicken with Turkish Cheese Pancakes (page 343).

The chicken itself pairs wonderfully with a crisp, dry, snappy, and citrusy Assyrtiko from the Greek island of Santorini.

SERVES 4

2 lemons, cut into ⅛-inch slices,
    seeds removed

¾ cup plus 1 tablespoon olive oil

6 tablespoons butter

Salt and pepper to taste

2 whole chickens, cut in half and deboned

2 terra-cotta bricks, like those found
    at a garden store, wrapped 3 times
    in aluminum foil

8 tablespoons za'atar

1. Make the lemon confit. In a small saucepan over very low heat, cook the lemon slices in ¾ cup of the olive oil, slowly and gently (barely simmering) for about 1½ hours, or until soft and jamlike. Drain the oil off and discard because it tastes bitter. Cool for at least 10 minutes and then refrigerate for at least 20 minutes. The confit should be cool before you stuff the chicken; it can be made days ahead if kept covered in the refrigerator.

2. Cut the butter into 6 pieces and then into 12 pieces and then again into 24 pieces so that you have 24 small cubes.

3. Season the chicken with salt and pepper on all sides.

4. Create pockets under the chicken skin on both the thigh and breast with your fingers. Make the pockets as deep as you can without piercing all the way through to the other side.

5. Stuff 6 cubes of butter under the skin in each chicken half and then smear a tablespoon of lemon confit in the pockets. Press down on the skin so the butter and confit distribute evenly. The butter may spread only a little, and that's fine; the heat will melt it and the pressure from the bricks will force the butter to baste the meat as it cooks.

6. Place the chicken skin-side up and fold each half together, pressing the thigh meat up against the breast meat and forming a round shape.

7. In a large sauté pan (about 14 inches), heat 2 cubes of the leftover butter with the remaining 1 tablespoon of olive oil, over high heat. When the butter begins to brown, add the pieces of

chicken, placing them skin-side down into the pan. Be careful not to overcrowd the pan; you will need to cook the chicken in two pans or in two batches. Place the bricks on top of the chicken pieces. It's okay if some chicken sticks out from under the bricks; you can move the bricks around as the chicken cooks.

8. Reduce the heat to medium-high and cook the chicken until it's brown and crispy on one side, for about 8 minutes. Remove the bricks and turn the chicken pieces over. Add the remaining butter pieces to the pan and arrange the bricks on top again. Cook for another 8 to 10 minutes on this side, or until the chicken is just cooked through.

9. Remove the bricks from the pan. When cool, you can remove the first two layers of foil from the bricks and re-wrap them for later use.

10. Place the chicken onto a large platter, skin-side up. Sprinkle each piece generously with za'atar and serve.

☙ Variation

You can also use 4 deboned, skin-on chicken breasts and 4 deboned, skin-on chicken thighs for this recipe, preparing them as above. Although you won't be able to create marbled meat, this variation still makes a delicious chicken dish.

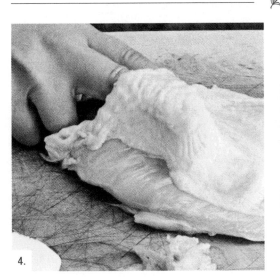

4.

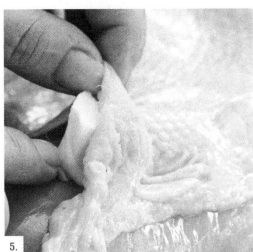

5.

DRIED HERBS: MINT, OREGANO, AND ZA'ATAR

9

FRESH HERB COMBINATIONS
Parsley, Mint, Dill, and Sweet Basil

Every summer, I work with an herb farmer named David Gilson, from the Herb Lyceum in Groton, Massachusetts, who grows beautiful fresh herbs. After much deliberation, I choose what I want to grow for the season, and David starts the herb seedlings in his greenhouse. Once the weather allows, we transplant David's herbs into Oleana's garden patio—an area behind the restaurant where we offer outdoor dining from May through October. We gather the herbs out of our garden and use them fresh in our dishes throughout the summer season, and Oleana's customers enjoy the delicate, romantic herbal breezes that waft through the patio. The romance in fresh herbs is related to their perfume, fragrance, and calming effect. For good reason, summer is our favorite time of the year.

You can use fresh herbs, much like spices, to create exciting and bright layers of flavor in your dishes. The fresh herb combinations in this chapter work particularly well together: they complement one another but each herb retains its individual flavor and doesn't get lost in the mix.

The herbs in this chapter all have a high water content, which makes them bruise easily: they turn black if overchopped or prepared with a dull knife. Parsley and dill are more forgiving and can be finely chopped, but basil and mint need extra care. You don't need to worry about bruising if you're making pesto–fresh herbs ground with nuts and oil–but when cutting mint or basil, it's best to use the French technique called *chiffonade*. Translated from the French, chiffonade means "made of rags," and in culinary terms, it refers to finely cut strips or ribbons of leafy herbs or vegetables. To chiffonade your herbs, stack about 6 leaves together, roll them snugly, and then slice them as thin as you can using a very sharp knife. Parsley and dill are trickier to chiffonade because the leaves are smaller. I usually gather a small handful and scrunch the leaves up, holding them with one hand with loosely curled fingers and slicing them little by little.

PARSLEY

Parsley is the most commonly used herb in cooking because it complements most flavors, adding a bright, clean, green, and almost citrusy taste to food, yet never dominating it. Interestingly, the ancient Greeks never cooked with parsley because it was considered to be a symbol of death; they used it as a funeral herb and fed it to horses. It wasn't used as part of a meal until the Romans discovered that parsley cleaned their breath after feasts of wine and rich food.

There are two types of widely available parsley: flat and curly. Flat, or Italian, parsley looks a bit like celery tops and has a brighter and stronger flavor than curly parsley. Flat parsley has a fuller flavor and gives you more bang for the buck.

Parsley is full of lovely chlorophyll, making it great to add to blended soups or oils to create a bright green color. I like to whip parsley up in the blender with olive oil to make a vivid green oil to drizzle over pasta and soup. It will keep for up to a week if you add a tablet of vitamin C during the blending process. If you want to make a smooth pea soup greener, add a handful of parsley while puréeing.

As the Romans discovered, parsley diminishes breath odor from strong foods like garlic. Garlic and parsley are the perfect complements and work wonderfully in combination on breads, in salads, and with meat dishes. Of course, the famous French snail dish, escargot, would not be the same without this combination added to melted butter.

Parsley lends itself to most soup and sauce bases because it brightens but doesn't dominate other flavors. Combined with mint, parsley is the key ingredient in the Middle Eastern tomato salad called tabouleh.

MINT

This fresh-tasting herb comes in many varieties, each with different flavor tones, including pineapple, apple, lemon, basil, licorice, and ginger. For cooking, I prefer to use plain spearmint, and I always choose leaves that are smooth and narrow rather than crinkly or fuzzy. Peppermint is not used much for cooking but lends its flavor to candies and chewing gums.

In Greek myth, the beautiful nymph Minthes was transformed into a plant by jealous Proserpina, wife of Pluto. Pluto could not undo the spell, but he was able to give the homely plant its delightful fragrance. Ancient Romans used mint to freshen their rooms.

Mint grows wild all over the world, but especially in the warm, dry climates around the Mediterranean. Italians mix mint with garlic and toss them together with roasted baby potatoes. In Arabic cooking, mint is often used to flavor lamb, eggplant, cucumber, and stuffed grape leaves. Turks use fresh mint combined with parsley and dill—a staple Oleana herb blend—in chopped vegetable or bean salads.

Mint pairs particularly well with lamb: the famous green jelly that is traditionally served with roast leg of lamb is a classic.

DILL

The fronds of dill look similar to fennel, but dill is a much stronger herb and has a parsleylike aroma and a hint of anise.

When used modestly, dill is refreshing and can be paired with all sorts of foods—white cheeses, yogurt, white sauces, chicken, fish, eggs, salads, and many vegetable preparations. Dill is classically combined with smoked salmon and capers, and it's perfect with yogurt and cucumber sauces. My favorite herbs to combine with dill are parsley and mint, but dill mixed with a little cilantro or fresh coriander is equally addictive.

Dill is native to the Mediterranean and southern Russia. The Romans regarded dill as a symbol of vitality and used it to decorate the food given to gladiators. Medieval cooks believed it had magical properties of warding off evil and enhancing aphrodisiacs. The word *dill* is believed to have come from the old Norse word "dilla," which means to soothe or lull; the herb was thought to be a digestive with calming effects, and dill tea made from the dried, flowering stems of the herb was given to crying babies. Today, dill is used in many countries, but it's most popular in Scandinavian, Russian, Greek, and Turkish cuisines.

When buying fresh dill, look for bright bunches that don't show any signs of wilting.

SWEET BASIL

To me, the flavor of basil is summer. It's a natural with almost any vegetable, but there's just nothing like the mouthwatering combination of fresh basil and tomatoes, right out of the garden in late August.

Basil thrives in warm climates, and there are many varieties, including purple, cinnamon, black opal, Thai, and holy basil. Sweet basil, with its refreshing clove and anise tones, is the most popular for culinary use. Basil's taste is more subtle than its aroma, which is slightly peppery and minty, so you can use it in large quantities.

Basil is considered a sacred herb in India, and it's been used widely for millennia in Iran, Africa, Egypt, Greece, and Italy. Roman scholars considered basil to be an aphrodisiac; it was given to horses during mating season, and when a lady left a pot of it in a window, it was a signal that her lover was welcome. In Romania, a young man was considered engaged if he accepted a sprig of basil from a young lady.

Basil is now a staple in most Italian cuisines, especially in Liguria, where the precious Genovese basil—as well as pesto—originates. Just past the western outskirts of Genoa, the unique microclimate and the ideal soil favors the growth of this variety of basil, which is especially balanced in terms of taste and aroma. Genovese basil seeds are available through many seed catalogs, including Johnny's Seeds (see Resources, page 358).

I store my fresh basil, roots on, in a glass, with water just covering the roots. If the water touches the leaves, they'll rot quickly. Basil kept like this will last in room temperature for up to a week or more, and it makes your kitchen smell like summer. When basil is refrigerated, it suffers and wilts almost instantly. After all, basil loves heat.

RECIPES WITH FRESH PARSLEY, MINT, DILL, AND SWEET BASIL

Beet Tzatziki

This beet dish is my twist on classic Greek tzatziki, which is traditionally made with cucumbers and is part of every Greek mezze table. The texture of shredded roasted beets is just wonderful with garlic and yogurt.

There are three widely available beet varieties: red, golden, and candy-striped. Red beets work in this recipe, but they're intense, and I prefer to use a subtler beet. Red beets are vivid red and bleed their color easily, which makes for stained hands during peeling. They also have a strong, earthy flavor and tend to scare beet haters away. Golden beets have a sweet, subtle, honeylike flavor that turns beet haters into beet lovers. My favorite variety the are candy-striped beets, called *chioggia* in Italian, with beautiful pink and white rings that swirl throughout.

I like to roast rather than boil my beets because roasting intensifies the sugars and makes for a more richly flavored dish. Boiling beets takes about half as much time as roasting, however, and it's fine to cook them that way if you're pressed for time. I've listed directions for both methods below.

If you want to make traditional tzatziki, use shredded cucumber instead of beets, and drain the water out by squeezing small amounts between the palms of your hands before mixing it with the rest of the ingredients.

The choice of yogurt is crucial in this recipe; it's best to use Greek-style yogurt, which is thicker and creamier than American brands. See page 331 for yogurt tips.

This beet tzatziki is wonderful served with Spinach Falafel (page 185) or grilled meats. It's great as one of many mezze or antipasti as a salad or vegetable course, served with Cranberry Beans Stewed with Tomato and Cinnamon (page 113) and Spinach Bundles with Warm Goat Cheese (page 180). It makes the perfect accompaniment for a light summer lunch with grilled salmon. And served with vegetable crudités and pita bread, it also works as an intriguing hors d'oeuvre.

⁓ MAKES 2½ CUPS ⁓

For the Beets

1 cup cooked, shredded candy-striped, golden, or red beets (about 4–5 golf ball-size beets)

Vegetable oil

Salt and pepper to taste

To Make Roasted Beets

1. Preheat the oven to 400° F.

2. Wash the beets.

3. Trim the root ends off of the beets so that they stand without rolling around.

4. Rub the beets with a little vegetable oil and place them in a small, heavy roasting pan or skillet. Sprinkle them with salt and pepper to taste, pour in ½ cup water, and cover them twice with foil. Four golf ball–size beets should take 45 minutes to roast. They should be tender when poked with a fork.

5. When cool enough to handle, rub the skins off with a paper towel or clean kitchen towel.

6. Grate the beets using the large holes of a box grater.

To Make Boiled Beets

1. Bring a medium saucepan of water to a boil over high heat. You should be able to fit 4 beets, covered with water, into the pan easily.

2. Wash the beets.

3. Trim the root ends off of the beets so that they stand without rolling around.

4. Drop the beets into the boiling water and turn the heat down to medium. Simmer for about 20 minutes, until the beets are tender when poked with a fork. Drain them into a colander.

5. When cool enough to handle, rub the skins off with a paper towel or clean kitchen towel.

6. Grate the beets using the large holes of a box grater.

To Make the Tzatziki

1. Place the garlic into a medium mixing bowl with the lemon juice and salt. Let it stand for about 10 minutes. This takes some of the heat out of the raw garlic.

2. Stir in the yogurt, olive oil, and black pepper.

3. Fold in the shredded beets and dill, and reseason with salt and pepper to taste if necessary. Serve the beets cold or at room temperature.

Grilled Peach and Pepper Salad

This recipe is a favorite in late summer, when peaches are best. I first tasted this combination in a small taverna outside Athens, where they served slices of roasted red pepper and grilled peaches spiced with cumin seed. I like to use fresh herbs to heighten the smoky flavors and bring out the brightness of the pepper and sweet peach.

It's perfect paired with Fried Haloumi Cheese (page 10) and is also wonderful with grilled swordfish. You also can serve this as a mezze or antipasti course with the Cranberry Beans on page 113 and/or with crumbled feta or blue cheese.

A glass of chilled Arneis, a white wine from the Piedmonte region which sometimes has a little fizz, is delicious with this salad. *Arneis* in the Piedmonte dialect means "a difficult and demanding person"–an appropriate name for a grape which is difficult to properly vinify. Arneis usually has a slight licorice flavor with an aroma of apple and pear.

SERVES 4 AS A MEZZE OR ANTIPASTI COURSE

2 ripe peaches, unpeeled	Salt and pepper to taste
1 teaspoon freshly squeezed lemon juice (about ⅛ lemon)	1 tablespoon fresh chopped dill
	1 tablespoon fresh chopped parsley
2 tablespoons extra-virgin olive oil	1 tablespoon fresh chopped mint
2 red bell peppers, roasted, peeled, and seeded (see page 97)	¼ to ½ teaspoon Aleppo chilies

1. Cut the peaches in half and remove the pits. Cut each half into halves again, and then each quarter into 4, making 16 pieces total. Toss the peaches with ½ teaspoon of the lemon juice and 1 teaspoon of the olive oil and set aside.

2. Cut each pepper in the same fashion as the peaches, making 16 pepper strips. Scrape off any remaining seeds or black skin with the back of a knife. Do not wash the peppers or you will wash away their natural oils and much of their flavor.

3. Place the pepper strips in a small mixing bowl and toss them with the remaining ½ teaspoon lemon juice and 2 teaspoons of the olive oil. Season them with salt and pepper and set aside.

4. Heat a medium nonstick pan over medium-high heat, until hot. Sear the peach slices on one side until they begin to caramelize and turn golden brown, about 2 minutes. Turn the slices over and brown the other side. Remove them from the pan immediately and place them back into the mixing bowl. If the skins bother you, you can remove them at this point. They should come off easily and leave a beautiful pink stain on the peach pieces.

5. Toss the peaches carefully, without breaking them up too much, with the remaining tablespoon of olive oil, the herbs, pepper slices, and Aleppo chilies.

6. Serve at room temperature arranged on a platter or in a glass serving bowl.

❧ Variation

You can grill the peaches in halves on a charcoal grill (see Grilling Tips, page 100) for about 4 minutes on each side. Remove the skins when the peaches are cool enough to handle and slice each half into quarters, giving you 8 pieces.

Chopped Romaine and Cucumber Salad with Yogurt Dressing

This crunchy, flavor-packed salad is inspired by the finely shredded romaine salads I ate in Greece, and is one of the most requested recipes at Oleana. The magic comes from the combination of the fresh parsley, dill, and mint. It's worth every bit of labor and love that goes into it.

This salad is richer than a simple green salad, so portions can be modest. Serve it with Deviled Eggs with Tuna and Black Olives (page 203) for a terrific light lunch and drink a Soave from Northern Italy.

~ SERVES 4 ~

For the Salad

1 large head of romaine, blemished outer leaves removed

1 English cucumber

¾ cup walnut halves, lightly toasted (See page 91)

1 cup roughly chopped arugula (about 1 small bunch), washed and dried well

1 tablespoon chopped fresh flat-leaf parsley

2 tablespoons chopped fresh dill

1 tablespoon chopped fresh mint

Salt and fresh ground black pepper to taste

¼ teaspoon Aleppo chilies

For the Yogurt Dressing

1 teaspoon finely minced garlic (about 1 large clove)

2 tablespoons freshly squeezed lemon juice (about ½ lemon)

1 tablespoon champagne or chardonnay vinegar (avoid acidic brands like Heinz)

1½ teaspoons sugar

½ cup Greek-style, whole-milk plain, or sheep's-milk yogurt

5 tablespoons extra-virgin olive oil

Salt and freshly ground pepper to taste

To Make the Salad

1. Wash the romaine leaves. Be careful to dry the greens thoroughly, or the dressing won't cling. Chop the romaine into ¼-inch shreds and place them in a large salad bowl.

2. Peel the cucumber and cut it in half lengthwise. Spoon out the seeds. Cut each half in half widthwise, making four long pieces, and grate the cucumber on the large holes of a box grater. Squeeze out any excess water with your hands.

3. Add the cucumber to the romaine. Add the walnuts, arugula, and herbs, and set aside or keep cold until you're ready to toss and serve.

To Make the Dressing

1. Make the dressing by combining the garlic with the lemon, vinegar, and sugar in a small mixing bowl. Let this mixture sit for at least 10 minutes to soften the sharpness of the raw garlic.

2. Finish the dressing by whisking in the yogurt and then the olive oil, little by little. Season with salt and pepper.

3. Just before serving, add half the dressing to the salad, season with salt and black pepper, and toss. Romaine is thick and crunchy and needs more dressing than a delicate lettuce. Taste the salad, and if the dressing's too light, spoon on more. Sprinkle with Aleppo chilies and serve immediately.

🌿 Mincing Garlic Very Finely without a Press

Peel the garlic and cut the clove in half lengthwise. Remove any sprout or germ because it's not digestible and can be a little bitter. Place the flat side of the garlic down on a cutting board and mince it, using the back of a chef's knife (the exact opposite side from the blade side)–smashing and chopping and crushing all at the same time. Then go back over the garlic with the sharp side of the knife to make an even finer mince.

Sliced Summer Tomatoes with Basil and Walnut Tabouleh

Tabouleh is an herb and bulgur salad popular in many eastern Mediterranean countries. I like to use fine bulgur instead of coarse because I find that fine bulgur absorbs more flavor and is softer and less chewy. Most Arabic tabouleh is made with lots of mint and parsley and a little bulgur to bind the herbs. My version showcases the bounty of a late-summer harvest: it bursts with the flavors of basil, tomatoes, and peppers fresh from the garden.

This healthful dish is perfect for a light lunch on its own or as a salad before a main course with dinner.

It's lovely served with a glass of Ligurian Vermintino. This wine is zesty and light and has a slightly savory quality. Pesto is a specialty of Liguria, and so it appropriately works well with these flavors.

⌐ SERVES 6 ⌐

¼ cup freshly squeezed lemon juice
(about 1 lemon)

¼ cup finely minced red onion
(about ½ small onion)

2 teaspoons finely minced garlic
(about 2 large cloves)

Pinch of salt plus more to taste

½ cup fine bulgur

2 bunches fresh sweet basil, preferably
Genovese variety, leaves only, washed,
(about 38 to 40 leaves)

2 tablespoons chopped fresh flat-leaf parsley

1 cup lightly toasted walnuts plus a few pieces
for garnish (see page 91)

¾ cup extra-virgin olive oil

Pepper to taste

2 large or 3 medium heirloom tomatoes
(see page 269) or another good vine-ripened
tomato, such as beefsteak

1. In a small mixing bowl, combine the lemon juice with the onion, garlic, and pinch of salt. Let the mixture sit for about 5 minutes, until the rawness of the onion softens and it turns pink.

2. Stir in the bulgur, adding 2 tablespoons of warm water. Let this stand for 10 minutes, until the bulgur swells and it is tender, not crunchy.

3. Using a food processor fitted with a metal blade, chop the basil leaves with the parsley, 1 cup walnuts, and the olive oil until the mixture is a bright green paste. Season with salt and pepper.

4. Stir in the bulgur mixture until well combined. Let this sit for 5 minutes to give the bulgur a chance to bind and absorb the flavors.

5. Just before serving, use a sharp or serrated knife to cut the tomatoes across the top into 16 round slices, about ½ inch thick. Capture any juices that run off the tomatoes to stir into the tabouleh.

6. Arrange the tabouleh in an even layer on the bottom of a large serving platter, spreading it thin and even with a knife or spatula. Top the tabouleh with the tomato slices in an even layer, slightly overlapped. Sprinkle the tomatoes with salt and pepper and top them with a few crushed walnut pieces. Serve immediately at room temperature.

Jerusalem-Style Carrot Salad with Hot Goat Cheese Crottin

I was inspired to create this dish at the Casablanca restaurant in Cambridge by the many Jewish recipes that combine carrots and pine nuts. It's also a variation on a salad I made in cooking school in France, showing off the contrast between bright herbs, sweet carrots, and bold garlic. In France, I didn't include pine nuts, but I like to add them to give this salad a Middle Eastern flair.

This salad is great any time of the year, but make sure you can find good-tasting carrots. They should be crisp and sweet and bright orange, with no black spots or rot.

You will also want to find aged goat cheese for this recipe, because it is firmer than young goat cheese and works well for pan frying. I like crottin de Chavignol, which is made in France. The name can pose a problem, since *crottin* literally means "horse dung" (the cheese is shaped into two-ounce mounds that bear an unfortunate resemblance to their name), but it is delicious. You can find goat cheese crottin in specialty cheese shops or online at www.zingermans.com.

Try drinking a Bianco di Custoza from the Veneto region of Italy with this dish. It's a white blend, composed primarily of Garganega with a crisp, dry, light result that has green qualities and pairs well with most vegetable dishes.

—∿ SERVES 4 ∿—

1 heaping teaspoon finely chopped garlic (about 1 large clove)

¼ cup freshly squeezed lemon juice (about ½ lemon)

1 tablespoon white wine vinegar

Pinch of salt plus more to taste

Pinch of sugar

1 tablespoon Greek-style or plain whole-milk yogurt

4 tablespoons extra-virgin olive oil

Pepper to taste

2 cups peeled carrots, grated on the large holes of a box grater (about 3 medium carrots)

4 tablespoon pine nuts, lightly toasted (see page 91)	4 goat cheese crottin de Chavignol
	½ cup flour
1 tablespoon chopped dresh flat-leaf parsley	1 egg, beaten with 2 tablespoons milk or water
1 tablespoon chopped fresh mint	2 tablespoons olive oil
2 tablespoons chopped fresh dill	Toasted pita chips (page 122)

1. In a small stainless steel or glass mixing bowl, let the garlic sit with the lemon juice, vinegar, a pinch of salt, and the sugar for about 5 minutes to soften the sharpness of the raw garlic.

2. Slowly whisk in the yogurt and 4 tablespoons extra-virgin olive oil. Season with salt and pepper.

3. In a large mixing bowl, combine the carrots, pine nuts, and herbs. Stir in the yogurt dressing and season with salt and pepper. Let this stand for about 10 minutes to let the flavors marry.

4. Preheat the oven to 200°F for keeping the crottin warm.

5. Split each crottin in half, widthwise, to make 8 pieces. Roll the cheese in the flour, and shake off any excess. Dunk the floured cheese into the egg mixture and roll the cheese in flour again,

shaking off any excess. Repeat this process for all 8 pieces of cheese so that they are lightly coated and ready for frying.

6. Heat the 2 tablespoons of olive oil in a large sauté pan, over medium heat. When the oil is hot, add the goat cheese and cook for about 4 minutes on each side, until the cheese is golden brown. Remove the cheese from the heat. Keep the crottin warm by covering them or placing the pieces in a very low oven (200°F).

7. Just before serving, divide the carrot salad onto 4 small salad plates. Top each pile of carrot salad with 2 pieces of hot goat cheese crottin and serve immediately, so that the cheese is warm and soft inside and can melt over the carrots as it's split into and eaten. Serve with pita chips to pass around.

Fatoush: Chopped Vegetable Salad with Crispy Pita, Yogurt, and Tahini

Served throughout the Middle East in hundreds of variations, *fatoush*, which means "moistened bread" in Arabic, is a wonderfully healthful tossed salad made with chopped vegetables and toasted or fried crushed flatbread. Fatoush is great to serve when you want to make salad a more substantial part of a meal, especially in the summertime, with the bounty of fresh garden vegetables.

Most traditional fatoush are made with romaine, but I leave that out and focus on the fresh chopped tomatoes, peppers, onions, and radishes. You can add other crunchy vegetables, like fresh fennel and even green beans or cauliflower. Winter versions could include endives or other bitter greens.

In the summer, when purslane—yes, that invasive weed—is thriving, I like to add the fresh leaves to my fatoush. Purslane is praised all over the eastern Mediterranean for its crunchy texture and thick leaves that hold up in a salad without wilting too quickly. Purslane is also the most heart-healthy green you can eat; it contains beneficial omega-3 fatty acids and is a good source for essential amino acids and noradrenaline. You can find purslane in Middle Eastern markets during the summer months or even in your own backyard. It's not a good idea to forage for purslane in an urban area, though, because the soils are usually highly contaminated. If you know a farmer, ask about purslane and he will be overjoyed to sell some of his weeds—or even give them away.

Since the bread soaks up the delicious juices from the chopped vegetables and tomato, the key to a good fatoush is in crisping up the pita so that it won't get soggy or mushy but will be slightly chewy after sitting for 10 minutes. I also like to make a thick yogurt and tahini sauce and serve it underneath the chopped salad; it's a rich and creamy surprise at the bottom of the bowl.

I sprinkle the top with a little sumac to brighten the lemon flavor even more. The lemon vinaigrette makes as excellent dressing for any green salad.

A cold pilsner goes perfectly with this fatoush.

—◠ SERVES 8 ◡—

¼ cup tahini (see recipe note on page 17; mix it well before measuring)

1 cup Greek-style or plain whole-milk yogurt

½ teaspoon plus 1 tablespoon freshly squeezed lemon juice (about ½ lemon)

Salt and pepper to taste

2 tablespoons Spanish sherry vinegar

Zest of ½ lemon

¼ teaspoon sugar

1 teaspoon Dijon mustard

⅓ cup extra-virgin olive oil

2 tomatoes (any heirloom variety or beefsteak) or 24 cherry tomatoes

1 English cucumber or 2 Lebanese cucumbers (available at Middle Eastern markets)

1 green bell pepper

4 radishes

¼ cup finely minced red onion (about ½ small)

¼ cup chopped fresh parsley

2 tablespoons chopped fresh mint

2 tablespoons chopped fresh dill

1 small bunch purslane or arugula or ½ head romaine, washed, thick stems removed, and dried thoroughly

2 cups toasted pita chips (page 122)

2 teaspoons sumac

1. Make the tahini sauce by combining the tahini, yogurt, and ½ teaspoon of the lemon juice in a small mixing bowl and whisking until smooth and creamy. Season it with salt and pepper and set it aside.

2. Make the vinaigrette by combining the vinegar, the remaining 1 tablespoon lemon juice, lemon zest, sugar, and Dijon mustard in a small mixing bowl. Whisk in the olive oil, little by little in a slow, steady stream, until the vinaigrette thickens or emulsifies. Season the vinaigrette with salt and pepper and set it aside.

3. Chop the tomatoes into ½-inch cubes or split the cherry tomatoes in half and place them in a large mixing bowl.

4. Peel the cucumber and split it in half lengthwise. Remove the seeds by scraping them out of the middle with a small teaspoon. Cut the cucumber into ½-inch slices, and then chop them into a ½-inch dice. Add the cucumber to the mixing bowl with the tomatoes.

continued

PARSLEY, MİNT, DİLL, AND SWEET BASİL

5. Cut the green pepper in half and then in quarters. Remove the seeds and ribs and slice each quarter into ½-inch strips. Chop each strip into a ½-inch dice and add them to the cucumber and tomato.

6. Cut the tops and bottoms off of the radishes so they rest on a cutting surface without rocking. Slice them in half and then into quarters. Slice each quarter in half so that you have a ½-inch dice, and add them to the bowl of vegetables.

7. Stir in the onion and the herbs and season with salt and pepper.

8. Chop the greens into ½-inch shreds and add them to the salad.

9. Crush the pita bread with your hands so that you have bits of pita about the same size as the chopped vegetables.

10. About 10 minutes before serving, toss the vegetable salad with the vinaigrette and crushed pita and reseason the salad with salt and pepper.

11. Place 2 tablespoons of the tahini sauce on the bottom of each salad plate or bowl and top with the fatoush. Sprinkle ¼ teaspoon of sumac over each salad and serve.

BEAUJOLAIS VERSUS BEAUJOLAIS NOUVEAU

Theresa Paopao, Wine Director at Oleana

Gamay from Beaujolais is a versatile wine that pairs beautifully with many dishes. Many people are familiar with Beaujolais Nouveau, which is very different from the other wines coming from this region. Beaujolais Nouveau is more of a celebration than a serious style of wine. It's always the first wine of the current harvest, usually only 2 months old, and always released on the third Thursday of November. It's a guarantee that around the world people are drinking fresh and juicy Beaujolais Nouveau on that Thursday. They drink this juice to taste the grapes of this year and predict the year's vintage as great, good, or fair. The more substantial wines of Beaujolais Superieur AC and Beaujolais-village AC are released the following spring, and these are the wines to pair with food.

Eggplant Soufflé

Each summer from late July through September, when my husband Chris harvests eggplant, I celebrate by making this delicious soufflé. Eggplant is a Mediterranean staple, and it grows there in some regions year-round. But for most of the year in New England, eggplant has to travel a long way to get to us, and the miles and travel time make the flesh flabby and bitter. We compensate for that by salting the eggplant after cutting it, letting it weep away some of the bitterness, and then wiping it dry just before cooking. With farm-fresh eggplant, there is no need for salting and wiping. The flesh of freshly harvested eggplant is bone-white, sweet, and creamy, and its blackish-purple skin is tight and super shiny.

I love this light and creamy preparation, which never fails to turn skeptics into eggplant lovers. In making a good soufflé, you'll need a buttered and floured soufflé dish (or eight 6-ounce ramekins) and a thick eggplant base into which you'll fold the whites. You can make the eggplant base up to 3 days before making the soufflé.

At Oleana, we serve this soufflé with Baby Sole with Crab and Raki, an anisette-flavored liqueur (page 270).

⌐ MAKES 1 LARGE OR EIGHT 6-OUNCE SOUFFLÉS TO SERVE 8 ⌐

2 large black bell eggplants

¼ cup salt plus more to taste

Pepper to taste

1 cup milk

Peeled outer layer of 1 onion,
  stuck with 2 cloves

1 bay leaf

4 tablespoons butter plus
  3 tablespoons softened butter

¼ cup plus 5 tablespoons flour

Freshly grated nutmeg to taste

½ cup grated kasseri cheese or
  Asiago cheese (page 206)

½ cup chopped fresh dill

4 eggs, separated

1. Trim the top and bottom off of each eggplant so that they can stand on a cutting surface. Peel each eggplant with a vegetable peeler and slice the flesh into 2-inch chunks.

2. Bring a large saucepan of water to a boil and add the ¼ cup of salt. Reduce the heat to medium-high and cook the eggplant for about 15 minutes, until soft and tender when squeezed with a pair of tongs. Drain the eggplant immediately in a colander.

3. Using a food processor fitted with a metal blade, puree the eggplant until smooth. Season the eggplant puree with salt and pepper; it may not need much salt because of the salty cooking water. You should have about 2½ cups of puree. Set it aside.

4. In a small saucepan, over medium-high heat, bring the milk to a boil with the onion and bay leaf. Turn off the heat and let it stand at least 10 minutes, to infuse the milk with flavor. Remove the onion and bay leaf.

5. In another small saucepan, over medium-high heat, melt 4 tablespoons of the butter until it starts to foam. Whisk in ¼ cup plus 1 tablespoon of the flour. Cook for 2 to 3 minutes, whisking, until the mixture is a golden brown color, but not dark.

6. Add the hot milk and whisk vigorously. At this point, the mixture should be thick, like dough

(this will bind the eggplant). Season the thick white sauce with nutmeg and salt and pepper.

7. Stir in the kasseri cheese, dill, and egg yolks.

8. Combine the white sauce with the eggplant purée.

9. Preheat the oven to 400° F.

10. Using a large whisk and large mixing bowl or an electric mixer, beat the egg whites until stiff peaks form.

11. Fold the egg whites into the eggplant mixture (see page 135). Set the this aside while preparing the soufflé dishes.

12. Butter eight 6-ounce soufflé dishes or one 1-quart soufflé dish evenly with the 3 tablespoons softened butter. Dust each dish or the large dish with the remaining 4 tablespoons flour and shake out any excess.

13. Fill each small dish or the large dish ¾ of the way up to the top with the eggplant soufflé mixture and bake for about 20 minutes, until golden brown and tall. The soufflé should be a little soft in the middle but not soupy.

14. Serve the soufflé immediately, before it falls (it will fall after about 6 minutes).

Istanbul-Style Artichokes

My good friend Ferda Erdinc, who owns Istanbul's Zencefil restaurant, taught me how to make this traditional Turkish specialty. One spring during artichoke season, Ferda and I were walking down the streets of the Jewish neighborhood in Istanbul, where vendors had their artichoke carts out on corners. Their giant wheelbarrows overflowed with these gorgeous thistles, and we couldn't help but buy a few. We watched the vendor clean them for us right there, rubbing them with a little lemon to keep them from browning on the way home.

Ferda prepared this recipe in her home kitchen that evening, and we ate them with a crispy tomato-rice dish. The artichokes can be served as part of a meal with fish or red meat or as one of many mezze before a meal.

⌁ MAKES 6 ARTICHOKES ⌁

6 whole artichokes	1 cup extra-virgin olive oil
Salt and pepper to taste	1 cup dry white wine
2 tablespoons flour	12 cloves garlic, peeled and cut in half
¼ cup honey	4 scallions, root ends trimmed and finely chopped
¼ cup freshly squeezed lemon juice (about ½ lemon)	¼ cup chopped fresh dill

1. Preheat the oven to 375° F.

2. Trim the stem end halfway off of each artichoke with a serrated knife, and then cut the top third of each artichoke off. Pull off the dark green outer leaves with your fingers, stopping when you can see the tender yellow leaves.

3. With a paring knife, clean and shape the base of the artichoke by trimming it down and removing most of the dark green color. You'll want to keep the shape of the artichoke but pare it down uniformly.

continued

4. Split each artichoke in half lengthwise and remove the fuzzy insides by scraping them out with a small teaspoon.

5. Season both sides of each artichoke with salt and pepper and then place the artichokes cut-side down in a heavy roasting pan or Pyrex dish.

6. In a small mixing bowl, whisk the flour with the honey, lemon juice, and olive oil and pour this mixture over the artichokes.

7. Add the wine and garlic to the pan and cover it tightly twice with foil.

8. Bake the artichokes for 30 to 40 minutes, until they are cooked through. Some of the liquid will evaporate and slightly glaze each artichoke.

9. Sprinkle the artichokes with scallions and dill and serve them warm or at room temperature with any extra braising liquid for dipping and extra salt and pepper.

REAL TOMATOES

I'm excited that after years of tasteless, pale, and uniform tomatoes, farmers are growing real tomatoes again. Tomatoes stopped being real tomatoes at some point in the 1950s, when agribusiness and food transportation became priorities in the United States. Farmers started growing new hybrid tomato varieties throughout the country, because they were consistent in size and shape and could be shipped cross-country without suffering. But in this process, the best features of tomatoes–tender skin, juicy flesh, and burst-in-your-mouth flavor–were lost. Thank goodness that some farmers are now starting to reverse that trend, planting beautiful, mouthwatering tomatoes of all colors, sizes, and shapes.

The term *heirloom* refers to many fruits, vegetables, and grains, including beans, apples, squash, wheat, and tomatoes. Heirlooms are open-pollinated plants (non-hybrids) that were bred over generations for qualities such as flavor and viability in local growing conditions. Heirloom varieties usually have a history or folklore of their own.

Farmers charge more for heirloom tomatoes–up to $8 apiece in some markets– because of their low yield and because they are highly perishable. But those who have tasted an heirloom tomato know they are worth every cent.

There are many heirloom varieties, so ask to taste them all and choose the ones you like best. For flavor, I like brandywine tomatoes; for color and juiciness, I like German Johnson; and for acidity, I like Valencia. All three of these contain a lot of water, and so they're best for eating raw or making gazpacho. They're also delicious in flavoring rice and bulgur, and I make a tomato purée for those dishes, using renowned Mediterranean food expert and author Paula Wolfert's technique. I split the tomato in half and remove as many seeds as possible with a small spoon. Then I hold the tomato half in one hand and, with the cut side facing out toward the large holes of a box grater, I grate the tomato until there's nothing left but skin. Finally, I strain out the water and add the purée to risotto, pilaf, and pasta dishes.

Don't refrigerate your tomatoes unless they are overripe. Refrigeration can change a tomato's texture, making it slightly mealy, and can alter its flavor and reduce its fragrance.

Baby Sole with Crab and Raki

We've had this elegant dish on the menu at Oleana since we opened in the winter of 2001. I was inspired to create it after I had a delicious meal at a fish restaurant on the Asian side of Istanbul, where I dined on creamy eggplant with crab that was broiled with raki. I also sipped on raki as I ate, and discovered that the liqueur matches perfectly with the flavors of eggplant and crab.

Raki, also called *Arak*, is a fennel-flavored liqueur similar to Greek ouzo that brings out the wonderful flavors in this dish but won't overwhelm it. If raki is unavailable, you can substitute ouzo or even the French pastis or pernod. If raki or ouzo doesn't appeal to you for sipping, try a clean pinot gris from Oregon, with ripe stone fruit flavors.

Serve Eggplant Soufflé (page 265) with this delicate fish dish.

⌒ᴧ SERVES 6 ᴧ⌒

1 cup heavy cream	Salt and pepper to taste
½ pound Maine or Dungeness crabmeat	Six 4- to 5-ounce sole or flounder fillets, boned and skinned
1 plum tomato, quartered and seeds removed	
1 tablespoon chopped fresh parsley	1¾ to 2 cups fish fumet (page 161)
1 tablespoon chopped fresh mint	½ cup raki or ouzo
1 tablespoon chopped fresh dill	4 tablespoons butter

1. Preheat the oven to 375° F.

2. In a small heavy saucepan, over medium heat, bring the cream to a boil and reduce the heat to low. Simmer for about 12 minutes, until the cream is thick and reduced by half.

3. Meanwhile, drain the crabmeat in a colander and press on it, extracting as much water as possible without tearing up the meat.

4. Chop the tomato into a small dice and place it in a medium mixing bowl with the crabmeat.

5. Add the fresh herbs and gently stir in the cream, seasoning the mixture with salt and pepper. The thick cream should bind the crabmeat but not make it soupy or too creamy.

6. Season both sides of the fillets with salt and pepper and place them; skin-side up, into a baking dish or roasting pan.

7. Place 2 to 3 tablespoons of the crab mixture on the bottom third of each fillet and roll the fillet over and around the crab mixture, making 6 roulades. Make sure the roulades are tightly rolled for a nice presentation.

8. Add the fish fumet and raki to the pan and bake the fish for 16 to 18 minutes, until it is just cooked through.

9. Remove the fish from the baking dish and set it aside under foil to keep it warm. Reserve your pan juices in a small saucepan.

10. Just before serving, heat the saucepan with pan juices over high heat. Boil the juices until they reduce by a little more than half and are slightly thickened and concentrated, 12 to 15 minutes. Reduce the heat to medium-low and slowly whisk in the butter, 1 tablespoon at a time. When the butter is incorporated, remove the saucepan from the heat and season the sauce with salt and pepper.

11. Pour the sauce over the fish and serve immediately. You can also pass the sauce around the table in a gravy pitcher for guests to pour themselves.

Trout Spanakopitta with Avocado and Salmon Roe

This dish is a fun, modern twist on two classic Greek mezze: spanakopitta and taramasalata. *Spanakopitta* means "spinach pie" in Greek, and instead of phyllo filled with the traditional spinach and feta cheese, I like to fill rainbow trout with a creamy spinach mixture, seasoned with plenty of fresh dill. Crisping the trout skin as much as possible mimics the crisp and flaky pastry used in traditional spanakopitta.

Taramasalata is a potato purée with carp roe that is smeared on pita bread and eaten before a meal. I like to make the purée with avocado and stud it with little pink salmon eggs. Each one bursts a little sea salt into a mouthful of creamy, rich avocado.

Gamay is perfect for this dish, with its fruity notes of cherries and black pepper spices. The tannins are low and the high acidity complements the richness of the trout. Look for a Beaujolais (see page 264) from the villages of Julienas, Chenas, Morgan, or Moulin a Vent. These provide the deepest, most aromatic red.

⌐∿ SERVES 6 ∿⌐

Ice cubes	½ cup feta
Salt and pepper to taste	1 egg
2 pounds spinach, large stems removed and washed	½ cup Greek-style or plain whole-milk yogurt
1 bulb fennel	6 rainbow trout, boned but left whole (6 to 8 ounces each)
6 tablespoons olive oil	2 avocados, peeled, halved, and scooped out
1 onion, finely chopped	1 tablespoon freshly squeezed lemon juice (about ½ lemon)
2 teaspoons finely chopped garlic (about 2 large cloves)	1 cup flour
2 tablespoons chopped fresh dill	5 tablespoons brown butter (page 108)
2 scallions, minced	4 teaspoons salmon roe or caviar
1 teaspoon ouzo or raki (optional)	

1. Prepare a medium mixing bowl with ice water.

2. In a large saucepan, bring 4 quarts of water to a boil. Add salt. Add the spinach and cook until wilted and tender, 1 to 2 minutes. Drain the spinach into a colander and then set it in a bowl of ice water to shock and cool it quickly.

3. Drain the spinach into the colander again and squeeze out as much water as possible with your hands. Squeezing small amounts at a time works best. Roughly chop the spinach and set aside.

4. Trim off the long fennel fronds and remove the tough outer layer. Cut the fennel into quarters and remove the core. Slice the fennel lengthwise and then chop it into to a fine dice.

5. In a medium skillet over medium-high heat, heat 1 tablespoon of the olive oil and add the onion and fennel. Cook for 4 to 6 minutes on medium-low heat, until the onion is translucent. Stir in 1½ teaspoons of the garlic and all of the spinach and cook for 5 minutes more.

6. Place this mixture in a medium mixing bowl and stir in the dill, scallions, and ouzo (if using).

7. Using a food processor fitted with a metal blade, purée the feta, egg, and ¼ cup of the yogurt. Stir this into the spinach mixture and season with salt and pepper.

8. Remove the heads from the trout and lay them open with the tails toward you, on a work surface. Season each fillet with salt and pepper.

9. On the top half of each fillet, spread ½ cup of the spinach mixture. Fold the fillets in half the short way, forming rectangles. Set aside.

10. Using a food processor fitted with a metal blade, purée the avocados with the remaining ½ teaspoon garlic and ¼ cup yogurt, the lemon juice, and 2 tablespoons of the olive oil, until smooth and creamy. Season with salt and pepper. Set aside.

11. Preheat the oven to 350° F.

12. In a medium skillet, over high heat, heat 1 tablespoon of the olive oil. Lightly dredge the trout fillets in flour and shake off any excess. Brown the trout in the skillet for 2 to 3 minutes on each side. You can probably fit 2 fillets at a time in the skillet. After both sides are brown, place them on a heavy baking sheet and wipe the skillet clean with a paper towel. Repeat the browning process until you've browned all the trout.

13. Place the trout in the oven. Bake the trout for another 5 to 6 minutes to cook it through and to assure that the spinach mixture is hot. The trout should be crispy on the outside and creamy on the inside.

14. Drizzle the trout with brown butter and serve each piece alongside a few heaping spoonfuls of avocado purée dotted with salmon roe.

10

OREGANO,
SUMMER SAVORY, SAGE,
ROSEMARY, AND THYME

The Mediterranean herbs in this chapter are hardy; they are stiffer, stronger, and more concentrated than "soft" herbs such as parsley, dill, and mint. Hardy herbs contain less water than soft herbs and don't bruise as easily when chopped. They should be chopped finely and used sparingly: too much in one mouthful can overpower a dish.

Sage and rosemary are used most frequently in the central Mediterranean region, whereas oregano, summer savory, and thyme have more of an eastern Mediterranean flavor. These herbs are often interchangeable and blend very well; in combination they create complex layers of flavor. They work on just about anything from fish to meat to vegetables, but there are perfect marriages: sage with squash or pork, oregano with tomato, rosemary with lamb, thyme with mushrooms or potato, and summer savory with olives.

OREGANO

Oregano, which means "joy of the mountain" in Greek, is a bold, savory, peppery perennial with round leaves that is native to the Mediterranean region, where it grows abundantly.

The flavor of *rigani*, or wild Greek oregano, which grows in the rocky hillsides, can vary greatly depending upon climate and soil conditions. In the United States, dried Greek oregano is sold in markets, but it has lost much of its wild, robust flavor. Oregano is used liberally in Mexican cooking, but Mexican oregano, a member of the Verbena family and not the Origanum family, is a shrub and has a very strong flavor, too strong for my taste.

A fresh oregano and basil combination is a familiar ingredient in pizza and pasta sauces here in the United States, mostly because it pairs so well with tomatoes. Oregano is also great with eggplant, zucchini, beef, lamb, pork, garlic, feta cheese, and other bold foods. In addition, I like to use it on fresh tomato salads, with fried green tomatoes baked with Parmesan cheese and tomato sauce, and with a bubbly casserole of shrimp and feta cheese.

SUMMER SAVORY

Summer savory is an annual herb with long, leggy stems and oval leaves. It's better to cook with than its hardy, woody counterpart, winter savory, which is favored by gardeners for its full shape. Native to the Mediterranean, summer savory was introduced to England by the Romans, who thought its strong fragrance to be an aphrodisiac. Summer savory was one of the first herbs to be brought to America by

the Pilgrims, and it is still a traditional ingredient in Thanksgiving stuffing.

Summer savory, which also can be used as a mild substitute for oregano, is wonderful in pickle brines and in salads, with tomatoes or in smooth green tomato soup. It's also perfect with egg dishes, beans, lentils, and peas. Summer savory is sometimes sold as za'atar in Middle Eastern markets.

SAGE

Sage is a hardy perennial with wiry, greenish-purple stems that become woody as the plant ages. The pungent leaves are wide, silvery-green, and downy soft, and they smell fresh and almost piney. Sage tastes herbaceous and sharp with subtle eucalyptus undertones; it should be used with a careful hand so as not to overwhelm a dish. Its botanical name, *salvia*, is derived from the Latin *salvere*, which means "to save" or "to heal," and the herb is still used medicinally, as it has been for millennia.

Sage is native to the northern Mediterranean coastal areas of southern Europe and it still grows wild on the hills of Dalmatia, the Croatian region on the Adriatic Sea that is famed for the quality of its sage.

There are hundreds of different varieties of sage, many used for garden decoration and fewer used for cooking. Garlic sage really tastes like garlic and is wonderful tossed with pasta. Pineapple sage is fun to dry and then steep in water; it makes a light and delicious chilled tea.

Because of its astringency, sage pairs well with heavy, fatty foods; it cuts right through pork, goose, and duck. I also like to combine sage with mushrooms and squash, add it to rich brie soup with fried oysters, and sprinkle it over eggplant, onions, dumplings, potatoes, beans, and peas. Fried sage leaves in butter is a great garnish for fish. Frying it softens the flavor, which will better suit fish.

Rosemary

Hardy rosemary is a sun-loving perennial that can grow upright or creep and spill over retaining walls. Both varieties have woody stems and leathery, needle-shaped leaves. Rosemary's fragrance is piney, cooling, and slightly minty. Its flavor is astringent, woody, peppery, warming, and minty. It is a strong herb and, like sage, must be used carefully or in small amounts, because it can overwhelm other flavors in a dish.

Rosemary is native to the Mediterranean region, and its botanical name means "dew of the sea." It thrives in sandy, well-drained soil and misty, sea-spray–filled air.

Ancient Greek scholars believed that rosemary's aroma improved their memory and helped keep their minds clear, and so they wore rosemary sprigs behind their ears. Rosemary's association with memory, lovers' fidelity, and remembrance has stayed with us through the ages, and this idea is succinctly captured in the Shakespeare's *Hamlet*: "There's rosemary, that's for remembrance; pray, love, remember." On a personal note, I wore rosemary in my hair on my wedding day to remember my father, Gary Sortun.

Rosemary counters the richness in meats such as lamb, pork, and duck. It's the perfect partner for garlic. The Italians love it, and often butchers will tie a strand of rosemary with cuts of lamb. Even though rosemary thrives in eastern Mediterranean countries, it is not used for cooking; cooks in the Middle East find the herb to be too overwhelming.

My favorite uses for rosemary are in breads, with roasted potatoes, and combined with garlic for lamb and rabbit dishes. I also use just a little to lift the fragrance from the walnuts and green olives in my Potato Risotto (page 294).

Thyme

There are more than one hundred varieties of thyme, many of them hybrid garden plants that creep out between stone or brick. I prefer cooking with plain garden thyme and English thyme, as they are the most straightforward and savory. Lemon thyme is also wonderful because of its bright scent and lemon notes.

Thyme is a perennial that may vary widely in appearance depending its soil and climate. Generally, it is stiff and bushy with stalks that are covered by pairs of small, narrow, elliptical leaves. Its aroma is warm, spicy, and pungent. Thyme adds depth and warmth to dishes.

Thyme is indigenous to the Mediterranean region. The Egyptians used it in the embalming process. The word *thyme* derives form the Greek *thymon*, meaning "to fumigate," and indeed the Greeks burned this herb during religious ceremonies.

The Armenians make tea with thyme, and the French use it to make bouquet garni: an aromatic package with bay leaf, parsley, and other herbs that flavors almost all French sauce and soup bases.

I use thyme more than any other herb because it adds warmth without overwhelming a dish. It's great with chicken, meat loaf, bacon-rich soups, potatoes, corn, and in any kind of cooked bean preparation. It also pairs very nicely with fish recipes, such as Cod with Truffled Leek Sauce (page 289).

RECIPES WITH FRESH OREGANO, SUMMER SAVORY, SAGE, ROSEMARY, AND THYME

Melon and Tomato Salad with Mozzarella and Oregano

This very Mediterranean salad features sweet melon and acidic tomato in a divine combination with fresh oregano and lightly brined cheese. In Turkey, melon is eaten with salty feta as a classic summer mezze. In Greece, tomato and melon salads also feature feta, black olives, and fruity olive oil.

Melon and tomato are very similar in structure, texture, and even taste; melons are just more floral and sweet and balance out the more acidic tomato. This recipe is perfect in August, when you can buy melons and locally grown tomatoes at the farmers' market. For this recipe, it's crucial that the tomatoes and melons be at their best.

A delicate white wine such as a Frascati, from the area southeast of Rome would pair well with this dish.

—⌐ SERVES 6 AS A SALAD COURSE ⌐—

1 small ripe cantaloupe

2 medium heirloom tomatoes or another good vine-ripened tomato variety, such as beefsteak

1 tablespoon roughly chopped fresh oregano leaves (2 to 3 sprigs)

4 tablespoons extra-virgin olive oil

2 tablespoons sherry vinegar

Salt and pepper to taste

2 balls buffalo-milk mozzarella (about 12 ounces total)

½ teaspoon Urfa chilies (optional)

½ crusty French baguette

1. Cut both ends off the cantaloupe so that it stands up on cutting surface without rolling. Using a sharp chef's knife, trim off the skin, starting at the top and working around the middle towards the bottom, following the shape of the melon. Try to remove only the skin.

2. Cut the peeled melon in half lengthwise and scrape out the seeds with a small spoon. Cut each half lengthwise into ½-inch-thick slices. Cut each strip in half and then dice the melon into a ½- to ⅓-inch dice. Place the diced melon in a sieve over a medium mixing bowl to let the juice drain off, for about 5 minutes.

3. Meanwhile, dice the unpeeled tomatoes the same size as the melon by slicing them into rounds and then into strips and then into a dice.

4. Pour the melon juice into a glass and chill it, reserving it for drinking later.

5. Add the tomatoes to the sieve with the melon pieces and let them drain for about 5 minutes.

Discard the tomato juice or reserve it for another use.

6. Place the tomatoes and melon into the medium mixing bowl and gently stir in the oregano, olive oil and vinegar. Season the salad with salt and pepper.

7. Cut each ball of mozzarella into 6 slices and arrange the pieces so that they slightly overlap on a serving platter. Season the cheese with salt and pepper.

8. Just before serving, place a heaping spoonful of chopped melon and tomato over each slice of mozzarella. Sprinkle with Urfa chilies and serve with crusty French bread.

❦ Variation

Substitute 12 ounces of French sheep's milk feta or barrel-aged cow's milk Greek feta for the mozzarella. Slice the cheese into ¼- to ⅓-inch-thick slices. It's okay if it crumbles a little bit.

Nookie's Pickles: Green Tomato, Turnip, Cucumber, and Pear Variations

Nookie, who served as Oleana's sous-chef for more than 4 years before moving to Spain in the late summer of 2005, grew up in a Jewish household in New York City, where his love for pickles began. When he was a good boy, the deli owners in his neighborhood let him fish a pickle out of their barrels for a treat.

Nookie brought his passion for pickles to Oleana, and started creating his signature condiments with the abundance of fresh vegetables we were lucky to get during peak harvest at my husband Chris's farm. Nookie would make big batches of pickles that we served with grilled meats, Chicken and Walnut Pâté (page 146), and Spinach Falafel (page 185). In late fall and winter, when the farm was quiet, Nookie would pickle pears or turnips instead; in the spring, he'd use ramps or wild leeks. The staff got addicted to Nookie's condiment specialty and altered the vegetables according to the seasons.

Pickles are a key condiment in Mediterranean cuisine; they're eaten as snacks and with grilled lamb or beef. See the suggestions below for pickle-making in different seasons.

⟶ MAKES 2 QUARTS PICKLES ⟵

---

2 pounds vegetables (see suggestions below)

½ cup salt

1 cup white wine vinegar

2 bay leaves

1 tablespoon brown mustard seed

2 tablespoons black peppercorns

½ cup whole garlic cloves, peeled and smashed (about 1 whole large head)

1 large bunch summer savory or fresh thyme, washed and roughly chopped

---

1. If you're using cabbage, pears, onion, or green tomatoes: cut the vegetables into ½-inch wedges. If you're using ramps or green garlic: leave them whole and wash them. If you're using Brussels sprouts: split them in half. If you're using turnips, carrots, or pumpkin: peel and slice them into ½-thick sticks. If you're using beets: peel and cut them into ½-thick wedges. If you're using cucumbers: leave them whole and follow the instructions for making cucumber pickles below.

2. In a large saucepan over high heat, combine 8 cups of water with the salt, vinegar, and all the herbs and spices and bring to a boil. Reduce the heat and simmer for 5 minutes.

3. Place the vegetables in a nonreactive glass or stainless steel bowl and pour the simmering brine over them. Cover the bowl with a clean kitchen towel and leave them at room temperature for 3 hours. You can also cover them with plastic wrap, but make sure to poke a hole in the wrap so that steam can escape. Refrigerate the pickles overnight. They will be ready to eat after 24 hours and will last up to 2 weeks.

❧ Vegetable Suggestions

Winter: *cabbage, turnips, beets, carrots, Brussels sprouts, pears*

Spring: *ramps or wild leeks, turnips, beets, green garlic (the first growth of mild garlic in the spring, which looks like a thin leek)*

Summer: *green or unripe tomatoes, turnips, onions, thick-skinned cucumbers such as lemon cucumbers or pickling cucumbers*

Fall: *pumpkin, Brussels sprouts, carrots, cabbage, beets, cauliflower*

❧ Making Cucumber Pickles

Select thick skinned, small cucumbers such as pickling cucumbers or lemon cucumbers. Boil the brine and simmer it as described in step 2 above. Cool the brine for 3 hours at room temperature before pouring it over the cucumbers. Let the brined cucumbers stand in the refrigerator, loosely covered, for 1 week; they will be "half-sours" at that point and they're delicious. At the 1-week mark, pour off half the brine and add water to replace it. You can then keep the pickles, now considered "full sours," for up to a month in the refrigerator.

OREGANO, SUMMER SAVORY, SAGE, ROSEMARY, AND THYME

Brie Soup with Fried Oysters and Sage

I've served this recipe at Oleana every New Year's Eve, and it's always a big hit. It's not inspired by the Mediterranean, but rather by a New Orleans restaurateur named Anthony Uglesich.

When I went down to the Big Easy to visit my mother, who's lived there for years, I would try to fit my days around a big lunch at Uglesich. The restaurant was housed in a rundown neighborhood next to the central business district, but it offered the best New Orleans-style food in the city.

At Uglesich, Anthony served an oyster brie soup that made me break my rule of serving only Mediterranean dishes at Oleana. This recipe is dedicated to Anthony and his wife Gail for the many great meals I've had with them. Anthony and Gail retired in the spring of 2005. You can check out the *Uglesich Restaurant Cookbook* for great recipes including Oyster Brie Soup.

Try pairing this soup with a rosé champagne (see page 357).

Serves 8 as a main course

For the Rich Veal Stock	For the Soup
5 pounds veal bones	1½ sticks butter
¼ cup tomato paste	1 cup flour
1 Spanish white onion, roughly chopped	10 cups rich veal stock
2 large carrots, roughly chopped	1 wheel brie (about 1 kilo or 2 pounds), trimmed of most of the rind
1 rib celery, roughly chopped	¼ cup heavy cream
1 head garlic, split in half horizontally, skins left on	1 tablespoon chopped fresh sage
	¼ cup brandy or cognac
	1 tablespoon freshly squeezed lemon juice (about ¼ lemon)

To Make the Rich Veal Stock

1. Preheat the oven to 425°F.

2. Place the veal bones in a heavy roasting pan and roast them for about an hour, until browned.

3. Add the tomato paste and chopped vegetables to the roasting pan, toss to combine, and continue roasting for 30 minutes.

4. Transfer the contents of the roasting pan to a large stockpot (that can hold 2 gallons) and fill it with 8 quarts of water. Bring this to a boil over high heat and skim off any foam that forms on the surface. Lower the heat to maintain a gentle simmer and cook for 5 to 6 hours, skimming fat from the surface every hour or so.

5. Strain the stock through a fine-mesh sieve. Cool and refrigerate the stock for up to 3 days or freeze it for up to 1 month. Makes 1 gallon.

To Make the Soup

1. In a large saucepan over medium-high heat, melt the butter and cook it for a few minutes until it starts to bubble and just begins to turn brown. Make the roux by stirring in ¾ cup of the flour and whisk until it forms a smooth paste. Cook for 2 to 3 minutes, whisking constantly.

2. Add the veal stock, whisking to incorporate the roux and thicken the broth slightly. Bring to a boil and reduce the heat to low, simmering for about 15 minutes.

3. Break up the brie into chunks and stir it into the soup, allowing a few minutes for it to melt. Add the cream, chopped sage, brandy, and lemon juice.

4. Allow the soup to cool for 20 minutes or so and then place it in small batches in a blender or use a handheld emulsion blender. Be careful using the blender when puréeing hot soup; the heat causes expansion and can pop the top off. You must hold the top firmly and only fill the blender ½ full. Start the blender on the lowest possible speed. If using an emulsion blender, you can blend the soup right in the pot. Blend the soup until smooth.

5. Strain the soup through a fine sieve or china cap to remove little bits of brie rind and make the soup as silky as possible. Season the finished soup with salt and pepper and set it aside over very low heat.

continued

OREGANO, SUMMER SAVORY, SAGE, ROSEMARY, AND THYME

6. About 20 minutes before serving, heat the oil in a medium saucepan over medium heat, until it reaches 350°F. You can check the temperature with a thermometer or you can tell when it's hot enough if one drop of tap water sizzles when flicked into the oil. If the oil smokes, it's too hot; you can then reduce the heat to very low and let it cool off.

7. Meanwhile, in a small mixing bowl, mix together the remaining ¼ cup flour with the cornmeal and paprika. Add the oysters and shake them around in the dredge until they are coated. Place them in a sieve and shake off as much excess flour as possible.

8. Drop the whole sage leaves into the hot oil, one at a time, and carefully stand back: the oil will spatter from the water in the sage. Fry the sage leaves until the oil becomes quiet and the leaves are crisp and slightly translucent, about 2 minutes. Remove the leaves with a slotted spoon and drain them on a paper towel. Sprinkle the leaves with salt and set aside.

9. Drop the oysters into the oil in batches of 8. Fry them until they are golden brown and crispy on the outside and soft and creamy on the inside, about 4 minutes. Remove them with a slotted spoon and drain them on a paper towel. Repeat the frying process until all the oysters are fried.

10. Meanwhile, warm 8 soup bowls under hot tap water or in a 200°F oven for a few minutes.

11. Arrange 4 to 5 oysters in the bottom of each soup bowl and top each with a fried sage leaf.

12. Ladle hot soup into gravy pitchers or small water pitchers and pass them around the table to pour over the oysters and sage. You can also ladle the soup into each bowl yourself, just before serving. But remember that the longer you wait to add the soup, the crisper the oysters will stay.

Green Tomato Soup with Summer Savory

This summer favorite is my interpretation of a traditional Greek recipe that my friend Gökcen Adar and I once discussed during a ferry ride across the Bosporus.

Green tomatoes are unripe, and their flesh is tart and meatier than ripened tomatoes. While they are practically inedible raw, they soften and keep their shape when cooked. Look for green tomatoes just before tomato season starts: usually late June for New England.

⤙ Makes 8 cups to serve 8 ⤚

---

6 tablespoons butter

½ cup flour

1 small onion, roughly chopped

6 cups roughly chopped green tomatoes
   (about 1 pound)

Salt and pepper to taste

2 tablespoons chopped summer savory leaves
   plus a few sprigs for garnish or basil
   to substitute

¾ cup fresh flat-leaf parsley leaves

⅓ cup crumbled feta cheese
   or grated kasseri cheese

2 heaping tablespoons Greek-style
   or plain whole-milk yogurt

2 teaspoons freshly squeezed lemon juice
   (about ¼ lemon)

⅛ teaspoon freshly grated nutmeg

---

1. In a large heavy stockpot or saucepan over medium-low heat, melt the butter. When it starts to foam, make a roux by adding the flour and cooking for a minute while stirring or whisking. Do not brown the roux.

2. Stir in the onion to coat and cook, stirring for 4 to 5 minutes, until the onion begins to soften.

3. Stir in the tomatoes and cover with 4½ cups of water. Season with salt and pepper. Increase the heat to high and bring to a boil.

4. Reduce the heat to medium-low. Add the summer savory leaves and simmer gently for 30 minutes, stirring occasionally to keep anything from sticking to the bottom, until the tomatoes are

continued

soft. Remove from the heat. With a slotted spoon, remove ½ cup of the cooked tomatoes, chop them finely, and set them aside for a garnish. Allow the soup to cool for at least 20 minutes.

5. Carefully purée the soup in a blender with the parsley leaves, cheese, and yogurt, until smooth. You will need to do this in 2 to 3 batches, depending on the size of your blender. Strain the soup through a china cap or fine sieve into a medium saucepan. This will make the soup ultrasmooth.

6. Gently reheat the soup and taste it for seasoning. Add lemon juice, salt, and pepper. Ladle the soup into bowls. Garnish with nutmeg, a sprig of summer savory, and a spoonful of reserved tomato. Serve immediately.

Fried Green Tomato Parmesan

Because of the movie with the same name, I had always thought that fried green tomatoes were an American dish straight out of the south. After eating many delicious plates of them at Uglesich, my favorite New Orleans restaurant, I was inspired to research green tomatoes in other cuisines. My friend Lydia Giambarella from the Calabria region of Italy, told me that she prepared green tomatoes similarly in her hometown. I have since found recipes from Greece, Turkey, and all over the Mediterranean that use green tomatoes. This one is my favorite.

Serve this bubbly casserole with a salad in the summer for a vegetarian meal or as a side dish with grilled meat.

An earthy, medium-bodied red wine, like a Chianti Classico, is just right with this dish.

SERVES 8 to 10

4 large green unripe tomatoes

Salt and pepper to taste

1½ cups all-purpose flour

3 eggs, beaten with 1 tablespoon water

2 cups fine unflavored or plain bread crumbs, such as the Japanese Panko brand (see page 156)

1 to 1½ cups olive oil

2 balls fresh buffalo-milk mozzarella (about 12 ounces total), sliced into ¼-inch slices

2 tablespoons finely chopped fresh oregano or summer savory

4 cups tomato sauce with caramelized butter (see Grilled Skirt Steak, page 26)

¼ cup freshly grated Parmesan cheese

OREGANO, SUMMER SAVORY, SAGE, ROSEMARY, AND THYME

1. Preheat the oven to 350°F.

2. Trim the top and bottom of each tomato so that it sits on a cutting surface without rolling. Cut the tomatoes into ½-inch slices. Each tomato should yield about 4–5 slices, depending on the size of the tomato, and the slices should lie flat.

3. Lay the tomato slices out on a cutting surface and sprinkle each generously with salt and pepper.

4. Set up 3 trays or medium mixing bowls, as follows. Add the flour to one and season with salt and pepper. Add the beaten eggs to another and season with salt and pepper. Add the bread crumbs to the last bowl.

5. Dredge a slice of tomato in the flour bowl and shake off any excess. Drop it into the bowl with the beaten egg to coat it, and shake off any excess. Coat each side of the tomato in bread crumbs and set it aside. Bread the rest of the sliced tomatoes in the same fashion.

6. After all the tomatoes are breaded, heat ¼ cup olive oil in a heavy, large, nonstick pan over medium-high heat. Brown the breaded tomatoes for about 3 minutes on one side. Add another ¼ cup olive oil to the pan and turn the tomatoes over, cooking for 3 to 4 more minutes, to brown the other side. Remove the tomatoes from the pan and place them on a baking sheet, lined with paper towels to drain. Repeat the browning process, until all the tomatoes are fried.

7. Place a layer of fried green tomatoes in a large, heavy baking or casserole dish in an even layer, slightly overlapped. Use 8 to 10 slices or about half the tomatoes.

8. Top this layer with half of the slices of sliced mozzarella cheese. Sprinkle with salt and pepper.

9. Stir the oregano into the tomato sauce. Spoon 2 cups of the sauce over the tomatoes and mozzarella cheese.

10. Place the final layer of green tomatoes on top and then top this with the remaining mozzarella. Season with salt and pepper.

11. Top the casserole with the remaining 2 cups of tomato sauce and sprinkle it with the Parmesan cheese.

12. Place the casserole dish on a heavy baking pan or tray to capture any juices that bubble over during baking. Bake the casserole for about 20 minutes, until the cheese is melted and the casserole is hot and bubbly. Serve immediately.

Cod with Truffled Leek Sauce and Sweet Potater Tots

This dish was inspired by ingredients from the south of France, but I added a twist: the shredded potatoes are like the tater tots I ate as a kid, and they're remarkably easy to make. It's a special late fall or winter recipe when expensive black truffles are in season and leeks are good.

Cod is caught in both the Atlantic and Pacific, and so it's readily available on both U.S. coasts. Ask your fishmonger for cod cut from the thick, head end of the fish, so that you can cut it into 2-inch-thick fillets.

I smother the cod fillets with sautéed leeks and black truffles, and then wrap it all up in parchment paper before cooking. The little paper packages steam the cod and collect the juices of the fish that will melt into the leeks.

All the fresh herbs mentioned in this chapter pair with the leeks and cod, but thyme and sage work particularly well with truffles. If fresh black truffles (see Resources, page 358) are not available, jarred truffle shavings will do and so will the infused oils that are more widely available.

A light red wine is delightful with this dish, despite the notion that you should only drink white wine with fish. Try a Valpolicella from Italy, or, if you prefer white, a French chardonnay works very well.

SERVES 4

Four 6-ounce portions cod,
   cut from the thick, head end

Salt and pepper to taste

4 leeks, white part only, root end trimmed

2 tablespoons butter

2 tablespoons olive oil

¼ cup dry white wine

2 tablespoons fresh chopped thyme
   or sage or a combination of both

4 sheets parchment paper

4 tablespoons winter black truffle shavings
   (fresh or jarred) or 2 teaspoons black
   truffle oil

1 sweet potato, peeled and halved

1 large baking potato, peeled and halved

3 tablespoons cornstarch

Pinch of sugar

2 teaspoons salt

4 cups canola or vegetable oil for frying

1. Sprinkle each piece of cod on both sides with salt and pepper and set aside.

2. Cut the leeks into ¼-inch slices and wash them well. Drain the leeks in a colander and pat them as dry as possible with a paper towel.

3. In a large sauté pan over medium-high heat, melt the butter with the olive oil until the butter just begins to brown. Add the leeks and sauté them, reducing the heat to medium if they start to brown. Cook the leeks for about 6 minutes, until they are soft and tender but not mushy.

4. Add the wine, salt and pepper, and 1 tablespoon of the herbs.

5. Cook for 4 more minutes, until the wine has almost evaporated and its sugars have slightly glazed the leeks. Remove from the heat and set aside.

6. Cut 4 squares of parchment paper, roughly 12 × 12 inches.

7. Place a piece of cod on the top quarter of each square. Top each piece of fish with 2 tablespoons of the leek mixture and a tablespoon of black truffle shavings or ½ teaspoon of black truffle oil.

8. Fold the bottom of the parchment paper over the cod so that the ends of the paper line up and the cod is at the bottom of the fold. Starting from one end of folded parchment paper, pinch the corner and start folding the paper in toward the fish in a rollover motion, ending at the other corner of parchment paper and enclosing the cod in a tight, shell-shaped package. Set the cod packages on a heavy baking sheet and keep them refrigerated while preparing the tater tots.

9. Place both of the potatoes in a medium saucepan and cover them with at least an inch of water. Turn on the heat to high and bring them to a boil, then reduce the heat to medium. Simmer the potatoes for about 12 minutes,

until al dente; they should feel slightly firm when pierced with a knife. Run cold water over both potatoes to cool them through. Don't drain the potatoes; let them cool down slowly in the cold water so that they stay intact. This will take about 8 minutes. Then drain the potatoes well.

10. Preheat the oven to 375° F.

11. Grate the potatoes using the large holes of a box grater.

12. Place the potatoes in a medium mixing bowl and combine them with the cornstarch, sugar, 2 teaspoons salt, and the remaining 1 tablespoon herbs. Season with salt and pepper to taste.

13. Take up about 2 tablespoons of potato mixture in your hand and crunch it into a tater tot shape. Continue this process until all the potato mixture is gone. Set the tater tots aside.

14. About 20 minutes before serving, place the fish in the oven and roast for about 12–14 minutes. The bags should be full of air and touching the underside; the fish should feel firm. Let fish rest in bag for 5–10 minutes.

15. Meanwhile, heat the canola oil in a large, heavy saucepan over medium-low heat. The temperature should reach 350° F: hot enough so that when you drop a tater tot in, it sizzles. Fry each tater tot, stirring them after about 30 seconds of frying with a pair of long tongs to keep them from sticking to the bottom, for 4 to 5 minutes, until golden brown and crispy.

16. Using scissors, cut open the cod packages by making crisscross incisions on the uncrimped, flat part of the package. Be careful not to get burned from the escaping steam. Pull the cut bag open with your fingers. Serve the cod in the paper–telling guests not to eat the paper even though it is truffle-rich and tempting–with tater tots on the side.

8.

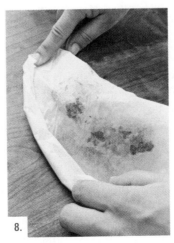

8.

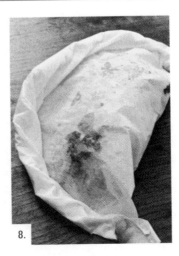

8.

JUST-DUG POTATOES

I've been asked many times what my favorite food is. My answer is always the same: just-dug potatoes. My first just-dug potato experience was during a visit to the Farm School in Athol, Massachusetts, where children and adults learn about farming in two separate programs. The Farm School invites kids from different backgrounds and schools to stay in their bunk house and work on the farm for a few days. Depending on the time of year and the ages of the students, kids can gather eggs from the chickens, feed the pigs, clear the woods, build a shed, harvest vegetables, weed, or plow–all as part of their field trip experience.

On the day I visited, the kids were harvesting potatoes, and I dug with them. I loosened each side of a row of soil with a pitchfork, and then the kids and I stuck our hands in the dirt and pulled out potatoes. I learned that potatoes are not a root but rather a growth on a stem; sitting in the soil, they look just like eggs in a nest. The instructor said, "This is where French fries come from," but I couldn't tell if the kids believed him. We all went into the dining hall and ate a lunch that the kids prepared from freshly harvested vegetables. It was exhilarating to watch these kids connect to their food and the land. For more information on the Farm School, see page 358 in the Resources section.

After my Farm School experience, I returned to the restaurant with my bag of just-dug potatoes. I was glowing so much that my staff asked if I had been drinking! I couldn't wait to get into the kitchen and start experimenting with the recipe I had been carrying around in my head: just-dug potato "risotto." I peeled the potatoes and minced them into tiny bits as small as rice granules. I cooked them with pitted green olives, walnuts, rosemary, and cream until the potatoes absorbed the cream, like risotto. Everyone in the kitchen tasted the results, and we all agreed that there was almost nothing better.

Just-dug potatoes are sweet and earthy: the sugars are concentrated and have not yet turned into starch. You can see the sugars: they stick to your knife as you cut the potatoes. Just-dug potato skins are thin, and they thicken when stored. When you wash just-dug potatoes, the skin will almost completely come off.

Just-dug potato season starts in the height of summer in New England and continues through fall. Potato farmers dig their crops at different stages, depending on variety, staggering of crops, and desired size. Even after a week of storage, potato starches change and the skins thicken. Stored potatoes are still delicious, but their flavor and texture have been altered.

Just-dug potatoes are great for roasting or preparing like a risotto or boiling and eating as is. They don't make a good mashed or puréed potato.

Potato Considerations

It's important to consider that different potatoes have different textures, and some varieties work better in certain dishes than in others. Here's my list of potato considerations:

Baking or Idaho or russet potatoes – Because these potatoes are so starchy, they dry out easily, giving old-fashioned baked potato wedges or steak fries the perfect crispiness. They also absorb butter, cream, and olive oil easily, which makes them work well for mashed potatoes or any potato purée, gnocchi, and dauphine potatoes (potato purée that is piped through a pastry bag and then broiled). With thicker skinned potatoes, peeling is usually necessary.

Fingerling potatoes – These long, thin potatoes are sweet and firm-textured. They hold their shape when cooked, which makes them great for roasting or adding to stews. The skins are delicious when left on.

Red bliss potatoes – Because they hold their shape so well, this white and sugary variety is great for cold potato salads and for grilling and roasting. And because they are pale and somewhat bland, they really soak up vinaigrettes.

Yukon gold potatoes – When shredded, this butter-flavored variety is starchy enough to stick together and fries up extra crispy, which makes it ideal for shredded potato cakes or latkes. Yukon golds are also perfect for scalloped potatoes or pommes Anna (a layered potato cake with clarified butter).

Kennebec potatoes – These potatoes develop skins thick enough to last in storage. They are also good for baking and are better peeled.

❧ Rules of Thumb for Cooking Potatoes

As for any vegetable that grows underground, start cooking potatoes in cold or warm water. If you drop potatoes into boiling water, they may explode and leave you with potato soup. When potatoes reach boiling temperature slowly, the starch develops a gelatin-like film that slows water absorption; your potatoes will be soft and tender without falling to pieces.

If your potatoes have sprouted or turned green, peel them deeply enough to get rid of the affected areas. At this stage, potatoes harbor toxic alkaloids that can give you an upset stomach.

Potato Risotto with Green Olives, Walnuts, and Rosemary

This recipe is a fun alternative to risotto, and it's particularly delicious with just-dug potatoes. I created this dish after enjoying the unparalleled just-dug potato experience, described on page 292.

Fresh rosemary complements potatoes well, and I use a little to brighten the floral tones that the olives and walnuts give. The other herbs mentioned in this chapter will also work as a substitute if rosemary is not one of your favorite tastes.

The combination of green olives and walnuts is truly Mediterranean. It's important to use really good-quality green olives–such as Picholine or Lucques, both from the south of France–that are sweet and floral and not meaty or too briny. The olives should cut through the rich cream and delicately flavor but not overpower the potatoes.

I like to use buttery, creamy Kennebec or Yukon gold potatoes in this recipe but any favorite potato will work. Chopping the potatoes into a very small dice requires some preparation time but is well worth the effort. The French culinary term for a very small vegetable dice is brunoise, and it's about an ⅛ inch. The potato dice absorbs the cream as it cooks and resembles the consistency of a creamy risotto.

Serve this dish with grilled or roasted meats or with a salad as a substantial vegetarian meal in the summer or early fall. Drink a glass of Sancerre rouge, a red wine from the Loire Valley made from Pinot Noir.

⟜ SERVES 4 ⟞

8 to 10 golf ball-size potatoes, washed (peeled, only if skin is thick)	¾ cup pitted, coarsely chopped Picholine or Lucques olives
2 teaspoons olive oil	4 tablespoons coarsely chopped walnuts, lightly toasted
2 shallots, peeled and finely minced	1 teaspoon chopped fresh rosemary
2 cups heavy cream	2 tablespoons freshly grated Parmesan cheese
Salt and pepper to taste	

1. Cut the potatoes into ⅛- to ¼-inch slices and then julienne each slice into strips a little thicker than a matchstick (⅛- to ¼-inch wide). Dice the julienne into a *brunoise* or very fine dice and place them into a medium mixing bowl. You should have about 4 cups.

2. In a medium-large, nonstick sauté pan over medium-high heat, heat the olive oil until hot and stir in the shallots. Cook for 2 minutes, stirring, and then add the potatoes. Stir to coat with the shallots.

3. Add the cream and season the mixture with salt and pepper.

4. Reduce the heat to low and simmer for 15 to 20 minutes, until the potatoes are tender and have absorbed all the cream. Check the seasoning and add more salt and pepper if needed.

5. Stir in the olives, walnuts, and rosemary. Thin out the mixture with a spoonful or two of water if the potatoes are too thick. Cook for 2 to 3 minutes longer to allow the olives and walnuts to warm up and release their fragrance.

6. Sprinkle with Parmesan cheese and serve immediately.

Maria's Shrimp Saganaki Flambéed with Ouzo

This recipe is from the kitchen of my dear friend and amazing home cook, Maria Hatziiliades. Both Maria and her husband Max are from Greece. Maria's shrimp are a great dish to bring to a summertime party: they're easy to make, can be served as a light meal, are delicious served hot or at room temperature, and guests can't get enough of them.

The ouzo is a must: it adds a sweet, slight fennel flavor that can't be duplicated. Serve this dish with a spicy Malagousia from Greece. If this wine is too difficult to find, try its Italian relative, Malvasia.

SERVES 4 AS A MAIN COURSE OR 6 AS A FIRST COURSE

1 white onion, peeled and cut into ½-inch dice

1 green bell pepper, seeded and cut into ½-inch dice

1 red bell pepper, seeded and cut into ½-ince dice

6 plum tomatoes, peeled, seeded (see page 104), and coarsely chopped

5 tablespoons extra-virgin olive oil

2 teaspoons chopped garlic (about 2 large cloves)

1 tablespoon chopped fresh oregano or summer savory

Salt and pepper to taste

12 large shrimp (U-10 or 10 to a pound), peeled and deveined

1 cup sheep's milk French feta or creamy-style feta

¼ cup ouzo

1. Place the onion and peppers in a large skillet with the tomatoes and olive oil and cook them over medium-high heat for 4 to 5 minutes, until the onion begins to soften. Reduce the heat to low and simmer the vegetables for 20 to 25 minutes, until the vegetables are soft.

2. Preheat the oven to 375° F.

3. Stir the garlic and oregano into the vegetable mixture and cook for a few minutes more. Season with salt and pepper.

4. Pour the vegetable mixture into a casserole dish and nestle the shrimp into it in one even layer. Sprinkle with feta.

5. Bake uncovered for 20 to 25 minutes, until the shrimp is cooked through and the casserole is bubbly.

6. Just before serving, place the casserole on a low burner until the mixture starts to bubble again. Add the ouzo and carefully light the casserole with a match, standing back a little in case the flame goes high. Bring the casserole to the table and allow the flames to burn off, leaving only the flavor of the ouzo, before serving.

OREGANO, SUMMER SAVORY, SAGE, ROSEMARY, AND THYME

Sage-Rubbed Pork with Red Rice and Beans

This is my Mediterranean spin-off of pork with rice and beans, a favorite dish in Latin countries. Fresh sage is an herb that pairs really well with pork and turkey; it's good with rich red and white meats because it cuts through fatty flavors and brightens the taste.

I love using flageolet beans, available at gourmet and whole foods markets, because they're delicate, fragrant, and naturally sweet and buttery. Even though I usually shy away from dried herbs, I like to toss the beans with herbs de Provence (see Resources, page 358). This high-quality fresh blend of rosemary, cracked fennel, thyme, basil, tarragon, and just enough lavender imparts a floral aroma that doesn't overpower.

In this recipe, I like to use red rice from the Camargue region of the south of France, a marshland that butts up against the Mediterranean coast between Marseille and Montpelier. The high natural salt content in the Camargue's soil makes growing most crops a challenge, but rice can handle high levels of salinity. Camargue rice has been granted a Protected Geographic Indication by the European Community, recognizing its uniqueness and its connection to the region. You can find American-grown varieties, but Camargue red rice is superior (see Resources, page 358). It is an earthy, gutsy unmilled short-grain rice, brownish-red in color, nutty in flavor, and firm and slightly chewy in texture. It's excellent paired with sage and other strong flavors. As a short-grain rice, it is not meant to fluff and separate and should be slightly sticky when cooked.

Enjoy a pinot noir from Burgundy with this dish.

⌐ SERVES 6 ⌐

2 small bunches sage, leaves only

4 cloves garlic

¼ cup lemon juice
(about ½ lemon)

7 tablespoons olive oil

2½ pounds boneless pork loin

2 cups flageolet beans, soaked overnight in plenty of water in the refrigerator

Salt and pepper to taste

2 teaspoons herbs de Provence

2 cups red rice from the Camargue

1 small Spanish onion, finely chopped

1. Using a blender, make a sage rub by puréeing the sage leaves with garlic, lemon juice, and 4 tablespoons of the olive oil.

2. Rub the pork loin on all sides with the sage rub and let it stand at room temperature for 1 hour before roasting to impart flavors.

3. Preheat the oven to 400°F.

4. Bring 8 cups of water to a boil in a medium saucepan, over high heat. Drain the soaked flageolet beans through a sieve or colander and add them to the boiling water, stirring. Reduce the heat to medium and simmer the beans for about 18 minutes, until tender but not mushy. Drain them in a colander or sieve and place them in a medium mixing bowl. Season them generously with salt and pepper and stir in 1 tablespoon of the olive oil and the herbs de Provence. Set aside.

5. Season all sides of the pork loin generously with salt and pepper.

6. Put the pork loin in a roasting pan and place it in the oven, uncovered; after 10 minutes, reduce the temperature to 350°F. Continue to cook the pork for 20 to 30 more minutes, depending on the thickness of the pork loin, until a meat thermometer reads 140 to 145°F, so the pork will be pink or medium. Leave the thermometer in and let the pork rest for at least 10 minutes, so that it reaches an internal temperature of 150°F. Add a cup of water to the roasting pan to loosen any bits of carmelized juice and roll the loin around in the juices to glaze it.

7. Meanwhile, bring 8 to 10 cups of water to a boil over high heat in a large saucepan.

8. Add the red rice and onion and stir. Reduce the heat to medium and simmer uncovered for about 40 minutes, until the rice is tender. Drain the rice well in a colander and put it back into the saucepan. Stir in the remaining 2 tablespoons of olive oil, using a fork so that the rice fluffs. Season the rice with salt and pepper.

9. Spoon a cup of rice in the center of each plate and make a well in the center to hold a ¼ cup of beans.

10. Slice the pork loin into 12 to 18 thin slices and lay 2 to 3 slices over the beans and rice and serve immediately.

⚽ 11 ⚽
FLOWER POWER

Cooking with Nasturtium, Orange Blossom, Rose, Chamomile, Lavender, and Jasmine

Like herbs and spices, edible flowers have been used throughout the Mediterranean region for millennia to add perfume, flavor, and intrigue to dishes of all kinds. Flowers and their essences grace carrot salads, teas and lemonades, custards, goat cheeses, and sangria. The combinations are endless.

Arabs are famous for using roses and orange blossoms—which they distill to make rosewater and orange-blossom water—in pastries and savory and sweet dishes. North Africans make rose-scented chili pastes. In Lebanon and Syria, they add rose petals to spice blends for pilafs and roasted meats, particularly game birds and lamb.

NASTURTIUM

Nasturtiums rank among the most common edible flowers, and the sunset-bright and pleasant flowers come in many varieties, ranging from trailing to upright. The blossoms have a mild, sweet flavor that gives way to spice, similar to watercress. It's fun to stuff whole nasturtium flowers with smoked salmon mousse or chop them and whip them into soft butter to melt over corn cakes or corn on the cob. The peppery leaves have a wonderful, velvety texture and work very well, like arugula, in salads.

ORANGE BLOSSOM

Orange blossoms are the flowers of love. Highly scented and full of essential oils, they are traditionally used as adornments in wedding ceremonies.

The blossoms impart an invigorating citrusy, bittersweet flavor that is balanced by a toasty, caramel note, making them perfect with savory dishes such as squash, carrots, sweet potatoes, and in stews with chicken and dried fruits.

Seville oranges are fragrant, bittersweet, and native to Asia. The Moors introduced these oranges to Spain in the eighth century, and the country remains the sole grower, with England taking 90 percent of the crop to make marmalade. The rest of the crop is used to make liqueurs and orange-blossom water, which is a by-product of the distillation process.

The trick with orange-blossom water is to create intriguing flavor by using very little and giving the merest hint of fragrance. Too much orange-blossom water, like rosewater, described below, will make your food smell like a garden or a bar of soap.

Orange-blossom and rosewater are added to sugar syrup and then drizzled over fruit and pastries or added to drinks. You can also use them to add an exotic Middle Eastern flavor to lamb, chicken with white wine and grapes, and rice dishes.

ROSE

June is a lucky month at Oleana: we receive Eva Sommaripa's rose petals, which she handpicks from the beach roses in Westport, Masshacusetts. Beach roses are soft in texture and sweet and gentle in flavor, and when used with a careful hand, they add honey-like sweetness to many dishes. You can use dried rose petals–which you can find in Middle Eastern markets–in spice mixes for pilafs or grilled meats like chicken and lamb or game birds like quail.

Maura Kilpatrick, our pastry chef, uses Eva's harvest to make rose petal jam, which we then freeze and use throughout the year. Maura uses the jam to soak beignets–a kind of French pastry similar to doughnuts–as well as glaze fruit tarts and flavor frozen desserts and custards.

Rosewater has been used in Middle Eastern cuisine since the tenth century, and it still flavors pastries, dried fruit, pistachios, almonds, baklava, halvah, ice cream, and rice pudding. It also lends it lovely flavor to lassi, an Indian yogurt drink.

Both orange-blossom and rosewater essences are sold in Middle Eastern stores and some specialty food stores. Rosewater sold in pharmacies is not suitable for cooking.

CHAMOMILE

Chamomile flowers are small and daisylike and have a sweet, applelike, honeysuckle flavor that brings comfort and relaxation. The flowers are lemony and wonderful when you're aiming for more subtlety than orange blossoms or rose petals. At Oleana, when we want to flavor our desserts with flowers other than the standard rose and orange blossoms, we use chamomile to impart a gentle, honeylike sweetness.

Chamomile is used in Asian cuisine, but not much in the Arabic world. Chamomile tea is the most common use, and the French also use the flowers to scent white chocolate and honey desserts.

LAVENDER

Lavender is most often associated with sweets, but today many chefs are taking the French example and adding the herb to savory dishes. The French include lavender in their blend called herbes de Provence, and just a touch adds a beautiful floral aroma and romance to a chicken dish or rice pilaf.

Lavender is a member of the mint family and is similar to rosemary, sage, and thyme. It tastes sweetly of fresh-cut wood and rosemary, and it adds a pleasant accent to a wide array of foods. Try it in sweet or savory baked goods, with chicken and lamb, potatoes, herbal teas, jams and jellies, and as a flavoring for vinegars and honey. Ground lavender with granulated sugar adds a twist to dessert recipes and is also a wonderful way to sweeten lemonade.

Although the woolly leaves are fragrant and edible, the pretty purple flowers and buds are the best for cooking. Use a light hand when seasoning with lavender; too much gives an astringent taste.

JASMINE

Jasmine flowers are intensely sweet and fragrant and, like chamomile, are traditionally used in making tea. Maura Kilpatrick, the pastry chef at Oleana, infuses them into sweet sugar syrups, which she uses to flavor berries and ice cream. She makes her infusions with the dried whole blossoms, which you can usually find in specialty tea stores.

RECIPES WITH NASTURTIUM, ORANGE BLOSSOM, ROSE, CHAMOMILE, LAVENDER, AND JASMINE

Grano with Greek Yogurt and Orange Blossom Honey

I ate this elegant breakfast almost every day when I was in Sicily, where grano grows everywhere. *Grano*, which means "grain" in Italian, are the polished, whole berries from durum semolina wheat. Commercial yogurt companies in Sicily sell grano mixed with yogurt on the shelves in supermarkets and to hotels. It's a delicious alternative to oatmeal in the morning. See page 88 for more information on grano.

I usually cook a big batch of grano, since it takes awhile, and then I freeze it in small portions in plastic bags. This way, I can just pull a bag of grano out the night before and use it to create a healthful and elegant parfait the next morning.

You'll want to choose your favorite honey for this recipe–one with a floral fragrance. I like to use subtle, delicate linden blossom honey (available at www.formaggiokitchen.com), but orange-blossom and clover honey work very well.

Another fun alternative is to layer this parfait with a sweetened homemade apricot or peach purée; see variation below.

✦ SERVES 4 ✦

½ cup grano, soaked in 3 cups of water overnight

1 teaspoon salt

1¼ cups orange or linden blossom honey

4 cups Greek-style or plain whole-milk yogurt

1 cup fresh berries (such as raspberries, blueberries, blackberries, or strawberries), washed and dried well

1. Drain the soaked grano in a colander or sieve and then place it in a small saucepan with 4 cups of water over medium-high heat. Bring the grano to a boil and reduce the temperature to medium-low and simmer it for 40 to 50 minutes, until it is tender but still a tiny bit chewy.

2. Drain the cooked grano in a colander and place it in a small mixing bowl; at this point, you should have almost 2 cups of grano. Stir in the salt and ¼ cup of the honey. Allow the mixture to cool to room temperature for at least 20 minutes.

3. Spoon ½ cup of the yogurt into the bottom of each of 4 parfait cups or little glass bowls. Spoon 3 tablespoons of grano over the yogurt and then top each with 2 tablespoons of honey. Sprinkle about 2 tablespoons of berries over the top of each.

4. Repeat another layer of yogurt, grano, honey, and berries. Serve chilled or at room temperature.

✿ Variation with Peach or Apricot Purée

Split 6 well-washed peaches or apricots in half and remove the pits. Place the fruit in a saucepan large enough to fit the pieces in a double layer at the most. Simmer the fruit on low heat for about 40 minutes, until the fruit softens and is juicy. Cool the fruit for at least 20 minutes and then purée it in a blender for about a minute, until very smooth. Strain the fruit through a fine sieve or a food mill to remove pieces of skin. Use in the purée in place of honey in this recipe.

Wilton's Corn Cakes with Nasturtium Butter

Wilton Osorno, the sous-chef at Oleana, makes scrumptious corn cakes called *arepa* that he grew up eating in Don Matias, Colombia. Arepa are a staple in Colombian cooking, and the cakes are served with meals instead of bread in many variations: some are puffy and some are flat, they can be eaten with loads of butter and cheese or plain, and they can be made with different varieties of corn. Arepa are perfect to make and eat when fresh, local corn hits the farmer's markets in August and September.

Seasonally, nasturtiums are usually at their peak at the same time as corn, and I love using the flowers in concentrated butters to smear on these savory pancakes. Nasturtium flowers are lemony, a little peppery, and bright with color and also make a beautiful addition to a summer salad. Nasturtium butter freezes well, so you can enjoy the flavor after flower season is long gone. The butter is also delicious on grilled fish and corn on the cob.

Serve these arepa as a side dish with grilled or roasted salmon or as hors d'oeuvres. They pair wonderfully with a glass of dry sherry or a light-style beer, like Corona, with plenty of lime.

MAKES 8 MEDIUM-SIZE CORN CAKES TO SERVE 4 TO 8

2 cups fresh sweet corn
  (about 4 to 6 ears)

1 white onion, finely chopped

½ cup chopped scallions (about 4)

¼ cup brown sugar

3 whole eggs

¾ cup flour

1 tablespoon heavy cream

Salt and pepper to taste

1 stick plus 2 tablespoons salted butter,
  at room temperature

2 cups nasturtium blossoms, washed, dried,
  and finely chopped

1 tablespoon chopped fresh basil

1. Using a food processor fitted with a metal blade, purée the corn, onion, and scallions for 2 to 3 minutes, until the mixture is finely chopped and starts to become creamy.

2. Place the puréed corn cake batter in a medium mixing bowl and stir in the brown sugar and eggs. Stir in the flour and finally the cream. Season with salt and pepper and set aside.

3. In a medium mixing bowl, use a whisk to combine 1 stick of the butter with the nasturtium blossoms and basil and season with salt and pepper. Whip this mixture for a few minutes with the whisk, until the flowers are well incorporated and the butter is light and fluffy and stained with bits of flowers.

4. In a large nonstick skillet or heavy cast-iron pan over medium-high heat, melt 1 tablespoon of the butter, until it starts to brown. Add ¼ cup of the corn cake batter at a time to form 4 arepa or however many your pan can fit. Lower the heat to medium and cook the arepa on one side until golden brown, about 4 minutes. Flip the arepa with a spatula and cook the other side for another 4 minutes.

5. Remove the arepa from the heat and place a tablespoon of nasturtium butter on each to melt over the hot cakes.

6. Make 4 more arepa with the remaining batter, repeating the same process with the remaining tablespoon of butter. Serve them immediately, warm or hot.

Zucchini Fritters with Nasturtium Aioli

These tasty fritters are inspired by classic Turkish zucchini pancakes called *mucver*. I've eaten these fritters in Greece, and they are eaten as a mezze all over Turkey.

I like to incorporate shredded nasturtium leaves into the zucchini batter to enhance the delightful peppery flavor. Add a western Mediterranean twist to this recipe by serving the fritters with a homemade garlic mayonnaise–or aioli, which in old Provencal dialect means "garlic sauce"–further flavored with lemony nasturtium blossoms. Adding yogurt makes the aioli softer, lighter, and creamier.

Aioli is wonderful served as a dip for or spooned on top of grilled vegetables and fish on a hot summer night. I also love to stir a spoonful of aioli into my boiled potatoes that I've roughly mashed with a fork and seasoned with salt and pepper.

These fritters can be served as a mezze with Dunia's Iced Tea (page 329) before a meal or as an accompaniment to grilled meat, fish, or vegetables for a main course.

⟶ MAKES 12 SMALL FRITTERS TO SERVE 4 TO 6 AS A MEZZE ⟵

For the Zucchini Fritters	For the Aioli
2½ cups grated zucchini (about 1 pound)	2 large cloves garlic
1 teaspoon salt	2 egg yolks
1 medium red onion, peeled and grated	⅛ teaspoon salt plus more to taste
1 tablespoon chopped fresh dill or mint	1 teaspoon Dijon mustard
1 tablespoon chopped nasturtium leaves (2 or 3 leaves, depending on the size)	1 cup canola oil
Black pepper to taste	1 teaspoon lemon juice
½ cup flour	1 cup packed, washed, and dried nasturtium blossoms
2 eggs	2 tablespoons Greek-style or plain whole-milk yogurt
½ cup olive oil for frying	Pepper to taste

To Make the Zucchini Fritters

1. Place the grated zucchini in a colander, sprinkle it with 1 teaspoon of the salt, mix it, and allow it to sit for 15 minutes.

2. Remove the excess moisture from the zucchini by squeezing it between the palms of your hands. Place the zucchini in a large mixing bowl.

3. Add the onion, dill, nasturtium leaves, pepper, flour, and eggs. Mix the ingredients well to form a thick batter.

To Make the Aioli

1. Place the garlic in a food processor fitted with a metal blade, and chop until the garlic is very finely minced. Make sure to scrape the sides of the bowl once. Add the egg yolks, 1/8 teaspoon of salt, and mustard, and puree for a minute, until smooth and creamy. With the motor still running, slowly pour in 1/2 cup of the canola oil. Add the lemon juice and continue to purée with the motor running. Add the remaining 1/2 cup canola oil, little by little, until you have a mayonnaise that is slightly thinner than the consistency of commercial brands. Add the nasturtium blossoms and yogurt and blend until smooth and creamy. Season with salt and pepper. Set aside.

2. Heat the olive oil in a heavy skillet over medium heat. When the skillet's hot, drop heaping tablespoons of the zucchini mixture into the oil and fry the fritters until they're golden brown on both sides, about 3 minutes on each side. Drain the fritters on paper towels.

3. Serve immediately with a small spoonful of aioli on each fritter.

Ruth Ann Adams's Rhubarb Rose Jam with Quail

Ruth Ann Adams is the chef at Cambridge's Casablanca restaurant in Harvard Square. She and I were teammates at a "battle of the sexes" cooking contest in Boston in 2005 in which we had to create dishes using mystery ingredients. Ruth Ann's mystery ingredient turned out to be quail, and she prepared this dish. I loved the innovative combination of sweet rose and tart rhubarb, which cuts through the rich quail meat, and so did the judges. We won the contest.

Quail is a small, slightly gamey dark-meat bird that makes a great first course because each bird provides only a few ounces of rich, flavorful meat. You can use Cornish game hens or squab as a substitute, but remember that these birds are slightly larger; you need only four Cornish game hens or squab in this recipe. It's important to use the dried rose petals with a light hand so that you won't overwhelm the meat.

In New England, rhubarb is in season from early spring through the fall; it grows and regrows all summer long.

Serve this recipe with Rice Cakes (page 65) and a glass of dry Gewürztraminer.

⌒ SERVES 6 AS A FIRST COURSE ⌒

---

4 pounds rhubarb stalks, washed, peeled, and cut into medium dice (about 8 cups)

¾ cup sugar

½ ounce dried rose petals, washed

Pinch of salt plus more to taste

1 tablespoon chopped lemon confit (see Crispy Lemon Chicken, page 245)

6 quails

3 tablespoons extra-virgin olive oil

Pepper to taste

---

1. Prepare a charcoal grill (see Grilling Tips, page 100).

2. Cook the rhubarb and sugar in a large saucepan over medium heat for 15 to 20 minutes, stirring occasionally. The rhubarb should be soft, but somewhat chunky.

3. Add the rose petals and a pinch of salt, and let the jam continue to cook on low heat for about 10 more minutes. The petals should melt into the jam, leaving only a little texture.

4. Remove the jam from the heat and stir in the lemon confit.

5. Split the quail in half and rub them with the olive oil. Season all sides of the quail with salt and pepper.

6. Grill the quail for a 3 to 5 minutes on each side.

7. Serve the quail immediately with ⅓ cup of rose jam alongside as a condiment. You will have some leftover jam to freeze.

NASTURTIUM, ORANGE BLOSSOM, ROSE, CHAMOMILE, LAVENDER, AND JASMINE

Chamomile Berry Soup with Chamomile Sabayon

Sabayon is a French word meaning a sweet egg or custard sauce flavored with wine. Oleana's pastry chef Maura Kilpatrick serves this sweetly scented light fruit dessert in the summer months, when berries are at their best. Maura has a talent for creating decadent desserts that satisfy the palate but aren't heavy. This is one of those desserts.

Maura recommends seeking out the best chamomile tea that you can find. It's best to buy loose tea leaves full of whole chamomile blossoms, which look like tiny daisies, and should be very fragrant.

Maura also suggests adding a mild and versatile chamomile grappa made by Paolo Marolo. If you can't find it through your local wine shop or on the Internet, you can use a decent standard grappa instead.

The chamomile and berry syrup can be made up to 3 days in advance.

◅ SERVES 8 ▻

For the Soup

1 cup loose chamomile tea

2 cups sugar

1 tablespoon freshly squeezed lemon juice
(about ¼ lemon)

1 strip lemon zest taken off with a peeler;
zest only and no pith (see page 72)

Ice cubes

2 cups fresh cherries, pitted and cut in half,
or frozen cherries

1 cup blueberries, washed and dried well

1 cup blackberries, washed and dried well

1 cup raspberries, washed and dried well

1 cup fresh red currants, washed and dried well

2 teaspoons Paolo Marolo's chamomile grappa
or regular grappa

For the Sabayon

Ice cubes

¾ cup heavy cream

6 egg yolks

¼ cup sugar

1 cup strongly brewed chamomile tea

To Make the Soup

1. In a medium saucepan, bring 4½ cups of water to a boil. Remove from the heat and stir in the loose tea. Let the tea steep for 30 minutes, and then strain it through a fine sieve.

2. Place the tea in a medium saucepan and add the sugar, lemon juice, and lemon zest. Bring this to a boil over high heat and then reduce the heat to low, simmering for 5 minutes to sweeten and concentrate mixture into a light syrup.

3. Meanwhile, fill a large bowl with ice and place another smaller bowl inside it.

4. Pour the hot syrup into the bowl over ice to cool.

5. Add the fruits in stages from the strongest to the most fragile, so that they stay intact. If you don't follow these instructions, your soup will be too mushy. Start with the cherries. After you've added them, stir the mixture for a few minutes and then let it sit for 5 minutes. Add the blueberries, stir for 1 minute, and rest for 5 minutes. Add the blackberries, stir for 1 minute, and rest for 5 minutes. You will add the raspberries and red currants to the soup just before serving.

6. Stir in the grappa.

7. Taste the soup for sweetness. The fruit should have sweetened up the syrup. Place the fruit in syrup in the refrigerator to chill completely, about 45 minutes.

To Make the Sabayon

1. Meanwhile, make the sabayon by bringing a medium saucepan of water to a boil over high heat, and then reduce the heat to low.

2. Prepare a large bowl of ice and set it aside.

3. Using a handheld mixer or KitchenAid, whip the heavy cream to soft peaks and set it aside.

4. In a medium stainless steel mixing bowl that will fit on top of the pan of simmering water, whisk together the egg yolks, sugar, and strongly brewed tea.

5. Set the bowl on top of the pot of simmering water, making sure the bowl does not touch the water. Cook the mixture, whisking constantly, until it's thick, 5 to 6 minutes. The sabayon should have tripled in volume and it should hold its shape when it falls from the whisk.

6. Remove the bowl from the pot and place it in the big bowl of ice. Whisk until the mixture is cool, about 5 minutes.

7. Fold the cream (see Folding, page 135) into the sabayon and refrigerate it until serving time.

8. Just before serving, carefully stir the raspberries and currants into the bowl of syrup soaked berries.

9. Ladle a cup of berry soup into each bowl and top it with ⅓ cup of soft sabayon over the center of each bowl.

Palace Bread: Syrup-Soaked Bread Pudding with Thick Cream and Pistachios

This sweet, sticky dessert, called *ekmek kadayifi* in Turkish, is based on an Ottoman recipe that was passed along the trade routes from Egypt to Syria. I tasted many versions of palace bread in the Arabic markets in Watertown, Massachusetts, and then I enlisted Maura Kilpatrick's help in perfecting a version for Oleana. Maura's palace bread is more caramely than the traditional Ottoman recipe, and it's the best I've ever tasted.

Be sure to serve your palace bread with plenty of mascarpone cheese, giving your guests enough to taste a little with every bite. Although it's rich, the tart quality of the cheese will offset the intense syrup of the soaked bread.

Palace bread is one of Oleana's signature desserts, and when it reappears on the menu, regular customers come in just for its return.

— SERVES 8 —

3¾ cups sugar	1 large baguette (about 12 ounces) cut into four 6-inch pieces, crusts trimmed and removed
1¼ cups mild honey	
1 tablespoon rosewater	1 cup mascarpone cheese, at room temperature
1 tablespoon freshly squeezed lemon juice (about ½ lemon)	½ cup finely chopped, lightly toasted pistachios (see page 91)

1. In a large, shallow saucepan or sauté pan big enough to hold the loaf of bread, combine the sugar and 1 cup of water. Bring this to a boil over medium-high heat.

2. Stir in the honey, bring to a simmer, and reduce heat to medium-low. Continue cooking until the honey-syrup darkens to light amber. This will take about 18 minutes.

3. Add the rosewater and lemon. At this point, the syrup should be quite thick.

4. Put the bread in the pan and carefully push it down into the syrup with the back of a ladle. Ladle the syrup on top. Slowly simmer the bread in the syrup for 30 to 40 minutes, continuing to submerge and baste the bread with syrup.

From time to time, carefully add small amounts of water to thin the syrup and prevent it from becoming too dark and sticky.

5. When the bread has turned a translucent amber color all over, remove the pan from the heat and set it aside to let the bread cool slightly and absorb most of the remaining syrup.

6. Transfer the bread to a cutting board and, with a serrated knife, cut it into 8 squares and then again into 16 small triangles.

7. Serve 2 pieces of bread on each plate, topped with 2 tablespoons of mascarpone cheese and a generous tablespoon of chopped pistachios over the mascarpone.

4.

5.

7.

NASTURTIUM, ORANGE BLOSSOM, ROSE, CHAMOMILE, LAVENDER, AND JASMINE

Poached Nectarine Stuffed with Nougat Glacé

Nougat glacé, or frozen nougat, is a traditional dessert in the south of France that shows Arabic origins in the use of honey and nuts. I've eaten dozens of nougat glacés in Nice, but I always find the texture to be too dry and crumbly to resemble ice cream. Oleana's pastry chef Maura Kilpatrick has created a delightfully light and fluffy twist on the French original, spiking the meringue with bits of candied orange and pistachio and using just a touch of orange-blossom water to enhance its Arabic flavors.

This recipe makes an amazingly light ice cream at home, and you don't even need an ice cream maker. You can stuff it into poached nectarines or peaches when they are in season. It's important to wait for good, ripe fruit. Or you can simply serve the nougat on its own with fresh fruit on top.

The pistachio praline and candied orange can be made up to week in advance, stored in an airtight container.

If you like sweet wine, try pairing this dessert with a delicious orange muscat from California.

⤙ Serves 8 ⤚

For the Candied Orange	For the Pistachio Praline
1 orange	1 tablespoon butter, softened
1 cup sugar plus more for coating strips	¾ cup sugar
	½ cup pistachios, toasted and roughly chopped

To Make the Candied Orange

1. To remove the peel from the orange, cut the orange into quarters and peel away the orange segments, reserving the orange for eating. Cut each quarter peel into ¼-inch strips.

2. In a small saucepan, blanch the orange peels by dropping them into boiling water. Bring the water back to a boil and then drain the peels. Repeat the blanching process 3 more times; this removes bitterness and softens the peels. After the fourth time, remove the peels and drain all the water out except for about ¼ cup, or enough to coat the bottom of the pan.

3. Add 1 cup of the sugar and turn the heat to medium-high. After a few minutes, the mixture should become syrupy. Let this boil without stirring about 5 minutes. You may need to swirl the pan around to prevent the sugar from clumping.

4. After 5 minutes, test with a spoon for stickiness. If the syrup sticks to the spoon, it is ready. Add the peels and stir carefully to coat them.

5. Using a fork, lay the peels out across a wire cooling rack in single layer. Dry them for 10 minutes.

6. While the orange peels are still warm, toss them with enough sugar to coat them (tossing 3 or so at a time) and return them to the rack to dry for another hour.

7. Dice the peels into small pieces. Set aside.

To Make the Pistachio Praline

1. Line a baking sheet with foil and rub it evenly with the soft butter.

2. Combine the sugar and ¼ cup of water in a small saucepan, stirring until the sugar dissolves.

3. Place the pan over medium-high heat and cook without stirring until the mixture turns golden brown.

continued

NASTURTIUM, ORANGE BLOSSOM, ROSE, CHAMOMILE, LAVENDER, AND JASMINE

4. Remove the mixture from the heat and quickly stir in the pistachios.

5. Immediately pour the mixture onto the buttered foil. After about 10 minutes, when the praline has cooled and hardened so that you can handle it, break it into 1-to 2-inch pieces and then finely chop it into bits. Set aside.

To Make the Nougat Glacé

1. Using a handheld mixer or KitchenAid with a whip attachment, whip the cream to soft peaks and set it aside in the refrigerator.

2. Combine the honey, corn syrup, and ½ cup of the sugar in a medium saucepan. Place the mixture on medium-low heat, stirring to dissolve the sugar. Cook the honey mixture to 250°F, using a candy thermometer to check the temperature.

3. While the honey cooks, prepare the egg whites. Using a handheld mixer or KitchenAid with a whip attachment, whip the egg whites on medium speed until foamy. Increase the speed and slowly add ¼ cup of the sugar. Keep whipping until the egg whites are smooth and shiny but not stiff, then reduce the speed to medium-low. If the egg whites stiffen before the honey is ready, reduce the speed to low.

4. With the mixer on low, pour the sugar syrup into the egg whites. Increase the speed to high and whip this mixture for 5 to 7 minutes, until the egg whites are cool and very stiff.

5. Fold (see page 135) the whipped cream into the egg whites, ⅓ at a time. Keep folding until the mixture is smooth.

6. Fold in the orange peel, pistachio praline, pistachios, and orange-blossom water.

6.

7. Place the nougat glacé in a plastic container and freeze it overnight or for at least 6 hours.

8. Meanwhile make the poaching liquid by combining 6 cups of water, the remaining 2 cups of sugar, and the lemon juice in a medium saucepan.

9. Prepare the nectarines by cutting a thin slice off the bottom of each whole nectarine to flatten it so that it can stand without rolling. Using a sharp paring knife, cut into the top of each nectarine at an angle and cut around the side of the pit to the bottom of the nectarine. Push the pit out from the bottom with your finger. Trim any fruit stuck to the pits and add the pieces to the poaching liquid.

10. Bring the saucepan of poaching liquid to a boil over medium-high heat, stirring once to dissolve the sugar. Reduce the heat to a medium-low or a brisk simmer.

11. Add the nectarines, 4 at a time, and cook them until they're just tender when pierced with a knife, 5 to 6 minutes.

12. Remove the nectarines with a slotted spoon and set them aside to cool. Poach the remaining nectarines.

13. After about 8 minutes, when the nectarines are cool enough to handle, peel the skins off with your fingers. The peel should come off in large pieces and leave some rosiness on the nectarines.

14. Put 2 cups of the poaching liquid in a small saucepan over high heat. Bring to a boil and then reduce the heat to a simmer. Simmer the liquid for about 10 minutes, until reduced to 1 cup. Cool the liquid for about 10 minutes and then refrigerate it for an hour or overnight. You can strain and reserve the remaining poaching liquid to make a sweet syrup to add to iced tea or sparkling water.

15. To serve, place a whole nectarine on a plate and scoop about ½ cup of nougat into the center, so that it fills the nectarine and spills out a bit from the top. Spoon a few tablespoons of chilled syrup over the top and serve immediately.

Watermelon Granité and Frozen Yogurt Parfait with Real Rose Petal Jam

Melon and rose is one of my favorite summer combinations, especially when served up in a frozen treat on a hot day. Granité, which is a scraped ice, is a fun alternative to sorbet. Granité can be labor intensive: you have to scrape it little by little with a fork to give it a fluffy and not icy texture that dissolves instantly on your tongue. Granité is one of the oldest frozen desserts; Napoleon had snow shipped from Sicily's Mount Etna so that he could flavor it with fruit syrups.

Every June, Oleana purchases beach rose petals foraged by Eva Sommaripa, a farmer who lives in Westport, Massachusetts. Beach roses have a softer texture and lighter perfume than common roses, and we use them to make a heavenly rose petal jam—enough to last us at least 6 months in the freezer.

Maura Kilpatrick, Oleana's pastry chef, created this unique dessert. The watermelon granité also makes a great cocktail when combined with rum. All of the components must be prepared at least a day in advance and up to 3 days.

SERVES 8

For the Watermelon Granité

3 cups sugar

One 4½- to 5-pound watermelon, peeled, seeded, and cut into small chunks

Pinch of salt

Juice of 1 lime

For the Frozen Yogurt Parfait

2 cups whole-milk plain yogurt, preferably Greek-style

¼ cup heavy cream

Grated zest (see page 72) and juice of 1 lime

4 eggs, separated

¾ cup sugar

For the Rose Petal Jam

2 teaspoons rosewater

1 tablespoon freshly squeezed lemon juice (about ½ lemon)

3 cups pink beach rose petals, lightly packed

To Make the Granité

1. In a medium saucepan bring 3 cups of the sugar and 3 cups of water to a boil over medium-high heat. Boil for 3 to 4 minutes to dissolve the sugar and lightly thicken the syrup. Remove the syrup from the heat, pour it into a liquid measuring cup, and set it aside. You should have about 4 cups of simple syrup.

2. Use a blender to puree the watermelon in small batches. Strain the puree through a fine sieve into a medium mixing bowl, discarding the solids. You should have 3½ to 4 cups of watermelon puree.

3. Stir in 1 cup of the prepared simple syrup and taste the watermelon liquid for sweetness. Add another 2 to 3 tablespoons of the simple syrup, depending on desired sweetness. It should be sweet but not overly sweet.

4. Stir in the salt and lime juice from 1 lime.

5. Pour the mixture into a shallow baking pan or Pyrex dish and place it in the freezer for 1½ hours.

6. Stir the frozen pieces from the edges into the center of the pan with a fork. Repeat this stirring, every 30 minutes, for another 1½ to 2 hours. Be patient: the more you stir the granité, the lighter and fluffier the ice crystals will be when complete. You can store the granité in your freezer for 5 to 7 days.

To Make the Frozen Yogurt Parfait

1. Use a handheld mixer or KitchenAid with a whisk attachment, and beat the yogurt, cream, and lime zest and lime juice until soft peaks form. Set aside in the refrigerator.

2. Using a handheld mixer or KitchenAid with a whisk attachment, whip the egg yolks at medium speed, slowly adding ¼ cup of the sugar, until the yolks are pale yellow and thickened, for about 4 to 5 minutes. Scrape the yolks into a medium mixing bowl.

3. In another medium mixing bowl, whip the egg whites on medium speed until they become foamy or frothy, about 2 minutes.

4. Slowly and little by little, add the remaining ½ cup sugar and continue whipping until the egg whites form soft peaks.

5. Gently fold ½ of the egg whites into the egg yolk mixture. When combined, add the rest of the whites, folding as before.

6. Fold in the whipped yogurt mixture carefully, trying not to deflate the mixture.

7. Pour the yogurt into a plastic container and place it in the freezer for at least 4 hours or overnight. You will have more than 8 servings of frozen yogurt, but you won't be able to achieve sufficient volume doing the recipe with fewer eggs.

continued

NASTURTIUM, ORANGE BLOSSOM, ROSE, CHAMOMILE, LAVENDER, AND JASMINE

To Make the Rose Petal Jam

1. Combine the remaining 3 cups simple syrup, the rosewater, and lemon juice in a medium saucepan over medium-high heat and bring it to a boil. Add the rose petals, pressing them down with a large spoon.

2. Reduce the heat to medium and keep the syrup at a low boil for 25 to 30 minutes, until reduced by ⅓. To check for thickness, spoon some syrup onto a plate; if you can then run the spoon through the syrup and the line remains, remove the jam from the heat.

3. Cool the jam to room temperature for at least 20 minutes. Refrigerate the jam overnight in a small bowl or plastic container.

4. The next day, taste the syrup. If it's too sweet, add another squeeze of fresh lemon juice. You will have more rose jam than you need for 8 servings, so freeze the remaining cup or so for future use. Try it tossed with fresh local strawberries.

To Assemble the Dessert

1. Freeze 8 parfait cups or glass dessert dishes for at least 30 to 40 minutes.

2. Place a scoop of granité into each dessert dish and create a well in the center with the back of a spoon. Place a scoop of frozen yogurt in the well and top with a tablespoon of rose jam. Serve immediately.

SPICE: FLAVORS OF THE EASTERN MEDITERRANEAN

Frozen Jasmine Soufflé with Tropical Fruit Syrup

Maura likes to serve this impressive frozen soufflé in the winter, when there are no locally grown fruits. I've noticed that the tropical flavors cheer people up and out of their winter blues. So does the addition of light spices, which perks up the syrup and pairs with the exotic jasmine.

The recipe is actually easier to make than it appears, but it does take some time. It is a soufflé in that the egg whites create the airiness; the finished product is more like light ice cream. Once you have mastered the technique, you can play with the recipe by infusing the cream with other flavors, such as lavender, ginger, or mint.

You'll need to infuse the cream with the jasmine tea at least 1 day and up to 3 days before preparing the dessert. You will also need ten to twelve small soufflé molds that can hold 4 to 6 ounces or use professional ring molds; see Maura's suggestions on page 325.

Makes 1½ quarts to serve 10 to 12

¼ cup loose jasmine tea

2½ cups heavy cream

8 egg yolks

2⅔ cups sugar

3 egg whites

2 tablespoons light corn syrup

3 whole star anise pods

6 whole cloves

6 black peppercorns

½ vanilla bean, split in half lengthwise

Grated zest (see page 72)
and juice of 1 lime

Pinch of salt

2 kiwi fruits, peeled and
diced into ¼-to ½-inch cubes

1 pineapple, peeled and
diced into ¼-to ½-inch cubes

1 mango, peeled and diced
into ¼-to ½-inch cubes

NASTURTIUM, ORANGE BLOSSOM, ROSE, CHAMOMILE, LAVENDER, AND JASMINE

1. Prepare the jasmine cream by heating the loose tea and cream in a medium saucepan over medium-high heat until just boiling. Remove from the stove, cover the pan, and let the jasmine steep and infuse in the cream for at least 1 to 2 hours.

2. Strain the cream through a fine sieve into a small bowl or container and refrigerate it overnight.

3. Using a handheld mixer or a KitchenAid fitted with a whip attachment, whip the jasmine cream to form soft peaks. Refrigerate in a small bowl or container.

4. Place the egg yolks in a mixing bowl. Begin whipping the yolks on high speed.

5. Meanwhile, make the syrup by cooking ½ cup of the sugar, the corn syrup, and 2 tablespoons of water in a small saucepan over medium heat, stirring once to dissolve the sugar, for about 5 minutes, until the temperature reaches 245°F on a candy thermometer. Remove the syrup from the heat.

6. Reduce the mixer speed to low and pour the syrup over the yolks, trying not to hit the whisk but aiming for the side of the bowl. When all the syrup is incorporated, increase the speed to medium-high and beat until the mixture is pale yellow and has doubled in volume, and the mixing bowl is cool to the touch. This will take 4 to 5 minutes. Transfer the mixture to a large mixing bowl and clean the work bowl.

7. In the clean, dry work bowl, begin beating the egg whites on medium speed.

8. In a small saucepan over medium heat, make the simple syrup by boiling ½ cup of the sugar and ¼ cup of water, stirring once to dissolve the sugar. Continue to cook without stirring until the temperature reaches 245°F on a candy thermometer.

9. By this time the egg whites should be at soft peak stage. Decrease the mixer speed to low and slowly pour the simple syrup into the whites, trying not to hit the whisk and aiming for the side of the work bowl.

10. Once the simple syrup is incorporated, increase the mixer speed to high and beat the whites until they are soft-peaked and shiny and the bowl is cool to the touch. This will take 4 to 5 minutes.

11. Using a rubber spatula, fold the whipped jasmine cream into the egg whites and then fold this mixture into the egg yolks, half of it at a time.

12. When the mixture is combined, pour the soufflé into ten to twelve 4- to 6-ounce soufflé molds and freeze them overnight. See Maura's tips on molding frozen desserts below.

13. Place the star anise pods, cloves, and peppercorns in a plastic bag. Crush the spices with a rolling pin until they are coarsely broken.

14. Combine the spices with 4 cups of water and the remaining 1⅔ cup of sugar, the vanilla bean, and lime zest and juice in a medium saucepan. Bring to a boil over high heat, stirring once to dissolve the sugar, and then reduce the heat to medium-low. Simmer the syrup for 15 to 20 minutes. Remove from the heat and allow the syrup to steep and infuse for at least 1 hour at room temperature.

15. Strain the syrup through a fine sieve into a medium bowl to remove the spices, and add the salt.

16. Stir the fruit pieces into the syrup and chill for at least 1 hour before serving.

17. Just before serving, take the soufflés out of their molds by running them under hot tap water for a minute. Turn them out into shallow bowls and top each with ½ to 1 cup of fruit coated with plenty of syrup.

MAURA'S TIPS ON MOLDING FROZEN DESSERTS

1. Professional stainless steel rings or other individual molds are available at specialty stores such as Sur La Table, if you choose to invest in them.

2. As a substitute for these fancy rings, you can purchase PVC pipe from a hardware store and have it cut into 3-inch rings. PVC pipe cannot be used for baking, however. Lightly oil the PVC pipes with a neutral oil, such as canola, and then place them onto a baking sheet. Before filling the rings with soufflé mixture, line each ring with plastic wrap, so that you can easily remove the frozen soufflé from the ring mold.

3. You can also use a soufflé ramekin, but the frozen dessert can be difficult to remove from the mold. It's often better to serve the dessert in the ramekin than to try to remove it.

4. The last option–and aside from the professional rings, perhaps the best–is to use 3- to 5-ounce paper drinking cups. Tear them away once the soufflé is frozen.

NASTURTIUM, ORANGE BLOSSOM, ROSE, CHAMOMILE, LAVENDER, AND JASMINE

Strawberry Lavender Tart

This recipe is a celebration of the delightful combination of strawberries and lavender. It's worth waiting for your local strawberry season, which, in New England, runs from June through early July. Strawberries trucked across the country out of season from other locales are just not as good. If you've ever tasted a strawberry picked fresh out of the garden, you'll know that it's worth delaying your gratification until local strawberry season.

This tart is also good with raspberries, blueberries, cherries, and blackberries.

The pastry is finished by hand, so it's important to freeze the butter in small pieces for a half hour before making it. Freezing keeps the dough moist but crumbly and prevents it from becoming tough. The pastry can be made 1 to 2 days in advance.

The best tart pan to use for this recipe is one with a removable bottom and short, fluted edges.

You can pair this dessert with a sweet, slightly effervescent Brachetto d'Acqui wine from the Piedmonte region of Italy.

⌒∿ MAKES ONE 9-INCH TART TO SERVE 8 ∿⌒

For the Crust	For the Filling
1½ sticks cold unsalted butter	1½ cups heavy cream
1¼ cups plus 2 tablespoons flour	2 tablespoons dried lavender
½ teaspoon salt	½ cup sugar
1 teaspoon sugar	⅓ cup flour
3 tablespoons heavy cream	5 cups strawberries, washed, hulled, dried, and halved

For the Lavender Syrup

1 cup sugar

½ cup dried lavender

2 cups water

¾ cup honey

2 teaspoons freshly squeezed lemon juice
(about ¼ lemon)

For the Whipped Cream

2 cups heavy cream

2 tablespoons lavender syrup

To Make the Crust

1. Cut the butter into ½-inch cubes and freeze them for 20 to 30 minutes.

2. Combine the flour, salt, butter, and sugar in the work bowl of an electric mixer. Using the paddle attachment, mix on low speed, until the butter is the size of small peas.

3. Pour in the cream and continue to mix on low speed, just until the dough appears moist but still loose and crumbly.

4. Put the dough mixture on a lightly floured work surface and work it together with your hands to form a smooth ball. Don't work it any further than this, or the gluten will develop and it will become tough. You should be able to see little pieces of butter in the dough.

5. Press the dough into a flat disc and wrap it tightly with plastic wrap. Place the dough in the refrigerator to chill for at least 2 hours.

6. After the dough has chilled, let it sit at room temperature for about 5 minutes. Then, on a lightly floured work surface, begin rolling the disc, lifting and turning as you roll to prevent sticking and to achieve a circular shape. Roll the dough out to a ½-inch-thick circle that is 2 to 3 inches larger in diameter than your tart pan.

7. Lightly butter or oil the tart pan. Roll the dough over the rolling pin or fold it in half so that you can lift it and place it into the tart pan. Ease the dough into the pan, pressing it down to seal it into the bottom edge and against the sides. Trim the dough evenly with the top of the tart pan edges by rolling the pin over the top. Place the tart uncovered in the freezer to rest for at least 30 minutes to 1 hour before baking.

8. Preheat the oven to 350°F.

9. Completely line the bottom and sides of the tart shell with parchment paper or aluminum foil. Fill the lining up to the rim with dried beans or rice. These can be saved for your next tart. Make sure the beans or rice cover the entire tart pan from edge to edge. The weight will keep the pastry intact as it bakes.

continued

10. Bake the tart shell for 30 minutes. Remove the pie weights and cook for 5 minutes longer or until the crust on the bottom is no longer moist. Let the tart cool for at least 20 minutes.

To Make the Filling

1. Meanwhile, heat the cream with the lavender in a medium saucepan over medium heat, until just boiling. Remove from the heat. Cover the pan and let the lavender steep and infuse with the cream for at least 1 hour at room temperature.

2. Strain the lavender cream through a fine sieve into a large mixing bowl. Discard the herbs.

3. Whisk the sugar and flour into the cream, being sure to whisk away any lumps.

4. Add the berries and stir to coat all the berries with the cream mixture. Let them sit for about 10 minutes to absorb as much cream as possible.

5. Using a slotted spoon or your hands, scoop up the berries, letting some of the excess cream drain through the spoon or your fingers. Place the berries into the baked tart shell. Arrange them evenly and discard the excess cream mixture. You may have ¼ to ½ cup of cream left at the bottom of the bowl.

6. Place the tart on a heavy baking sheet and reduce the oven temperature to 325° F.

7. Bake the tart for 40 to 45 minutes. The tart will still appear moist.

To Make the Lavender Syrup

1. Meanwhile, make the syrup by combining the sugar, lavender, water, and honey in medium saucepan. Bring the mixture to a boil over medium-high heat, stirring once to dissolve the sugar, and reduce the heat to medium. Briskly simmer until the syrup reaches 235° F on a candy thermometer, 30 to 35 minutes.

2. Cool the syrup completely for about 30 minutes at room temperature and strain it through a fine sieve. Stir in the lemon juice. You will have about 1 cup of syrup, which is more than you need. It freezes very well and makes an excellent sweetener for homemade lemonade or iced tea.

To Make the Whipped Cream

1. Make the whipped cream by whipping the cream with a wire whip or an electric mixer on high speed until it forms soft peaks. Add 2 tablespoons of lavender syrup and continue to whip until combined.

2. When the tart has cooled completely, after about 30 minutes, serve each slice with a few spoons of lavender syrup drizzled over it. Top with whipped cream and serve.

Dunia's Iced Tea

My mother lives in New Orleans and frequents a Lebanese restaurant there called Mona's that serves a delicious Lebanese iced tea. My mother loves Mona's tea, and she implored me to figure out how to re-create it.

Tea is only served hot in Arabic countries—iced tea is an American invention. So with a little playfulness, I set out to experiment. I spoke to my friends Diala Ezzediene and Hashim Sarkis from Beirut, and they told me about jallab syrup, which is made from dates, raisins, and rosewater and has a natural caramel flavor similar to cola. The syrup sweetens the tea perfectly. You can find it at Middle Eastern stores and at www.kalustyans.com.

I named this delicious iced tea after Diala and Hashim's daughter, Dunia. *Dunya* means "the world" in ten different languages, including Arabic and Turkish.

Dunia's iced tea is refreshing and addictive year-round.

MAKES 8 SERVINGS

8 cups brewed black tea

1 cup jallab syrup

2 tablespoons freshly squeezed lemon juice (about ½ lemon)

Ice

8 mint sprigs, washed and dried well for garnish

4 tablespoons lightly toasted pine nuts (see page 91)

1. Allow the tea to set at room temperature for at least 1 hour after it has steeped.

2. Stir in the jallab syrup and lemon juice and taste. Add more jallab syrup depending on your preference for sweetness.

3. Fill 8 glasses halfway with ice. Drop a mint sprig into each and pour the tea over the tops, filling each glass.

4. Sprinkle the top of each glass with ½ tablespoon of pine nuts and serve.

NASTURTIUM, ORANGE BLOSSOM, ROSE, CHAMOMILE, LAVENDER, AND JASMINE

12
RICH, CREAMY FLAVOR
Nuts,
Yogurt, and Cheese

I include nuts, yogurt, and cheese in this book because, like spices, they play an important role in enriching foods throughout the Mediterranean. Pesto is a well-known example of a sauce that is thickened by nuts and enriched by cheese, but there are endless other examples waiting for you to discover.

Especially in the eastern Mediterranean region, nuts, yogurt, and cheese give depth, richness, and texture to sauces, pilafs, vegetable dishes, pastas, and soups without adding heaviness.

Nuts

Nuts play a crucial role in Mediterranean cooking: they add a layer of rich flavor to foods–much like cream and butter–but without all the heavy fat. I love butter and cream, but only in small amounts. Too much can ruin a meal, making me feel too full, too quickly.

Nuts are versatile, their uses are endless, and because they grow so abundantly in the Mediterranean rim, they are a staple of the cuisine. Natural nut oils blended with water can be made into milk, which forms the basis for Sicilian-style ice creams. Combined with olive oil, finely ground nuts can be used much like egg yolks to thicken a Turkish sauce called tarator that looks like thin mayonnaise. Crushed nuts can also be blended with bread crumbs to form picada, a Spanish thickener for soups and sauces, which is an Arabic version of the French butter-and-flour thickener called roux.

❧ Nuts Tips

1. *Store your nuts in the freezer in an airtight container to keep them super fresh.*

2. *Buy nuts in bulk; they tend to be fresher than prepackaged nuts.*

3. *Look for blond walnuts from Turkey, which you can find in Middle Eastern markets. They aren't as bitter as California walnuts.*

Yogurt

In the United States, we consider yogurt to be a low-fat or even nonfat diet food, available in multicolored convenience packs at the supermarket. For most of the rest of the world, though, yogurt is wonderfully thick and creamy, is combined with pastas and meat dishes, and is often homemade. Some Greek yogurts are as thick as cheese, and you can cut them with a knife. Labne, eaten on vegetable dishes throughout the eastern Mediterranean region, is a delicious strained yogurt that has the consistency of mascarpone cheese.

Yogurt tastes delicious, and it also has many health benefits. The "good" bacteria in yogurt aids in digestion and kills bad bacteria that can cause illness; this is why yogurt is often taken as a beverage in Middle Eastern countries and in India.

I've tasted just about every yogurt available in Boston, and my favorites are the Greek brands like Krinos (www.krinos.com) and one made with sheep's milk in upstate New York by Old Chatham Sheep Herding Company (www.blacksheepcheese.com). Sheep's milk is higher in fat than cow's milk, so the consistency is extremely creamy–more akin to European yogurts. The Greek brands are made with cow's milk and are the thickest, but with a texture so creamy that they appear to be whipped. If neither alternative is available, seek out a locally made yogurt. For Greek yogurt available online, try www.parthenonfoods.com. Another delicious, really thick and creamy brand is Total by Fage Company, available in both cow's and sheep's milk varieties at Whole Foods stores and Trader Joe's.

If a good whole-milk yogurt isn't available, you can use low-fat, as opposed to nonfat yogurt. Just be sure to add 1 tablespoon of heavy cream to every cup of yogurt to impart a whole-milk flavor.

You can make your own thick yogurt at home by straining whole-milk yogurt overnight in a colander or sieve lined with cheesecloth in your refrigerator.

It's also easy to make your own fresh, delicious yogurt from scratch (see Leslie's Homemade Yogurt, page 333).

RECIPES WITH NUTS, YOGURT, AND CHEESE

Leslie's Homemade Yogurt

Leslie Chaison, an organic farmer who lives in Massachusetts's Pioneer Valley, gave me her tried and true recipe. While the yogurt is forming, it's important to keep it at a consistent temperature (around 100°F), to ensure the growth of cultures.

↝ MAKES 1 QUART ↜

1 quart fresh, good-quality whole milk	2 heaping tablespoons plain whole-milk yogurt

1. Preheat the oven to 100°F.

2. In a medium saucepan, heat the milk, shutting off the heat just before it scalds. Let the milk cool to about 100°F.

3. Run hot water over a medium nonmetal bowl, such as a ceramic crock or glass mixing bowl, to warm it up. Dry off the bowl.

4. Pour the heated milk into the bowl. Using a whisk, add the yogurt to the milk, blending thoroughly.

5. Wrap a small bath towel around the outside of the bowl. Place this inside a large mixing bowl. Fill the large mixing bowl with very hot water, so that the water reaches almost to the top. Cover the smaller bowl with a lid or large plate.

6. Place the wrapped and covered milk and yogurt mixture into the oven and leave it there for at least 6 hours or overnight. The oven temperature needs to remain at a constant 100°F to 110°F (warming temperature). Do not leave the yogurt in the oven for more than 8 to 10 hours. The longer you leave it in the oven, the more sour it will taste. The refrigerated yogurt should keep for at least a week.

Armenian Bean and Walnut Pâté

This recipe was inspired by my friend Armen Mehrabyan, who lives in Armenia, where he grows and harvests wild herbs that he makes into teas and essential oils. Armen supplies many of Oleana's teas as well as some of our wild cooking herbs. He also researches ancient Armenian recipes, and he prepared this one–whipped beans and nuts in a bowl sprinkled with pomegranate seeds–during one of his visits to America.

I altered the recipe a little, because I like to serve it in a log that can be sliced and presented as a vegetarian pâté. At Oleana, we serve this dish with Shoushan's Homemade String Cheese (page 178) as a bread condiment or hors d'oeuvres.

Pomegranate season comes in the late fall and runs through the winter. When fresh pomegranates are not available, you can dot each piece of pâté with a drop of pomegranate molasses to impart a lemony tartness.

⟶ MAKES ONE 16-INCH LOG TO SERVE 8 ⟵

1 cup dark red kidney beans,
   soaked overnight and rinsed well

5 cups water

¼ white onion, roughly chopped

1 bay leaf

1½ cups walnuts, lightly toasted
   (see page 91), plus a few for garnish

½ teaspoon chopped garlic
   (about 1 small clove)

4 tablespoons butter

Salt and pepper to taste

1 tablespoon chopped fresh dill

1 tablespoon chopped fresh mint or basil

1 tablespoon chopped fresh flat-leaf parsley

¼ cup pomegranate seeds
   (about ½ pomegranate)
   plus a few for garnish

1. In a medium saucepan over medium-high heat, bring the beans to a boil with the water, onion, and bay leaf. Reduce the heat to medium-low and simmer for 40 to 50 minutes, until the beans are very tender. Skim off any white foam that forms at the top as the beans cook.

2. Drain the beans into a colander and discard the bay leaf.

3. While the beans are still warm, toss them with the walnuts, garlic, and butter in a medium mixing bowl. Add salt and pepper. You will need at least 1½ teaspoons of salt. Stir until everything is combined and the butter has softened and is evenly distributed throughout.

4. Purée the mixture in a food processor fitted with a metal blade, until smooth and creamy, 3 to 4 minutes. You should have a thick bean puree or paste.

5. In a small mixing bowl, mix the herbs together and then blend half of them into the beans.

6. Spread the purée ¼ to ½ inch thick onto a small baking sheet, lined with plastic wrap. Cool completely at room temperature, for at least 30 minutes.

7. Sprinkle the purée generously with the ¼ cup pomegranate seeds and remaining fresh herbs, and then roll the purée into a log from one end to the other, using the plastic wrap to help roll.

8. Wrap the log tightly in plastic wrap and chill it again for 2 hours or overnight.

9. Cut the log into ½- to 1-inch-thick slices and garnish with walnuts and pomegranate seeds.

7.

7.

8.

Maria's Feta Sauce with Shrimp, Melon, and Tomato

This is another recipe from the kitchen of my good friend, Maria Hatziiliades. Like most sauces, it can be put to many uses. Its wonderful combination of smoky, salty, spicy flavors makes it ideal for grilled vegetables, lamb, and beef. In the summer, I love to serve Maria's feta sauce with grilled shrimp and chunks of melon and heirloom tomatoes.

Serve a light, effervescent Gavi from the Piedmonte region with this dish.

MAKES ALMOST 3 CUPS SAUCE TO SERVE ABOUT 6

For the Sauce

1 to 2 jalapeños or
   1 small Hungarian hot pepper

14 to 16 ounces creamy French feta,
   roughly crumbled (2 cups)

½ cup extra-virgin olive oil plus
   about 1 tablespoon for brushing

¼ cup hot water

1 pinch salt

For the Salad

6 skewers

18 to 30 peeled and deveined shrimp

Extra-virgin olive oil

Salt and pepper to taste

2 to 3 brandywine, German Johnson,
   or other heirloom tomatoes,
   cut into 1- to 2- inch chunks
   (about 3 cups)

¼ seedless watermelon,
   cut into 1- to 2-inch chunks
   (about 3 cups)

1 tablespoon fresh chopped oregano
   or 2 tablespoons sliced fresh basil leaves

To Make the Sauce

1. Prepare a charcoal grill (see Grilling Tips, page 100).

2. Grill the peppers on all sides for about 3 minutes, until the skins have charred and blistered a little. Keep the grill going for the shrimp skewers. You can alternatively char the peppers on your stovetop, following the directions for roasting and peeling peppers on page 97.

3. When the peppers are cool enough to handle, peel them and remove some of the seeds. The more seeds you leave in, the hotter it will be.

4. Combine the peppers, feta, olive oil, hot water, and pinch of salt in a blender and purée until smooth and creamy, for about 2 minutes, stopping once to stir and scrape the sides.

To Make the Salad

1. Place 3 to 5 shrimp on each skewer. Brush the shrimp with a little olive oil on both sides and season them with salt and pepper.

2. Grill the shrimp for about 3 minutes on each sides, or until the shrimp are pink and no longer translucent, and cooked through.

3. Season the chunks of tomato and melon with salt and pepper.

4. Serve the grilled shrimp on a platter with the chunks of melon and tomato surrounding a bowl of feta sauce for dipping. Sprinkle with oregano.

Garlic and Almond Soup

There is a saying in Provence: "*Aigo bouido sauva la vido,*" which means "garlic soup saves lives." It is true that garlic has immune-stimulating properties, and it has been used for millennia to heal a range of ailments. Although this soup just may save lives, it's also plain out-of-this-world delicious.

I created this recipe in 1993 when I was the chef at Aigo Bistro in Concord, Massachusetts, and it has followed me from restaurant to restaurant ever since. It's a favorite of loyal customers and has become a signature dish. I was originally inspired by the Provencal soup called *aigo bouido,* which means "boiled garlic " in old Provencal dialect, and then I gave the soup a Spanish twist by adding a *picada*–a mixture of puréed almonds and bread crumbs–to thicken it.

It's important to use a blender to prepare this soup because the blade pulls in and gives a smoother and tighter purée, leaving no chunks of almonds or bread. The garlic becomes sweet, soft, and silky when it's roasted, making for a sweet, creamy soup. I like to garnish it with a parsleyed olive oil, which I make in the blender until the parsley liquefies and the natural chlorophyll turns the oil bright green. I also add a little vitamin C to the oil to help keep its vivid green color for up to a week.

Drink some rosé from Provence or Spain with this soup and serve it with Grilled Mushroom Banderilla (page 45).

⮜⮜ MAKES ABOUT 10 CUPS TO SERVE 8 ⮞⮞

6 whole heads garlic

4 tablespoons canola oil

Salt and pepper to taste

1 tablespoon butter

2 large onions, peeled, halved,
and cut into thin strips

½ cup dry bread crumbs (Panko Brand or plain
unseasoned, not sourdough)

1 cup blanched whole or slivered almonds
(no skins; see Note, page 340)

8 thin slices French bread or baguette

8 tablespoons extra-virgin olive oil

8 cups chicken stock, preferably homemade

½ vitamin C tablet (optional)

½ bunch fresh flat-leaf parsley
(about 1 cup)

1. Preheat the oven to 350°F.

2. Split the garlic heads in half widthwise, and season with salt and pepper. Place the cut sides down on a heavy baking sheet lightly coated with about 2 tablespoons of the canola oil.

3. Roast the garlic in the oven for 20 to 25 minutes, until the garlic is soft. Once the garlic is cool, after about 30 minutes, squeeze the garlic out of its skin. You should have about 1½ cups of squeezed garlic.

4. Over medium-high heat, melt the butter with the remaining 2 tablespoons of canola oil in a large, heavy sauté pan, until the butter begins to brown. Add the onions and sauté them over high heat until they begin to soften and become translucent, 7 to 10 minutes. Turn the heat down to medium-low and continue cooking, stirring occasionally, for about 20 minutes, until the onions are golden brown. Season with salt and pepper and set aside.

5. Spread the bread crumbs and almonds evenly on a baking sheet and bake until golden brown, about 12 minutes.

6. In a food processor fitted with a metal blade, process the almonds and bread crumbs until very finely ground. Place them in a mixing bowl and set aside.

7. Purée the onions and garlic in the food processor until smooth and creamy. Set aside.

8. Make the croutons by brushing the slices of French bread on both sides with approximately 3 tablespoons of the olive oil. Place them on a baking sheet in an even layer and toast them in the oven for about 6 minutes, until golden and lightly crisp. Set them aside to cool at room temperature. Reduce the oven temperature to 220°F to warm the soup bowls later.

continued

9. In a large saucepan over medium-high heat, bring the chicken stock to a boil. Reduce the heat to low and simmer, gently, for about 5 minutes.

10. Make the picada by placing 2 to 3 cups of the hot chicken broth in a blender with the almonds and bread crumbs and blend until smooth and creamy, about 4 minutes, creating the smoothest texture possible.

11. Scrape the picada into a medium mixing bowl and whisk in the garlic and onion purée, incorporating it to make a smooth paste. Whisk this mixture into the simmering chicken stock, and season the soup with salt and pepper. The soup should be smooth and creamy. If there are any chunks of nuts or it doesn't look smooth

enough, strain it through a medium sieve. Keep the soup warm on very low heat, until ready to serve.

12. Place the remaining 5 tablespoons of olive oil with the vitamin C tablet (if using) and parsley leaves in the blender and blend for 3 to 6 minutes on high speed, making a bright green oil. The parsley should completely liquefy, and there shouldn't be any flecks in the oil.

13. Warm 8 soup bowls in the 220°F oven for just a minute.

14. Ladle the garlic soup into warm bowls and top each with a crouton of toasted French bread. Drizzle 2 teaspoons of parsley oil over the top of each crouton and serve immediately.

❧ Note

If you can't find blanched almonds, you can bring 3 cups of water to a boil and add 1 cup of whole raw almonds, and continue to boil for 45 seconds to 1 minute. Drain. Allow to cool for a few minutes and then pop the almonds out of their skin one at a time by pinching the nut between your thumb and forefinger and middle finger. Spread the nuts out to dry.

Celery Root Skordalia

Traditionally, skordalia is a Greek potato and garlic purée that is served with just about anything–meats, vegetables, fish, and grilled bread–or as a common mezze. Like a garlicky mashed potato and lemon sauce, skordalia has the consistency of thick Greek-style yogurt.

As is frequently the case with Greek dishes, skordalia is all about garlic and lemon, and it doesn't always include nuts. I use the Arabic technique of adding nuts in this recipe, though, to make a "milk" by puréeing them with oil, lemon, garlic, and water. This technique creates a sublimely creamy consistency without the heaviness of cream or butter.

This twist on classic skordalia is perfect in the fall, when celery root is in season and garlic has finished curing. Celery root, or celeriac, tastes like a rich, nutty cross between celery and potato.

At Oleana, we also make this recipe in the spring, using Jerusalem artichokes and parsnips. For a luxurious variation, you can also stir in black truffle shavings or white truffle oil before serving to impart a heady late autumn aroma.

This skordalia tastes great at room temperature or even cold as a mezze, and it pairs well as a side dish with grilled beef kebobs or with roasted beets as a mezze or salad course.

MAKES ABOUT 6 CUPS TO SERVE 8

1 large or 2 small celery roots (2 to 2¼ pounds)

1 teaspoon plus 2 tablespoons salt

1 tablespoon whole-milk, plain yogurt,
    preferably Greek-style

2 baking or Idaho potatoes (about 1½ pounds),
    peeled and cut into quarters

¾ cup whole blanched almonds
    (see note, page 340)

1½ tablespoons garlic, roughly chopped
    (about 3 cloves)

1 tablespoon freshly squeezed lemon juice
    (about ½ lemon)

½ cup extra-virgin olive oil

Salt and black pepper to taste

1. Cut both ends of the celery root so it stands on a cutting board. Using a knife, peel it by following its shape, starting at the North Pole, rounding out at the equator, and ending at the South Pole. Shave it without cutting into too much of the vegetable. After peeling, rinse the celery root to remove any dirt and then cut it into eighths. Place the pieces in a medium saucepan. Cover them with warm water and 1 teaspoon of the salt. Bring to a boil and then reduce the heat to medium and simmer about 25 minutes, until tender. Drain the celery root, reserving 1 cup of the cooking water.

2. While the celery root is still hot, purée it in a food processor fitted with a metal blade, with the yogurt and 1 to 2 tablespoons of the reserved cooking liquid, until smooth and creamy, 3 to 4 minutes. Place the purée into a medium mixing bowl and set it aside.

3. Place the potatoes in a medium saucepan with enough water to cover them and 1 tablespoon of the salt, and bring them to a boil over high heat. Reduce the heat to medium and simmer the potatoes for about 18 minutes, until tender, and then drain them.

4. While the potatoes are still hot, mash them through a ricer or food mill and mix into the celery root. The ricer or food mill gives you a fine, fluffy purée.

5. Place the almonds, garlic, remaining cooking liquid, lemon juice, and olive oil in a blender with 2 teaspoons of the salt. Blend until completely smooth, for about 2 minutes, so that there are no bits of nuts left and the mixture is blond and creamy.

6. Fold the nut mixture into the potato–celery root mixture and reseason with salt and black pepper.

Turkish Cheese Pancakes

Called *gozleme* in Turkish, these pancakes are similar to quesadillas and are often stuffed with spinach as well as cheese. In the Taxim neighborhood of Istanbul, you can watch women roll out the dough and stuff the pancakes by hand in shop windows.

At Oleana, we use a pastry called *yufka*, which has the texture of a very thin tortilla, to make the pancakes. You can also substitute a thick, country-style phyllo, which is available at Middle Eastern Markets. Or you can try making it yourself with the recipe below.

At the restaurant, we serve these pancakes under our Crispy Lemon Chicken (page 245) with plenty of lightly dressed greens, such as arugula in the summer or frisée in the winter.

---∿ MAKES 8 PANCAKES TO SERVE 8 ∿---

For the Homemade Yufka Dough

1½ cups unbleached flour
  (8 ounces)

1 teaspoon salt

2 tablespoons extra-virgin olive oil plus
  a little extra for cooking crepes

8 pieces of waxed or parchment paper,
  cut into 6-inch squares

For the Filling

2 to 3 tablespoons butter

1 small white onion, finely chopped

1 cup ricotta cheese

4 ounces or ½ cup crumbled feta cheese

½ cup grated kasseri cheese

2 tablespoons chopped fresh parsley

1 tablespoon chopped fresh dill

1 tablespoon chopped fresh mint

Salt and freshly ground black pepper to taste

1 recipe homemade yufka or
  2 large commercial yufka sheets or
  8 sheets thick country-style phyllo

2 tablespoons olive oil

To Make the Homemade Yufka Dough

1. Sift the flour with the salt into a medium mixing bowl.

2. Make a well in the middle of the flour and pour in the oil and ⅔ cup lukewarm water. Using your hands to draw flour in from the sides, work the mixture into a sticky dough. Turn onto a lightly floured surface and knead well for about 3 minutes, until the dough is smooth and elastic.

3. Working on a lightly floured surface, divide the dough into 8 pieces. Roll each piece into a ball. Place the balls on a floured surface, cover them with a damp cloth, and leave them to rest for about 20 minutes.

4. Roll the balls of dough into flat rounds, using a lightly floured rolling pin, so that they are about 6 inches in diameter.

5. Heat a griddle or a large nonstick sauté pan over medium heat and wipe it with a little oil. Slap one of the flat rounds onto it. Use your fingertips to shift the dough about, making sure it browns and puffs up here and there. Brush the upper side with more oil, and flip it over.

6. While the second side is cooking, spread ¼ cup of cheese filling evenly over the cooked side. After about 1 minute, lift the pancake with its filling on to a piece of wax paper or parchment paper and roll it up into a cone. Wrap the paper around it to make it easier to hold, and eat it while it's hot.

To Make the Filling

1. In a small skillet, melt 1 tablespoon of the butter, add the onion, and cook over medium heat until the onion is soft and translucent, 6 to 8 minutes. Cool and set aside.

2. In a large mixing bowl, prepare the filling by combining the cheeses, onion, and herbs. Season with salt and pepper and set aside.

3. If you're making your own pastry, follow the recipe for yufka dough and pick up at step 4, below. If you're using commercial yufka, cut each sheet into 4 pieces. If you're using thick phyllo, brush each piece with a little olive oil and fold in half along the narrower dimension, then cut the folded piece in half so that you have 2 double-thick pieces about 4½ x 7 inches each.

4. Place ¼ cup of the cheese mixture in the center of each pastry and fold them up like envelopes.

5. Heat the remaining 1 to 2 tablespoons of butter in a large frying pan, over medium-high heat. When the butter starts to brown, place 2 to 3 pancakes (depending on the size of the pan) seam-side down and cook them for about 4 minutes, until golden and a little puffy. Flip the pancakes and cook for another 4 minutes Repeat the process until all pancakes are cooked, and serve hot.

3.

4.

5.

Ricotta and Bread Dumplings with Red Wine and Porcini Mushrooms

This is a classic bread dumpling recipe from Puglia, on the heel of Italy's boot. The people of that region have some of the longest life spans in the world–thanks to lots of olive oil, red wine, vegetables, dark leafy greens, fish, and very little red meat. I visited Puglia in 1988 with an organization called Oldways Preservation and Trust to study the diet.

The dumplings are a great way to use day-old bread. By soaking it in milk and kneading in eggs, ricotta, and Parmesan cheese, the stale bread turns back into dough. When cooked, the dumplings are light, soft, and a little crisp on the outside: perfect for soaking up the delectable tomato and porcini mushroom sauce.

Porcinis are rich, heady, meaty mushrooms that are amazingly versatile. Delicate enough to give grace to this elegant sauce, they're also vigorous enough to stand up to a steak or a rich glass of red wine.

At Oleana, we add escarole to the sauce in the fall, Bibb lettuce in the spring, and dark leafy greens like kale in the winter to make this dish into a full meal.

These dumplings pair well with a dark, earthy Mourvedre from Provence.

MAKES TWENTY-FOUR 1½-INCH DUMPLINGS TO SERVE 4 TO 6

For the Dumplings

1 large French baguette (about 12 ounces), some of the crust removed, cut in half and then into rough pieces (day-old bread is best because it absorbs more milk)

1 cup milk

½ cup heavy cream

1 whole egg

¾ cup fresh ricotta cheese

¾ cup freshly grated Reggianno or Grana Padana Parmesan cheese plus 4 tablespoons for garnish

⅛ teaspoon freshly grated nutmeg

Salt and pepper to taste

2 tablespoons butter

2 teaspoons olive oil

For the Sauce

2 teaspoons olive oil

¼ cup dried porcini mushrooms, soaked in hot
water for 15 minutes, drained and roughly
chopped, or ¼ pound fresh or frozen porcini
mushrooms, roughly chopped

1 leek, white part only, cut into ¼-inch slices,
then washed

1 cup dry red wine

1 teaspoon finely chopped garlic (about 1 clove)

2 cups crushed canned tomatoes or 2 cups
peeled, seeded, and roughly chopped fresh
plum tomatoes (about 12)

1 cup water or vegetable broth

½ head Bibb lettuce or escarole (about 1½
cups of torn leaves) or 4 to 6 leaves of kale,
stems removed, washed and roughly cut

Salt and pepper to taste

2 tablespoons butter

To Make the Dumplings

1. Place the bread pieces in a large mixing bowl and
toss them with the milk and cream. Push the
bread down with your hands and hold for about
1 minute, so that the bread absorbs most of
the liquid. Let the bread rest and soak for about
10 more minutes.

2. Squeeze as much milk as you can out of the
bread, a little at a time, between the palms of
your hands, until there aren't any more drips.
Discard the excess milk and cream.

3. Using a food processor fitted with a metal blade,
purée the bread until the mixture is a doughy

continued

4.

5.

consistency and starts to form a ball. It's not important that it is completely smooth; just process it for a couple of minutes until it rolls around the blade into a ball.

4. Place the egg, ricotta, Parmesan cheese, nutmeg, and about ¾ teaspoon of salt in a medium mixing bowl and whisk together until the egg and cheeses are completely incorporated and smooth. Stir in the bread mixture and season with black pepper. You should have a biscuit or soft cookie dough consistency.

5. Form 1½-inch balls from the dough, using a small ice cream scoop or tablespoon. Roll them between the palms of your hands into about 24 little dumplings. Line them up on a platter or baking sheet and flatten them slightly so that they are not completely round, about the size and shape of a large sea scallop. Cover and refrigerate them for at least 20 minutes.

To Make the Sauce

1. Meanwhile, heat the olive oil in a medium saucepan over medium-high heat. After a minute, add the mushrooms and leek and stir to coat them with the oil. Cook for 3 minutes or until the leek just begins to get limp.

2. Add the wine and bring to a boil, stirring and scraping the bottom of the pan. Reduce the heat to medium and simmer the wine and vegetables for about 10 minutes, until the wine has reduced

and thickened to coat the vegetables with a syrupy glaze.

3. Stir in the garlic, tomatoes, and water and continue to simmer for another 30 minutes. The mixture should thicken and reduce by one quarter.

4. Stir in the greens and continue to cook them until soft and tender, about 10 more minutes.

5. Season the sauce with salt and pepper and whisk in the butter. Set aside on very low heat to keep the sauce warm.

6. Preheat the oven to 350°F.

7. Melt 1 tablespoon of the butter with 1 teaspoon of the olive oil in a large, nonstick skillet over medium-high heat, until the butter begins to brown. Add about 12 dumplings, depending on the size of your pan, being careful not to crowd the pan too much. Cook the dumplings for 2 to 3 minutes on each side or until they have an even golden brown crust on both sides. Remove the dumplings onto a baking sheet and repeat the process, browning the remaining dumplings in the remaining tablespoon of butter and teaspoon of olive oil.

8. Bake the dumplings to warm the centers all the way through, for about 10 minutes.

9. Place 4 dumplings on each plate and spoon ½ cup of sauce over them. Sprinkle Parmesan cheese over the tops and serve immediately.

CHEESE

Italian and French cheeses such as brie, camembert, robiola, and the triple creams like St. Andre and mascarpone are high in butterfat, which means it's better to eat them by themselves rather than cook with them. Mediterranean-style cheese, such as feta, on the other hand, contains less butterfat, and lean cheeses are better suited for cooking.

Feta, the famous Greek curd cheese, is still made in the mountains of Greece by shepherds who use unpasteurized milk, much the way it was made thousands of years ago. Originally, feta was made with goat's or sheep's milk, but today much of it is made commercially with pasteurized cow's milk, which is firmer and easier to transport.

The milk, which is curdled with rennet, separates and drains in a special mold or cloth bag. The feta is then cut into large slices (*feta* means "slice "), which are salted and then packed in barrels filled with whey or brine. The feta cures in the brine or whey solution for a week to several months, which is why it is sometimes called "pickled cheese." Feta dries out rapidly when removed from its brine.

Feta cheese is white, usually formed into square cakes, and ranges in consistency from soft to semihard. It has a tangy, salty flavor that ranges from mild to sharp. Its fat content can range from 30 to 60 percent; most is around 45 percent milk fat.

Haloumi, a specialty cheese from Cyprus, is slightly firmer than feta; it's brined after it's folded with dried mint and cooked.

The breed of cow and the cow's diet–purple flowers and thistles or grain and plain old hay–dramatically affect the taste of cheese. Sheep's, goat's, and cow's milk all taste different and have varying amounts of butterfat, which also affects flavor.

I like to bring friends to the Middle Eastern and Armenian markets in Watertown, Massachusetts, to sample the fetas. Greek, domestic, Bulgarian, Turkish, and French– they're all delicious, and picking a favorite just comes down to a matter of taste.

It's worth seeking out imported or handcrafted cheeses; commercial varieties available at the grocery store are usually overprocessed, too salty, and dry. If you have a specialty cheese shop in your area, ask to taste the different fetas, ricottas, and kasseri cheeses.

I like to use cheese to enrich a dish instead of butter or heavy cream. I often use feta to bind spinach in making spinach pies, I whip ricotta with feta and kasseri cheese to stuff pancakes, I blend feta into sauces to make them rich and creamy, and I use ricotta as a binder in dumplings. Aged hard cheeses such as Parmesan can be finely grated and added to custards or milk-based sauces as well as sprinkled over pastas to season and enrich them.

Palace Pilav: Bulgur with Pine Nuts, Almonds, Pistachios, and Mulberries

In *The Ottoman Kitchen*, Sarah Woodward describes the kitchens in Istanbul's Topkapi Palace, where the Ottoman sultans reigned for four centuries. The palace was famous for its remarkable kitchens, the splendor of its banquets, and the massive amounts of food presented at them. She writes: "[The kitchens] give a clue to the excesses that marked the latter days of the Ottoman empire. The chimneys on their ten-domed buildings sit squatly above the second courtyard, opposite the harem. In the kitchens there are huge cauldrons being used to make this type of richly scented pilav that the sultans were reputedly so fond of." The cauldrons were so large that it took four men to lift them.

   Such luxurious pilavs as this one may well have been made in palace cauldrons. There are many versions of elaborate pilavs. This is mine. It is considered a special-occasion or fancy pilav because it is packed with nuts and berries and is enriched by the hazelnut aroma of brown butter. The addition of crushed toasted pasta is a typical addition to eastern Mediterranean pilavs.

Mulberries, which look like dried brown raspberries but taste like figs, are available at most Middle Eastern markets. You can also substitute chopped dried figs or golden raisins if you can't find mulberries.

   I like to use coarsely ground bulgur in this recipe, which is different from the fine bulgur used in the *kibbeh* and *köfte* recipes in this book. Fine bulgur gets mushy and doesn't hold up well in a rice dish; it is better suited for binding.

   It's important to toast the nuts in this recipe to draw out the oils and make the pilav taste rich. See Toasting Nuts on page 91.

   This versatile pilav is marvelous with chicken, beef, or lamb. You can also add some white rice to the bulgur for yet another variation. Kids love this pilav because of the sweet mulberries, which makes it easy to slip them a serving of whole grain.

⌒ SERVES 6 ⌒

1½ cups coarse bulgur

2 teaspoons olive oil

2 coils or nests of De Cecco brand angel hair pasta, crushed into ¼-inch small pieces measuring about ¼ cup

½ onion, finely chopped

4 tablespoons brown butter (page 106)

2¼ cups chicken broth or water

Salt and freshly ground black pepper

2 tablespoons pine nuts, lightly toasted

3 tablespoons lightly toasted, roughly chopped almonds

2 tablespoons lightly toasted, roughly chopped pistachios

¼ cup dried mulberries or chopped, dried figs

6 tablespoons plain whole-milk yogurt, preferably Greek-style

1. Soak the bulgur in warm water for 15 minutes and drain.

2. Meanwhile, in a large saucepan, heat the olive oil over high heat and add the pasta after a minute. Stir the pasta to coat it with oil, and immediately reduce the heat to medium. Continue to stir the pasta for 3 to 4 minutes, until it turns a caramel-brown color. This will happen very quickly.

3. Stir in the onion and continue to cook for another 5 to 7 minutes, stirring from time to time, until the onion has softened.

4. Stir the bulgur into the onion and pasta, adding 2 tablespoons of the brown butter.

5. Add the chicken broth and season lightly with about a teaspoon of salt and some pepper to taste.

6. Increase the heat to high and bring the liquid to a boil. Then reduce the heat to medium and cook vigorously for 5 minutes, then reduce the heat to low and simmer until almost all the liquid is absorbed, 7 to 10 minutes.

7. Remove the pan from the heat, place a clean, dry dishtowel over it, and press the lid down tightly on top. Leave the pilav to steam for 20 minutes. The cloth will absorb all the moisture, which will make bulgur fluffier and lighter.

8. Fluff the pilav with a fork, add the nuts and mulberries, and reseason with salt and pepper to taste.

9. Serve hot with a drizzle more of brown butter on each serving. You can add a dollop of yogurt on the side or you can make a well in the center of each serving and spoon some yogurt in the middle.

Fried Mussels with Turkish Tarator Sauce

Fried mussels, served on skewers and smothered with garlicky sauce, are plentiful on the streets of Istanbul. At the market near Taxim Square, vendors shuck mussels, drop them in batter, and then fry them with olive oil in large steel drums.

This dish is an Oleana staple. We serve the mussels with tarator sauce, an eggless version of mayonnaise, made by puréeing raw, blanched almonds with olive oil, lemon, and garlic. We make an extra-thick version, though, which coats the mussels better than traditional tarator sauce.

The blender is crucial in making this sauce smooth and creamy; the blade pulls the ingredients in, which creates a tighter, smoother sauce. A food processor, which has blades that push food out, is better used for chopping.

I like to cook with Prince Edward Island mussels that are farmed on poles. They are never sandy because they don't touch the bottom of the ocean, and they don't have much of a beard to remove either.

I also love to eat these mussels and tarator sauce in a po' boy sandwich between chunks of baguette. This dish is superb with a glass of well-chilled Spanish Cava, a sparkling wine from Spain.

— SERVES 8 —

For the Mussels

48 or 4 dozen mussels, a little more than a pound

1 cup dry white wine

1 clove garlic, skinned and smashed

4 to 6 cups canola or olive oil for frying

For the Tarator Sauce

¼ cup extra-virgin olive oil

2 teaspoons finely chopped garlic (about 2 large cloves)

½ cup blanched whole almonds

1 teaspoon freshly squeezed lemon juice (about ⅛ lemon)

Salt and freshly ground pepper to taste

For the Batter and Garnish

¾ cup flour

¾ cup cornstarch

1¼ to 1½ cups light-style beer, such as a Pilsner

2 teaspoons chopped fresh parsley

½ teaspoon salt

¼ teaspoon freshly ground pepper

8 leaves romaine lettuce

1 lemon cut into 8 wedges

To Make the Mussels

1. Wash the mussels in a colander and pull off the beards, starting from the pointy end and pulling down and out of the lip.

2. In a large pot, over medium-high heat, steam the mussels with the wine and smashed garlic for about 5 minutes, until the mussels open. Cool the mussels for at least 15 minutes, until they're a comfortable temperature to handle.

3. Pull the mussels out of their shells and set them aside.

To Make the Tarator Sauce

1. Strain the mussel-steaming liquid through a fine sieve and pour ½ cup of it in a blender, followed by the extra virgin olive oil, chopped garlic, almonds, and lemon juice, in that order. Purée the mixture for at least 3 minutes, until it is thick and completely smooth. There shouldn't be any almond chunks, and the sauce should be very creamy. Season the sauce with salt and pepper.

2. In a large saucepan, heat the canola on low heat until it reaches 350°F.

To Make the Batter and Garnish

1. Meanwhile, combine the flour and cornstarch in a medium mixing bowl and whisk in the beer, parsley, salt, and pepper.

2. Drop the mussels into the batter and fish them out with a fork, dropping them a few at a time into the hot oil. Fry the mussels until they're golden brown, for about 4 minutes. Place them on a towel to drain off excess oil, and season them lightly with salt.

3. Serve the mussels immediately on the romaine leaves, topped with plenty of tarator sauce and lemon wedges to squeeze over the top.

Sicilian Cremolata with Sugared Almonds

When my husband Chris and I were visiting Siracussa, Sicily, we ate a slice of warm, buttery brioche topped with a scoop of almond cremolata or gelato, which is normal fare for Sicilians in the morning during the hot summer months. It's so civilized to eat ice cream on warm bread for breakfast!

When I returned to Oleana, I told pastry chef Maura Kilpatrick about our breakfast treats, and she created this dairy-free, incredibly satisfying dessert that has floated on and off our dessert menu for more than two years. The almond-milk base is mixed with sugar before freezing and churning; the rich nut oils create a soft and creamy texture without eggs or cream.

You can make Maura's version at home without an ice cream churner, but you'll need to prepare the recipe a day in advance to allow time for the mixture to freeze before whipping. If you're lucky enough to own an ice cream maker, it will save you some time.

At Oleana, Maura sandwiches slices of brioche with chopped bittersweet chocolate, which she toasts in a sandwich press until the chocolate is melted. The gooey chocolate sandwiches are the perfect vehicle for absorbing the cremolata, little by little, as you eat.

—⌒ Serves 6 to 8 ⌒—

Cheesecloth	2 cups sliced almonds with skins on (7 ounces)
4½ cups slivered blanched almonds	
1 cup plus 6 tablespoons sugar	1 egg white

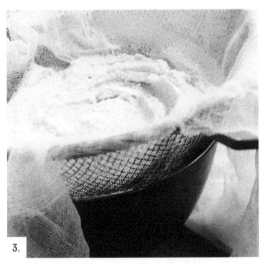

3.

6.

1. Place a strainer over a medium mixing bowl and line it with a double layer of cheesecloth, larger than the strainer so that the cloth overlaps the edges of the strainer. Cheesecloth varies in thickness and fineness of the weave, so if the layers of your cheesecloth look thin and loose, add a third layer.

2. Put 1½ cups of the slivered blanched almonds and 2 cups of water in a blender and process the nuts until they make a smooth liquid like thick milk, about 3 minutes.

3. Pour the almond milk into the cheesecloth-lined strainer. Stir the milk gently to help push it through the sieve and to make room for the second batch of milk.

4. Continue making almond milk by repeating the almond-blending process described in step 2 twice more, adding the mixture to the cheese-cloth both times.

5. Let the almond milk strain for 1 hour, stirring it occasionally with a large spoon.

6. Gather the cheesecloth around the remaining almond paste left in the cloth and twist the top, slowly squeezing as much liquid out as possible. Keep twisting and squeezing until you've squeezed as much out as you can. Discard the almond solids. You should have about 5 cups of almond milk. This can be made up to 3 days ahead of time.

7. Pour the milk through the unlined strainer back into the bowl and whisk in 1 cup of the sugar, until it dissolves, in about 1 minute.

8. At this point, you can use an ice cream maker to process the cremolata by following the manufacturer's instructions for making regular ice cream; then pick up at step 9, below. You can also freeze and process the cremolata yourself, as

continued

follows. First, freeze the almond milk overnight in a shallow baking pan or dish. The next day (or up to several days later), chip the frozen almond milk into small pieces and process about ¼ of the pieces at a time in a food processor fitted with a metal blade, for 20 to 30 seconds each time. Pulse the mixture once more, until it is smooth and turns white.

9. Transfer the cremolata to a container, stir it all together, and freeze it, covered, for at least 2 hours or overnight. If it loses its creaminess overnight, rechurn it in the food processor and freeze it for another hour before serving.

10. Put 6 to 8 glass ice cream dishes in your freezer for at least 20 minutes.

11. Preheat the oven to 300° F.

12. Make the sugared almonds by combining the sliced almonds with the remaining 6 tablespoons of sugar in a small mixing bowl.

13. In another small mixing bowl, whisk the egg white until foamy, for about a minute.

14. Toss in the almonds and sugar, and stir them so that they are completely coated in egg white.

15. Spread the almonds onto a parchment-lined baking sheet.

16. Bake the almonds for 25 minutes, or until they are lightly toasted and dried. You will have to touch them to make sure they are dry enough, as they will be shiny from the egg white and may look wet.

17. Cool the almonds completely for about 20 minutes at room temperature, and then break them into small pieces or clusters.

18. Before serving the cremolata, let it sit at room temperature for about 5 minutes, or until it is just soft enough to scoop.

19. Scoop the cremolata into frosty ice cream dishes and top them with a generous amount of sugared almonds.

PINK WINE IS NOT A BAD THING

Theresa Paopao, Wine Director at Oleana

If given a choice, I would happily drink only rosé champagne for the rest of my life, but I'm willing to bet that most people associate pink wine with something other than the world-class fermented grape juice that it actually is. Most Americans–at least those that fall in line at the tail of Gen X, like me–associate pink wine with wine coolers or other white zinfandel. Not wanting to be confused with cheap wine drinkers, we shun rosés. Besides, pink is frou-frou. It looks fabulous in a martini glass à la *Sex and the City*, but in a wine glass, somehow pink has less appeal.

More and more people, though, are beginning to drink rosé wines and discovering that 1) they can be dry and most of the time are; 2) they can be as complex and interesting as their red and white counterparts; 3) they are refreshing, especially on a hot summer day; but 4) they're not just for summer anymore–they're a great alternative to white during the winter when red just won't do; and 5) rosé goes with just about everything, from simple fish dishes to spicy barbeque.

Some really good French rosés can be found from Guigal. But rosés vary, and a trustworthy wine retailer can be your best guide as you experiment.

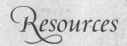
Resources

www.amazon.com
Persian saffron

www.arabiannights.ca
Arabic products
Coffee/spice grinders

www.auiswisscatalogue.com
Flash-frozen peeled chestnuts from Italy

www.blackwalnuts.com
Black walnuts

Corti Brothers
www.cortibros.biz
916-736-3800
Grano

www.cybercucina.com
Black truffles

The Farm School
www.farmschool.org

www.formaggiokitchen.com
Linden blossom honey
Maras chilies
Serrano ham
Urfa chilies

www.istanbulsupermarket.com
Red pepper paste from Turkey
Yufka dough

www.johnnyseeds.com
Heirloom seeds

Kalustyan's
www.kalustyans.com
800-352-3451
Aleppo chilies
Baharat spice mix
Chickpea flour
Egyptian mint
Fenugreek leaves
Grape leaves
Madras curry powder
Nigella seeds
Pomegranate molasses
Turkish coffee pots
Urfa chilies
Za'atar (green or Jordanian)

www.kellerscreamery.com
Plugra buter

www.krinos.com
Greek yogurt

Old Chatham Sheep Herding Company
www.blacksheepcheese.com
Sheep's milk yogurt

Oldways Preservation and Trust
www.oldwayspt.org

www.parthenonfoods.com
Greek yogurt

www.penzeys.com
Blue poppy seeds
Cinnamon
Herbs de Provence
Különleges paprika
Sweet curry powder

www.peopleswoods.com
Natural lump charcoal

www.salttraders.com
Smoked salt

www.sausagemaker.com
Hog casings

Sevan Bakery
www.sevanboston.com
599 Mount Auburn Street
Watertown, MA 02472
617-924-9843
Lamejun
Manti

www.thespanishtable.com
Hot paprika
Salt cod
Smoked paprika
Sun-dried paprika (bittersweet)

www.sunnylandmills.com
Grano

www.surlatable.com
Stainless steel ring molds

www.todarobros-specialty-foods.com
Cheese curds

www.tohum.com
Dark-roasted organic tahini
Dried mulberries
Heirloom chickpeas
Sun-dried pepper paste

www.tulumba.com
Basturma
Kurukahveci Mehmet Effendi, a Turkish coffee
Ohanyan's pastirma
Sumac

www.vtbutterandcheeseco.com
Crème fraiche
Cultured butter

www.vermontcountrystore.com
Indian sugar

www.zingermans.com
Goat-cheese crottin
Pomegranate molasses
Red rice from the Camargue

Acknowledgments

This book would not have been possible without many other people. I am deeply grateful for their encouragement, commitment, and support.

I'd like to thank my entire staff at *Oleana* for their hard work and for keeping the restaurant going strong while I wrote this book. I'd especially like to thank Wilton Osorno and Nookie, our sous-chefs; Maura Kilpatrick, pastry chef extraordinaire, who contributed many great recipes to this book; my business partner, Gary Griffin, for trusting me and allowing me to pursue my dreams; and our manager Theresa Paopao, for helping me pair wines so carefully with each dish. Thanks also to Christine Tobin for such enthusiasm, charm, and passion for food styling.

I'd like to thank my agent Lisa Ekus, who was my cheerleader and often my voice. Thanks also to the ladies at ReganBooks, especially Cassie Jones, for believing in this book and pushing me forward, and to Judith Regan, Tammi Guthrie, Richard Ljoenes, and Adrienne Makowski.

Thank you to writer Nicole Chaison, for coaxing out my ideas and then transforming them into clear words on the page.

Thank you to Susie Cushner, the most talented photographer I know, who believed in this project so deeply and, along with her team, made such artful pictures.

I am very grateful to Rosemary Jason and my dear friend Susan Turner for helping test recipes.

Thank you to Cliff Wright for being a rich resource of information and Mediterranean facts, and to Paula Wolfert, Nancy Jenkins, and Claudia Roden for being my mentors.

Thank you to Maria Hatzilliades, Ferda Erdinc, and Ayfer Unsal, who continue to inspire me, for allowing me to include their recipes and stories.

Thank you to my husband Chris Kurth, for putting up with me while I wrote, and for his editing, unconditional love, encouragement, support, and most of all, for the food he grows that inspires me to cook better and fresher every day.

Big thanks to Nora Huvelle and David Lubin for the use of their beautiful home in creating pictures. Thanks also to Jacquelyn and Greg Bokor for the same.

I'd like to thank all my friends that believed in this book and believed in the restaurant and contributed so much to its success: especially Sari Abul-Jubein, Vartan Nalbandian, Max Hatzilliades, Joanne Reeves, Maura Shepard, and Mike Toth.

And lastly, I'd like to thank all my customers, who have, over the years, continued to request this book and motivate me to write it.

Index

A

Abul-Jubein, Sari, x, 83

acorda: Portuguese bread soup
    with rock shrimp, 214–15

Adams, Ruth Ann, 310

Adar, Gökcen, 123, 285

Aigo Bistro, ix, 338

aioli:
    lemon, 50
    nasturtium, zucchini fritters with, 308–9
    toasted orange zest, 50

Aleppo chilies, 140–41
    recipes with Urfa, paprika and, 143–71

allspice, 102–3
    recipes with cinnamon, nutmeg and,
      105–39

almond(s):
    blanching, 340
    in celery root skordalia, 341–42
    couscous, veal tagine with Moroccan spices
      and, 162–65
    fried, halibut cooked in milk with
      cinnamon, spinach and, 123–24
    and garlic soup, 338–40
    palace pilav: bulgur with pine nuts,
      pistachios, mulberries and, 350–51
    sugared, Sicilian cremolata with, 354–56

in Turkish tarator sauce, fried mussels with,
    352–53

Anik, Michel, 152

appetizers:
    Armenian bean and walnut pâté, 334–35
    beet tzatziki, 252–53
    caramelized onion tart with poppy seeds,
      bacon, and dates, 182–84
    chicken and walnut pâté with smoky paprika,
      146–48
    chickpea and potato terrine stuffed with pine
      nuts, spinach, onion, and tahini, 110–12
    creamy parsnip hummus with parsley, 188–89
    deviled eggs with tuna and black olives, 203–4
    grilled mushroom banderilla, 45–46
    hot buttered hummus with basturma
      and tomato, 200–202
    muhammara: red pepper and walnut purée,
      153–55
    roasted red peppers with sesame seed
      vinaigrette, 195
    Serrano ham with blood-orange
      and fennel salad, 85–86
    smoky eggplant purée with pine nuts
      and Urfa pepper, 144–45
    spinach bundles with warm goat cheese, 180–81
    Swiss chard dolmas with Ayfer's rice, 117–19
    whipped feta with sweet and hot peppers, 149

❧ C ❧

couscous, almond, veal tagine with
    Moroccan spices and, 162–65
crabmeat:
    baby sole with raki and, 270–71
    egg-lemon soup with saffron and, 51–52
crackers, savory Turkish-style (crick-cracks), 176–77
cranberry beans stewed with tomato
    and cinnamon, 113–14
cream, heavy:
    in Arabic coffee pot de crème, 30–31
    in baby sole with crab and raki, 270–71
    folding custard and, 135
    in frozen jasmine soufflé with tropical
        fruit syrup, 323–25
    in maple sugar crème brûlée, persimmon
        pudding cake with, 136–39
    in nougat glacé, poached nectarine stuffed
        with, 316–19
    in potato risotto with green olives, walnuts,
        and rosemary, 294–95
    in salt cod fritters with red wine and sweet
        peppers, 157–60
    in scallop pizza with leeks and fennel seed,
        92–93
    in strawberry lavender tart, 326–28
crème brûlée, maple sugar, 139
crème fraîche:
    Bavarian, poached figs in spiced red wine
        with, 132–35
    in caramelized onion tart with poppy seeds,
        bacon, and dates, 182–84
    folding custard into, 135
    monkfish with ginger, seared greens and,
        53–54
cremolata, Sicilian, with sugared almonds,
    354–56
crepes, chickpea, 8–9
crick-cracks: savory Turkish-style crackers, 176–77
crust, for strawberry lavender tart, 326–28

cucumbers:
    and chopped romaine salad with yogurt dressing,
        256–57
    for Nookie's pickles, 280–81
    red lentil köfte with tomato, pomegranate and,
        12–14
cumin, 2–3
    recipes with coriander, cardamom and, 5–37
Cupia restaurant, 144
curry powder, 196–97
    homemade, 209
    recipes with turmeric, fenugreek and, 199–225

D

dates:
    caramelized onion tart with poppy seeds,
        bacon and, 182–84
    spiced, fried haloumi cheese with pear and,
        10–11
desserts:
    Arabic coffee pot de crème, 30–31
    black walnut baklava, 129–31
    chamomile berry soup with chamomile sabayon,
        312–13
    frozen jasmine soufflé with tropical fruit syrup,
        323–25
    künefe with champagne-cardamom syrup, 34–35
    molding frozen, 325
    palace bread: syrup-soaked bread pudding
        with thick cream and pistachios, 314–15
    panforte, 68–69
    persimmon pudding cake with maple sugar
        crème brûlée, 136–39
    poached figs in spiced red wine with crème
        fraîche Bavarian, 132–35
    poached nectarine stuffed with nougat glacé,
        316–19

jasmine, 300, 302
    frozen, soufflé with tropical fruit syrup, 323–25
    recipes for edible flowers and, 303–29
Jason, Rosemary, 170
Jerusalem-style carrot salad with hot goat cheese
        crottin, 260–61
Johansen, Betty, ix

❧ K ❧

kale, black, malfati in chestnut soup
        with moscato wine, 125–27
kasseri cheese:
    in eggplant soufflé, 265–66
    in moussaka, lamb steak with Turkish
        spices and, 166–69
    roast chicken stuffed with basturma and, 223–25
    sarikopites: Greek pastries with tuna,
        fennel and, 83–84
    shrimp with fennel, fenugreek and, wrapped in
        shredded phyllo, 206–8
    in Turkish cheese pancakes, 343–45
kibbeh, squash, with brown butter
        and spiced feta, 106–8
Kilpatrick, Maura, 34, 129, 132, 176, 301–2, 312,
        314, 316, 320, 323, 325, 354
köfte, red lentil, with tomato, cucumber,
        and pomegranate, 12–14
Kokkari restaurant, 28
künefe with champagne-cardamom syrup, 34–35
Kyriakides, Cassie, 220

❧ L ❧

labne (yogurt cheese), 80
    pecan, for endive and apple salad
        with grapes and sumac, 80–82

lamb:
    spoon, 22–23
    steak with Turkish spices and moussaka,
        166–69
    Turkish baharat spice mix for, 232
lamejun (flatbread), 95
    chicken, with roasted peaches, pistachio,
        and sumac, 94–96
L'Atelier restaurant, 206
lavash (thin bread), 94
    for chicken lamejun with roasted peaches,
        pistachio, and sumac, 94–96
    for spinach falafel with tahini sauce
        and pickled pears, 185–87
lavender, 300, 302
    recipes for edible flowers and, 303–29
leeks:
    scallop pizza with fennel seed and,
        92–93
    steamed mussels with smoky paprika and,
        150–51
    truffled, sauce, cod with sweet potater
        tots and, 289–91
lemon:
    aioli, 50
    in avocado hummus, fried squid with,
        17–18
    in champagne-cardamom syrup,
        künefe with, 34–35
    in creamy parsnip hummus
        with parsley, 188–89
    crispy, chicken with za'atar, 245–47
    -egg chicken soup with grano
        and sumac, 87–88
    -egg soup with saffron and crab, 51–52
    -olive oil sauce, halibut cakes with, 76–77
    in roast chicken stuffed with basturma
        and kasseri cheese, 223–25
    in steak tartare, Turkish style, 120–22

M

mace, 103

malfati (dumplings), black kale, in chestnut soup with moscato wine, 125–27

manaaeesh, Francisco's (flatbread with za'atar), 240–41

maple sugar crème brûlée, persimmon pudding cake with, 136–39

mascarpone cheese:
> in künefe with champagne-cardamom syrup, 34–35
>
> in palace bread: syrup-soaked bread pudding with pistachios and, 314–15

Maya, Rafael, 157

mayonnaise, in deviled eggs with tuna and black olives, 203–4

Mazy's jeweled rice, 58–59

Meddeb, Moncef, ix–x

Mediterranean Feast, A (Wright), 146

Mehrabyan, Armen, 110, 334

melon and tomato salad with mozzarella and oregano, 278–79

Middle Eastern five-spice, 109

milk, whole:
> in Arabic coffee pot de crème, 30–31
>
> in crème fraîche Bavarian, poached figs in spiced red wine with, 132–35
>
> halibut cooked in, with cinnamon, fried almonds, and spinach, 123–24
>
> in mashed potatoes with fenugreek, 216–17
>
> in moussaka, lamb steak with Turkish spices and, 166–69
>
> in ricotta and bread dumplings with red wine and porcini mushrooms, 346–48
>
> for salt cod fritters with red wine and sweet peppers, 157–60
>
> in veal tagine with Moroccan spices and almond couscous, 162–65

mint, dried, 228–29
> recipes with dried oregano, za'atar and, 231–47

mint, fresh, 248–50
> recipes with fresh parsley, dill, sweet basil and, 251–73

monkfish with ginger, crème fraîche, and seared greens, 53–54

Mooridian, Mark, 28

Moroccan ras el hannout (spice blend), 16

Moroccan-style sweet potato bisteeya, 42–44

Mourad, Mona, 20

moussaka, lamb steak with Turkish spices and, 166–69

Mozayeni, Mazy, 58

mozzarella cheese:
> curd, for Shoushan's homemade string cheese with nigella seeds, 178–79
>
> in fried green tomato Parmesan, 287–88
>
> in künefe with champagne-cardamom syrup, 34–35
>
> melon and tomato salad with oregano and, 278–79
>
> in pumpkin börek, 115–16

muhammara: red pepper and walnut purée, 153–55

mulberries:
> in Mazy's jeweled rice, 58–59
>
> palace pilav: bulgur with pine nuts, almonds, pistachios and, 350–51

mushrooms:
> grilled, banderilla, 45–46
>
> ricotta and bread dumplings with red wine and porcini, 346–48

mussels:
> fried, with Turkish tarator sauce, 352–53
>
> steamed, with leeks and smoky paprika, 150–51

N

Nalbandian, Vartan, 178

nasturtium, 300–301
> recipes with edible flowers and, 303–29

Q

R

T

U

V